FRACTURED FAMILY

by

Mark S. Cornwall

FRACTURED FAMILY

by

Mark S. Cornwall

All publishing information or other inquiries should be directed to Baby Boomer Publishing, P.O. Box 646, Summerland, California 93067.

Visit our website:

MarkCornwall.com

Dedicated to:

Suzan, Tod, Jack and Mary

FRACTURED FAMILY

TABLE OF CONTENTS

FRACTURED FAMILY

PART ONE

1969: My Too Funny Brothers

1.

Welcome to *The Snake Pit*

My sister and I sat home alone watching the 1948 movie *The Snake Pit.* It was on the 1960 *Late Night Movie* channel when I was nine and Suzie was thirteen. Our parents were out for the evening and our older brother, Tod, was in the Navy. I can't remember any other scene from the movie, but I was scared to death that there might be snakes in the pit when the female protagonist found herself locked up in Juniper Hill State Mental Hospital. It was where schizophrenic patients went to either "snap out of it" or die.

I failed to recognize *The Snake Pit* was a phantasmagoria of delusional horrors as shown through individual patients acting out, all at once. The mental patients in the movie were freaks. They ranged from the kneeling, begging kind, to the dancing aristocrat with a can-can dancer in the middle. There were those mumbling in tongues and those lost in this world and mad as hell about being in their strait jackets. Everybody's a lunatic in the *Snake Pit.* They are all left to feel abandoned and betrayed, fearful of violence, and confused as to who they are and why they're there.

It was creepy at age nine to think this hospital existed as depicted in the movie. My sister assured me these hospitals didn't exist anymore and were used for dramatic purposes only. She denied those kinds of people even existed. But boy, was she wrong. Because they did exist in San Bernardino at a place called Patton State Mental Hospital. And the patient thrown in the pit at just age twenty-three was my sister Suzan.

In this true-life adventure of Suzan Cornwall, she came to the insane asylum from a middle-class upbringing that included complex family issues shared with aunts, uncles and cousins—the whole fam-damily, if you get what I mean. Each family member had to suffer through Suzan's struggle to remain sane and stay out of incarceration.

But this isn't a story about Suzan being diagnosed as paranoid schizophrenic. It's a story about the impact that diagnosis had on our family, and the family's resistance to that diagnosis. It's the story of how each family member dealt with the stigma of the diagnosis, and why the stigma is never talked about. And it begins and ends with the fabled horrors of Patton State Mental Hospital.

This story is presented by each family member as they experienced living through the hell of having their sister incarcerated for being crazy. Mark, Tod, and Suzan, the siblings, each tell their story of 1969, the year the whole world was fragmented.

2. Patton's Fabled Horrors

I thought I could write a story with no heroes. But I couldn't think of a hero that didn't have faults. I could make one up, but what fun would that be, hearing about a hero better than you because they don't exist? No, I'll give you a real hero, by examining their faults. Someone with faults, but someone who we can still admire.

Take my sister, Suzie. She was a charmer alright, but that didn't make her a hero. In fact, she didn't become my hero until after she became mentally ill. She was no hero until she was diagnosed as a paranoid schizophrenic and locked up in Patton State Mental Health Hospital where she became pharmaceutically addicted to Thorazine. That's where the records show Suzan Annette Cornwall succumbed to mandated sterilization, and routine shock treatments. Yet still, she dreamt of having babies. Suzie was my hero because she survived it all.

The hospital was originally named the "Southern California Asylum for the Insane and Inebriates." Surely, you can feel the understanding based upon that christened name in 1893. You just throw the drunks in with the lunatics. It's all the same deviant behavior, isn't it?

Those were the days you were sent to the funny farm to relax. "Just chill out—you've had a nervous breakdown, you'll be fine." The Patton buildings made a grand landscape at one time. It had spiral peaks holding up the roof of this four-story Gothic-looking mansion turned government building. It was mixed with California bungalows sprawled across 300 acres of gently rolling hills, stacked with concrete and fenced in with barbed wire. It looked like an abandoned school yard with a broken merry-go-round.

This rural facility housed, fed, and buried thousands of mental patients sent there to use the same bucolic setting to cure their illnesses. That was the backward thinking of the day. They couldn't cure what ailed you, but they could secret you away so you couldn't fracture the family any more than you had been allowed—like the patients shouting epithets on the streets today.

The authorities took those afflicted with mental disease and kept them apart from those normally referred to as "sick or injured." That's where the stigma began, with isolation. Look, being a schizophrenic *is* different from having a broken leg or the flu, and quite frankly, cannot be tolerated by the family because of the inevitability of a break-up. Inviting your mentally ill sister to dinner is like inviting the Joker from Gotham City. You never know what you're going to get, but you can be certain it's disruptive.

Unlike a broken leg, mental illness carries a stigma that makes you want to punish the patient—yes, that's right, even though they 'know not what they do.' It's so sad to look at my sister and see nothing wrong with her, but I hear her accusing Aunt Betty of having hodgepodge written on her soul that's been vexed by the devil.

What does that mean? You tell me. It's obviously crazy. And it carries an intrinsic need for punishment because it hurts other members of the tribe. You want to punish Suzie as though she had some control over her disease and intentionally used it to hurt the ones she loved. Suzan, being diagnosed with paranoid schizophrenia, hurt her family in ways we couldn't understand because they made no sense. But we still had to deal with it. Nothing like this would have occurred if she'd been diagnosed with a broken leg.

Suzan continued hurting people with her disease. You wonder why, but there's no answer. It was something she was aware of when she wrote, "My heart aches, and my sorrows hurt the ones I tell." The price the government charged the taxpayer for Suzan to stop hurting her family was a life sentence in the snake pit. That was the stage of mental health in 1893, and that's what it was in 1969. And I bet that's the way it is today.

3. Meeting in the Snake Pit

"Hey Suzie, you lost your slipper," said Marshal, approaching from the rear. He's a tall, sinewy young fella, sporting a goofy grin, and wearing a holster around his waist like a cowboy. But instead of a six-gun, he's got a pack of Marlboros stuck in his quick draw holster. He was a friend of mine in high school.

"Oh, yeah, where'd you find it?" said Suzan.

"You just walked out of it, back there. It's got S. A. Cornwall written on the sole," said Marshal, handing her the soft satin shoe, like a ballet slipper.

"That's me...Hey, you got a smoke, cowboy?" said Suzan, eyeing the Marlboros in his holster.

"Sure do, and I got a striking resemblance to match," said Marshal, opening the flip top box with one hand.

"Aren't you clever. That's quite a gun belt," said Suzan, admiringly.

"The boys around here gotta learn there's a new sheriff in town," and with that he clipped the end of a wooden match with his thumbnail to set it aflame.

"You better be careful with those matches. Don't let the orderlies see them," warned Suzie.

"Didn't you hear me, I'm the new sheriff," said Marshal.

Suzan couldn't help but notice Marshal's tattoos on the three middle fingers of his hands. On his right fist was tattooed "MOM" and on his left fist was tattooed "DAD."

Suzan put the cigarette to her lips and took a long drag before asking, "What's with the tattoos—you got mommy and daddy issues?"

This is where she finds Marshal laughs a lot about things that are not so funny, random inappropriate laughter.

"I was trying to send a message to my parents. Think it got through? I don't. I was in military school, you know," laughed Marshal.

"When?"

"In high school."

"I thought you went AWOL from the Marines," said Suzan.

"Before that. I went to the military academy for a couple of years when I was in high school."

"That's sad. It's kind of dorky," said Suzan.

"Maybe that's why I got in so many fights."

"So, what's that make you? A fighter?

"I never won a fight," said Marshal, trying to be truthful. "Just defending myself. I keep trying... to defend myself. ...Think it's got something to do with my appearance?" To this he gave a hearty laugh.

"Yeah, you look sort of ...sort of...I bet everybody likes you, and if they don't, they're just jealous," said Suzie, "Maybe you should get some mental treatments."

"Oh, I ain't gonna get no treatments. No way, Jose. You go in one way... making a bunch of loud noises, and you come out a zombie." Marshal leaned in with his torso so passer-byes couldn't hear him, "Like what happened with McNulty. They shoved that metal spike so high up in his brain he hasn't been able to talk since."

Suzie, taking another long drag from her Marlboro, looked Marshal dead in the eye and said, "I'm breaking out of here."

"Right now?" asked Marshal.

"You heard about it, didn't you?" said Suzie.

"I don't think so."

"You watch the news? It's all over the news."

"I don't watch much T.V."

"Well, it's on breaking news. They know I'm breaking out of here," said Suzie.

"I wanna go with you."

"Okay then, we'll go tonight."

With that taken care of, they stopped to give it some thought. At that point an elderly patient shuffled up to Suzan and said, “Suzan, can I have what’s left of that butt you’re smokin?”

“Of course you can, Vivian, but Marshal won’t mind giving you a new one,” said Suzie.

Marshal didn’t mind and opened his pack for Vivian.

“Thanks, sonny,” she said, “You gotta match for that?”

Marshal laughed, “No, but I got a striking resemblance.”

Six months after this conversation, Marshal Mezey was declared sane by the “Lunacy Board” at Patton State Hospital and returned to work in the oilfields outside Bakersfield. There he met his untimely demise when he climbed out on a derrick without a safety harness and fell 110 feet to his death at age nineteen.

4. Patton's 125 Years of Service

Suzan entered the hospital long after it was renamed Patton State Mental Hospital in 1927. But locally, the hospital has always been known as Patton State "Insane Asylum," or to the patients within Patton it was called the "Snake Pit." When Suzie was committed to this cuckoo's nest, the wheel of mental health treatments were clearly a holdover from the dark ages of psychiatry, when mental health was treated by way of isolation.

Isolation was the first and only step towards treatment. Everything else called *treatment* sounds incredibly unhealthy. The schizophrenic patients couldn't be helped medically. There were no antipsychotic drugs in 1969 that could act as a cure. That's why they resorted to trying to scare the sweet bejesus out of the schizophrenic patient—to help them *snap out of it.*

Throwing a person in the snake pit was the only way they could make the patient see what would happen to them if they didn't get better. That's what happened to "V. Cunningham," the protagonist in Mary Jane Ward's *The Snake Pit.* The nurses in their starched white caps could only medicate their patients to keep them tranquil. Thorazine was the drug of choice that left the patient dry mouthed and dizzy.

The typical patient acted strangely when they got "excited", and the environment at Patton made them stranger.

The strangest ones, like my sister, were lost in this world. The snake pit was in the center of this massive cathedral where Suzie was left to languish with the perverts left over from the criminal justice system. The pit wasn't filled with just women either—men shared dormitories on the other side of the mental health campus.

Suzan had committed no crime, yet she was treated worse than a criminal. She was a danger to society and to herself. She was locked up with no privileges. You don't need a psychiatric degree to know how mixed-up a *paranoid schizophrenic* can be. That's as bad as it gets. She was made a ward of the State and ushered into a program of mandatory servitude in the snake pit for the mentally disturbed.

That meant either 1) She could be "restored" to her good sense through the fanciful therapy of country living (and fear of the snake pit), and after her peaceful retreat to the farm, she could be declared *sane* by the Lunacy Commissioner who was empowered to decide a patient's clarity; or, she remained incarcerated like a human being wrapped in a blanket of Thorazine and left to die in the bottom of the tomb for the insane. After that, Suzie would be buried on the hill with the other patients.

But before she died, she'd have to endure the pit. There are no locked doors inside the Cathedral where patients go to meet. There is no privacy anywhere in the hall. Men and women are allowed to roam freely through the hallways during the day, a sort of stock yard of destitute souls. The only locked doors in the whole building were those leading to freedom. There were no exits outside.

When I first visited Suzan at Patton State Mental Hospital, I drove across the grounds to park in the visitor parking lot. It was the worst reception possible for a young man visiting his mentally disturbed sister for the first time. As soon as I exited my car to approach the building, I heard voices echoing from inside. Voices of those trapped behind the thick walls. It was the constant anguish rising from the groan of patients.

Some were screaming at the top of their lungs. I could distinguish two or three voices crying out pitifully, "Help me!... Please help me. I'm begging you," as though his back was breaking from the torture. "Help me, I'm begging you!" The prisoners would scream their bloody heads off, but nobody came because they couldn't be helped. Medication time was over and they were still suffering.

This was a *general admission* insane asylum in 1969. The population of the infamous *Snake Pit* included every kind of mental patient from Alpha to Zulu, from eating disorders to identity disorders; every disorder that's disruptive and misunderstood. They were all admitted for treatment, and everybody was thrown in together. Whether they were alcoholics, drug addicts, epileptics, or suffered from down-syndrome, autism or dementia. These poor victims were patients of Patton, to be victimized again. I couldn't believe there were so many of them.

The criminally insane defendants found their way into the snake pit to avoid doing hard time. And the violent delusional criminals also grew amongst the general population, making this open-pit style of convalescence less safe for a mix of patients in the hall. By 1969, when my sister arrived, the criminal types had taken over the institution. That same element leaked into various treatments ordered by the staff. The doctors and nurses were in the dark about curing mental illness. They were teetering on trying almost anything. The treatments were appalling.

It's hard to imagine how some treatments might alleviate the pain of mental illness. Many therapies prescribed were strange and disturbing, if not downright cruel. For example, prescribing male and female circumcisions to cure mental illness, what's the connection? Or forcing a patient to endure hydrotherapy by strapping them inside a tub where they became susceptible to water boarding techniques.

Worse still was the fact Patton was one of the last Mental Health Hospital's in America to give up the most barbaric treatment of the twentieth century: the lobotomy. This was a surgical intervention of the brain where surgeons attempted to sever the connection between the two frontal lobes by using a transorbital lobotomy pick through the eye socket. The transorbital pick was an 18-inch metal spike used on 230 patients before it was discontinued. As the comic Tom Waits said, "I'd rather have a bottle in front of me, than a frontal lobotomy."

Suzan became a cog on the whole dark treatment wheel.

But what struck me was what they did to my sister. They stripped Suzie of her right to have a child. The doctors systematically used sterilization as a prophylactic treatment to stop mental illness from spreading throughout society. It was a policy to eliminate the possibility of a person like Suzie being born. Think eugenics. Would the world have been a better place without Suzan? All the patients in the snake pit were treated as though they were idiot bastards, with nobody in their corner to support them.

5. Then Came George

Suzan's journey began after she was deserted by every person she knew, including our parents, who left her to die on the steps of Suffolk County Mental Health Hospital, in New York. My parents had raised her as best they could, keeping her on the straight and narrow, then cut her off completely when they moved to Berchtesgaden, Germany, to pursue their own occupational dream in 1969.

Suzie was abandoned at Suffolk County Mental Hospital by our parents on the grounds there was nothing wrong with her. They said Suzie didn't want to work. She was twenty-three years old and that was old enough to know better. She had to work. If she couldn't work at anything, well, it was too bad for her. The old baptism by fire. Sounds harsh, doesn't it? Well, nobody said life was easy. But what did my parents think would happen to her? Honestly?

Our parents were living their dream of moving to Europe and teaching for the Department of Defense Educational Activity (USDESEA). That's the U.S. agency responsible for providing the American education throughout the free world. My mother wrote to Uncle George, after he accused my parents of child neglect by flying off to be headmasters of the American School in Berchtesgaden,

Germany, and abandoning Suzan in her fragile state with George and Betty. Berchtesgaden was Adolph Hitler's old home—the ultimate in victor's spoils for a couple from Bakersfield. Mary wrote, in retort to the accusation they were acting selfishly, "Is that really so selfish?"

It turned out Suzie could not work. It wasn't because she was "lazy" or had to have things "her way;" it was because she was at the tipping point of going insane. She was in the boat heading round the bend toward insanity. She didn't have the attention span to stay on any job. Within the hour she'd start thinking how her Aunt Betty and Uncle George, whose house Suzie was visiting on Long Island, were playing hodge podge with her soul, and hexing their own home using witchcraft. This *hexing* caused Suzie to call the police to have her aunt and uncle arrested for practicing witchcraft. These allegations made Suzie a difficult person to live with, and an impossible person to employ.

My uncle, who was a writer, wrote to my father in Germany, about Suzan's behavior:

George wrote, *"In her less but lucid moments, Suzan was sullen, resentful, defiant, and suffered from a well-defined persecution complex. She would lay on her bed all day drumming on the wall with her fingers and occasionally bursting into prolonged laughter that could only be described as eerie. Come the evening when she was fully rested, she would storm out of her bedroom and demand, "Take me to the airport and buy me a ticket for home. I'm leaving for California.'"*

Poor Aunt Betty and Uncle George. They would reject Suzan's idea because it meant once again, buy a ticket to where? San Francisco, Los Angeles, or Bakersfield. To do what? To be taken care of by whom? That was the big question.

"She'd go back to her room and wash her hair, incessantly, washing her long blond straight hair. Sometimes twice, one after the other. This is the strange behavior exhibited by Suzan, the difficult house guest, who refuses to even make her bed. But this barely scratches the surface of Suzan's weird veneer," my uncle wrote.

As she was choosing between sanity and insanity, our parents decided they would accept the assignment of their lives by taking the reins of a two-room kindergarten through eighth grade elementary school, located in Bavaria. It was located on a base with only thirty-five families. Berchtesgaden was a recreation area for the European forces. These military men oversaw the management of the six ski resorts in the area. As my mother was quick to point out, "We went there for a job, not a vacation."

At any rate, they hit the lotto when it came to their duty station. The Alpine mountains could not have been more ruggedly handsome. Berchtesgaden was where Adolph Hitler kept his residence with Eva Braun. He had a fondness for inspiring landscapes he painted as a young man. It was titillating to think about those rotten Nazis bastards running through the tunnels under the hotel resorts in fear of their lives.

II

THERE WAS CONFLICT

6. The Juggernaut of Conflict

Suzan Cornwall's breakdown came in 1969. That's when the conflict began between the Scullin family and the Cornwall family over what to do about Suzan. Suzan had gone to New York City to become a model and ended up sleeping in Central Park with no money. Aunt Betty and her family lived on Long Island, in Stoney Brooke, not far from New York City. Betty and Jack Cornwall were siblings, while Mary and George Scullin, the writer, were in-laws.

Everybody had an idea as to what should be done with Suzan, and all of them interrupted Mary and Jack's plan for their future. Mary wrote the following letter to Suzie as they were leaving for Germany early in 1969. They had spoken on the phone to Betty and George who they claimed were verbally abusive to them:

"Dear Suzie,

It was very upsetting for this situation to arise just before we were to leave for Germany. The movers were here when Betty called for the first time, and she and George went on their rampage. The apartment was almost empty. We couldn't possibly have made arrangements at this point to take you with us.

Besides, your place is not with us. You should be on your own. What Betty and George had to say as far as Daddy and I are concerned, was nothing but wine talking. We have offered you psychiatric help before—you must be the one that decides to do it. The fact that you didn't want to see the doctor should have shown Betty how you have faith in yourself. We know you are capable—all that is lacking is your will to do it. No one can create that for you. You've had plenty of guidance and counseling, all of which you disregarded because it wasn't your way—that is as it should be. You know yourself and what you want to do. No one can live your life for you.

"I hope by now you have been able to leave Betty's. I'm sorry we suggested you're going there but at least it's been a refuge. I think you are much more stable than they are, but that's really no excuse to show bad breeding by not cleaning up after yourself and laughing at Betty. No matter how hopeless it seems to be, clean and be proud of yourself. It's not your home. Will write from Germany—Love, Mother."

At that time, I was nineteen years old and living in Bakersfield, California where I was born and raised and had nothing to offer but a joint. It seemed like the world was coming apart at the seams every day. The war in Vietnam was raging, and I was trying to avoid the draft. King had been killed,

Kennedy was assassinated, and we were walking on the moon. It was a time of extreme societal unrest, and Suzan personified the times by teetering on the edge of a nervous breakdown.

My father had a different take on Suzie's situation. He saw it as Susie using "a convenient façade to escape from having to meet the responsibilities of taking care of herself," wrote my father to Betty. How Suzan's drumming her fingers on the wall, and washing her hair incessantly, had anything to do with a 'convenient façade' was beyond me.

The same can be said for summoning the police officers to arrest her aunt and uncle for practicing witchcraft. That sounds like the exact opposite of a convenient façade. But what do I know? Jack illuminates Suzie's problem in the following excerpts from a letter he wrote in response to his sister's allegations towards him. At the top of the letter my father wrote, "(Please Betty, Keep this confidential. Destroy.)" Obviously, she did no such thing.

"Dear Betty,

Your announcement of Suzie's behavior was not a surprise to us, because it has been a pattern for the last two years. She will not work, and she expects everyone to support her. I have looked into the possibility of forcing or coercing her to accept counseling, but she will not accept the idea. I have suggested treatment, but she will not listen to a thing I say. I have spent many hours trying to influence her way of life, but her reaction is always negative.

Since she is twenty-three years of age, an adult, she must, on her own free will, submit to the therapy. The only hope I have is that she will someday reach a point, as Bob did, [Bob was their alcoholic brother] and decide that she would be happier if she would just accept a simple life of working, day to day, and doing her best.

I feel that will come about eventually, if she has some help, but at the same time, be expected to do something for herself—like working. She could do many things, but she has this obsession about becoming a model. But in the meantime, all other work is beneath her.

Suzie is perfectly aware of this "operation", and she uses it on everybody. She does a beautiful job of getting her listeners to sympathize with her and make them believe what a bastard her dad is. If only a person could get this girl to sever the umbilical cord, she would be happy. Maybe this will come about while we are gone to Germany.

I have confidence in Suzie, and I know she is going to make it in spite of what she is going through now. The gold carat will shine through eventually, I'm sure. If only she would have confidence in herself. The gold carat will shine through eventually!"

It doesn't help "cut the umbilical cord" to hear your father not only questioning your integrity about being lazy, but to outright accuse your kid of running an "operation" whereby she scams people to support herself. To say that Suzan, your own flesh and blood, the poor girl with no money or clothes, goes around "scamming people" to get money, doesn't make any sense and I question my father's motivation.

The best excuse I have for Dad was that he didn't realize the gravity of the situation. He wasn't aware of how far around the bend Suzie had gone. He says he's seen this pattern of behavior happening over the last two years, and how Suzie's scamming people was used as a "convenient façade" to escape her responsibility of working.

That sounds literate, but what does it mean? If anything, she was being punished for her convenient façade, as though she beat somebody up with it. It was like she committed an assault on life with her convenient façade. The only place she was escaping to was the Suffolk County Psycho Ward.

What is Suzie supposed to do now that her parents had flown to Germany? She was staying with the Scullin's. Dad says, "You go to work." But she can't work. Dad says, "Yes, she can." Her employer says, "No, she can't." What the bloody hell?

When it comes to this stage in examining the options for Suzan, I would side with my Uncle George. He wrote the real problem was Jack didn't want some "handicap weirdo" around his entourage for fear people may query his own "impeccable position" in the education community. Jack was more worried about what people thought of Jack than his daughter's farewell. Mental disease was seen as taboo, just as it is now, a family secret that's not talked about publicly, or even amongst the extended family. Mums the word.

7. Uncle George Responds

Mental illness, as opposed to mental health, is still thought by some to be a shameful and disturbing phenomenon in the U.S. That's strange, because a fifth of the population has firsthand experience of dealing with the mentally disturbed. Somebody in their family is sick. It's not like a broken arm the doctor sets for eight weeks and you're healed.

Mental health issues can last forever, and it cast needless dispersions on both the victim and their family. The family's fear of the unknown spread rampantly. If my daughter's insane, who'd she inherit it from? Nobody knew. Jack wanted to escape that fear over his daughter. Having no balls to confront the issue head on, he chose to fly to Germany with Mother and escape the whole mess. That's how Dad planned to have no Suzan around, to complicate his life at his new job. And Uncle George knew it.

In response to another of Dad's letters, wherein he sarcastically wondered where George received his psychiatric training, George wrote back to him this classic line:

"Where, you wonder, did we receive our psychiatry training? From the painful disintegration of a mildly disoriented child, as she progressed more and more rapidly to a complete breakdown in the two-and-a-half months she was here. We wrote

to you, we called you, we pleaded with you, and I became furious with you because you refused to believe she was indulging in anything more than a few harmless delusions and eccentricities you were all too familiar with.

She was falling apart, and I told you so. But you chose to believe I had a snootful, and was arrogant, and ignorant, and could be dismissed by ignoring me completely. Me, you can ignore, permanently, but not your daughter. You claim she is 23, and a responsible adult. But no 12-year-old is less capable of fending for herself than Suzan".

As Susie approached her summit of susceptibility to schizophrenia, her mind already infected with paranoia, our father, perhaps led by wishful thinking she would improve, kept hem-hawing around. "I'll take care of this my own way," was his standard refrain to the question, "What are you going to do about Suzan?" Unfortunately, "Suzie drifted further and further around the bend, on an increasingly faster current", wrote Uncle George.

Just as her continued stay at the Scullin's became intolerable, Suzan managed to get picked up by the police and placed in the Suffolk County Mental Hospital's "non-voluntary security confinement" for an observation period of fifteen days. Suzan was in white water then; until she opened the flood gates to let the crazy flow over her, anointing her entire being. She finally arrived in the snake pit of New York State.

What blew her way down the river, and around the bend, out of sight, was the realization that every friend, every boyfriend she ever had, every girlfriend, and even her parents had abandoned her. There was no one left. She was stuck in Suffolk County Mental Ward in Stony Brook, New York, three thousand miles from home. It was while she was in that confused state that the disintegration of her mind proceeded inevitably to the end.

Suzie had been brought up bourgeois. She was as middle class as a casserole for Sunday dinner. She was the middle child between her older brother, Tod, and her younger brother, me. Interestingly, we three kids were born four years apart so my parents would never have two children in college at the same time. Brilliant! But they didn't consider they were creating a generational gap between each child. Big difference between a 19-year-old and a 10-year-old child. Such was the foresight of our parents to get their procreation plan to fit into their financial plan. From the very beginning our family's future was all planned out.

8. Yokuts Club Day Camp

Both Mary and Jack were schoolteachers in Bakersfield, California and they created the Yokuts Club Day Camp for children between the ages of 5 through 12 for their summertime recreation. The Yokuts Club grew to be fabulously popular for its unique ability to build character by using local Indian lore. And the Yokuts Club was nothing, if not a character-building organization. The result of their entrepreneurship with Yokuts was it made them more money during eight weeks of summer camp than they made teaching school all year.

Suzan became a big part of the Yokuts organization when she became a camp counselor at age sixteen. My father wrote to his sister Betty that, "Suzie was the best counselor I ever had in Yokuts for her age—the most dependable, capable, versatile, and well organized. She did much better than the adults who have worked for me. The most amazing fact of her charisma was the absolute command she kept of the situation. She was a leader and an officer even in college in Bakersfield, until she went to San Diego State. The wrong crowd fouled this kid up, yes, but why in the hell has this had more influence than her early training?"

This was from the same letter my father asked to be destroyed. Why? Obviously, it was taboo to talk about.

When Suzan was a freshman attending Bakersfield Junior College, she caught a lucky break. Her hair style in 1965 became the trademark for the Hippie generation. She was in the first wave of Hippies to invade San Francisco in 1967. Long, blond, straight, (and I mean straight) hair, past her shoulders, with or without bangs, was the hairdo of the day and every girl wanted it. Think Joni Mitchel.

Suzie's hair changed her life. She had always enjoyed a modicum of popularity, but this long straight hair put her into the generation my dad referred to as the "wrong crowd." Be that as it may, I guess I fell in with the wrong crowd too, the same as everybody who cared about humanity.

I don't know how much LSD Suzie took. But it was the drug of the day, and I don't think she took much, although I agree once is too much for some people. But it wasn't like Suzan took it by the handful like Jimi Hendrix was portrayed as taking, the way our parents portrayed the Hippy lifestyle. I saw her the year after the "Summer of Love," in late August 1968, when my buddy Bruce Jones and I visited her in Haight Ashbury. We traveled from Bakersfield to Boise State for our freshman year to play Bronco football on scholarship.

At the age of eighteen, both Bruce and I were impressed with my sister's boyfriend. Twenty-four years old, he had gone to the University of Idaho in Moscow on a tennis scholarship. His apartment was in the middle of the Haight, and he assured us the love was gone from the previous "summer of love" and was now replaced with methedrine. But this guy was not a hippy. He was a capitalist and entrepreneur—and a good one at that.

He dealt pot and hallucinogens, drove a black *Cayenne,* wore Berluti loafers, and had tickets to the 49'ers. Living in the epicenter of anti-materialism, he enjoyed being the most popular guy around with all the money and long hair to boot.

That was quite a feat in 1968 when only "freaks" had long hair. He shared with Bruce and me a sample of his wares, and that was the first time we'd taken a hallucinogen. STP was the name of it. We sat in the front row of the movie theater watching *2001: A Space Odyssey,* then went home and talked wildly about things we had never talked about before, all night long. It was still fun as I remember it today.

My sister had no interest in participating in any LSD games. I would have noticed. So, I eliminated that as the reason for her insanity, which was what everyone else accused her of. There was no evidence she even took drugs. In fact, she appeared guarded against hallucinogens, as though she'd experimented before and didn't like it. The same way a lot of people were in the sixties. She had enough to know she didn't want any more—a very sane decision.

So, something happened to Suzie between the summer of '68 and the summer of 1969. You wonder what role her environment played in driving her insane, living in a place like Haight Ashbury for two years during its most drug-ridden times. Thousands of kids did it, and they all came out alive and well. But not Suzan.

9. Uncle George Seethes

I may as well introduce our brother Tod, nine years older than me, making him a 27-year-old artist. You heard it right. I was there when Tod was told by a discriminating critic of his paintings that his Degree in Fine Arts from the University of California Santa Barbara, was "Worthless as Tits on a Boar!"

Nevertheless, Tod pressed on in life doing everything possible to be himself. Take him or leave him. Most people left him because of his get in your face personality. But he was a fine artist with his tiny oil brushes, just like our old man.

After I saw Suzie in San Francisco, Tod was getting a divorce in L.A. from Lisa Todd, the brunette sexologist on the T.V. show *Hee Haw.* It was she who answered questions in the bit, "Letters from the Lovelorn." Tod came to visit us at Boise State, during his own lovelorn days with Lisa.

He drove straight from Hollywood in his green mustang wearing black leather pants like Jim Morrison in Beatle boots. Tod always made a spectacle of himself, and it didn't go unnoticed in Boise, Idaho. He was the talk of the team in those leather pants.

So, there's my family of five. I injured my knee in the second game of the season which blew up my four-year scholarship. It also brought an end to the only job I knew, so now I was facing the world the same as Suzie. Alone, looking for work, staying at a friend's house in Bakersfield, and trying to stay out of trouble.

At least Suzie had graduated from the questionable 'Powell Modeling Academy,' paid for by my mother before she deserted Suzie. My Uncle wrote of my sister's brush with being a model this way:

"Suzie had a bona fide modeling contract in New York City, all but signed, sealed and delivered. She had checks amounting to hundreds of dollars due any day now from here, there, from her parents, among others. She was going to be rich and famous, and success was inevitable. But nothing ever materialized, and Suzie was left sleeping in Central Park before she made it to us out in Stony Brook, Long Island, a broken girl."

Uncle George wrote this letter to my father, dated August 29, 1969, concerning Suzie's mental health, then went on:

"The statement that really caused me to seethe and upset my writing schedule for a couple of days, [George was the author of Killer, the underlying story to Gunfight at the OK Corral] was Jack's determined repetition of, "I'll take care of it my own way!" That's a rather startling statement, like saying you'll take care of a shattered pelvis when you get around to taking a course in bone-setting. This girl can't wait."

To say Suzan caused hard feelings between my parents and the Scullin's would not be enough. Here's how Aunt Betty summed up my parents' cold response to their daughter's cry for help:

"It's all so appalling—even now I find it surprising to realize that of all the low-down individuals I have known in my time—and I've known plenty—you two are the worse."

Isn't it a shame that letter-writing has disappeared. How'd you like to pull a quote like that from a text on your phone from 55 years ago. Letters last forever, if you keep them.

Of course, we should let Suzie have the last word on what happened during those two and a half months it took to find her way into the Suffolk County Mental Ward. She wrote a letter from that ward to Uncle George, after she was labeled a paranoid schizophrenic.

It's a fine time to let Suzie speak from the grave, so to speak. She may have been insane, but her penmanship is perfectly neat and clear. Her individual letters were written by hand in a perfectly straight line, as though they were typed with a brush script font, on unlined yellow paper, folded over.

"Dear George,

Yep, the headlines are reading "Kin of missing officer." or was it "Kin of officer missing." And no one can find us. I'm still in this fucking mental hospital hopefully to be released Thursday. I'm telling you we're living under a fascist state. Well, they just barged into our home and locked me up as if I had committed a crime. God knows this kind of government is wrong and Capitalism is the only way to fly.

I'm telling you if this isn't ***straightened*** *out in court our country is headed toward a tremendous* ***boom.*** *I imagine you've heard plenty of this from Lori [Suzie's cousin Laurie]. Going to Drake is quite a privilege. As soon as I get some money together I'm planning upon going back to finish my formal education. Our country needs formality and without the crackpots everything runs smoothly. I wouldn't be here if it wasn't for a crack in the government heads. Maybe by Thursday we will all know about dogma.*

Love,

Suzan"

10. Tod Takes on Suzie

Tod has his own take on how Suzie got screwed up. He basically said the same things as our father, only through a different filter. Being four years older than her, he considered Suzie to be a "sophomore" flower child, and he was, of course, in the first wave of the Flower Power movement in 1967 San Francisco. But in reality, he was the last wave of the beatnik generation.

Tod wrote the following letter to Aunt Betty giving her his explanation of Suzie's condition:

"For Suzan it all began when she was 20 or 21 years old, after she flunked out of college and couldn't go home because 1) Dad was too authoritative, and 2) Suzan was too rebellious and head strong to compromise (but not strong enough to make it alone). Dad was terribly narrow minded, – how could she help it? I'm talking about the summer of '67 for Christ Sake, when the whole goddamn mass media couldn't get enough of the hippies, LSD, pot, meth, etc. Most of us got through it alright, but Suzie came through being kind of lost – all she'd done for a year was conflict with the old man. And that seemed to become her identity. She didn't have much going on, but then she spent the next year supposedly on her way to becoming a model. "Reaching for the stars," as she put it. She obviously didn't have what it

takes: money, clothes, contacts, and a lot of aggressive fortitude. She might have done okay if either Mother or Dad were really behind her and supported her during this venture. But they were just half-assed going along with it, expecting her to work part-time, etc. Suzie couldn't or wouldn't do this, and as you know, strongly resented them not giving her more money. They gave, but not enough, just enough now and then, in a crisis. Suzie had to continually convince them that she was in crisis mode.

Sickness and misery then became her misfortune. It became her way of survival whether it was Grandma Tucker, old friends, Mark or me. That's the way she got along from one hand out to the next. When the parents started to react against her "non-schemes" I told her so many times to get a job and forget them. But every job she got was plain drudgery, and she made sure the parents knew it, so they would take some pity on their poor middle-class daughter working like one of the "underprivileged." She knew they had the money and never gave up trying to convince them to get up off it. Like a lot of her girlfriends or acquaintances were getting more from parents who had less."

I suppose she could have been successful if she had been clever enough to sing the right song. But she couldn't stop sticking up for a lot of controversial bullshit carried over from the flower child days – like the feel of long hair on men. If my parents are forced to come to her rescue and forced to put in more time and money, better spent two years ago then that would be poetic justice. Great, back to the old pattern – Suzan finds herself once again in a time of crisis in her young life. Only this time it will be a little more genuine than the last. And this sort of thing will get more and more genuine each time it happens until it is the only truth she knows. I'd like to think there is another way to go. But what is it?"

I haven't seen Suzan for 4 months, but she was going through all the same changes when she was here visiting me. She changed her mind every day. She talked about becoming a model, but didn't make any effort to contact any of Lisa's photographers and finally jamming off to New York on borrowed money. The point is, I don't think she is that much worse. Because you are her aunt and sensitive to her situation, and at the same time aware of her father and what the relationship might have been, you are very vulnerable to Suzie's particular syndrome. And she probably likes the idea (subconsciously perhaps) that you have become concerned. She certainly didn't learn it from her parents. I just want to try to make you see the situation more objectively – or maybe I'm saying it more 'my way.' I'll cop to it."

First of all, I love my sister very much and have seldom been cold or hard with her, but even if she did come back to California. I would lay down the same ultimatum I told you to make on her – she must get one of the many jobs available in three days, or whatever time you want to set or she must turn herself in for psychiatric care. At which time my father should be informed. I'd say about a week of this 'State' business ought to snap the 'dazed innocent' into a realistic adjustment to the 'outside world.' If she stays longer, maybe they'll teach her a trade."

"Spoken like a true Nazi, you ignorant fuck!" I screeched at Tod, metaphorically. "You misinformed fool, you have no idea how her illness works! Teach her a trade? Where's the love?"

Tod was always willing to give his sometimes-lucid opinion; his hazy, opioid induced opinion of what was happening with Suzie. But this letter is the spitting image of our old man talking at us. "All you have to do," Tod/Dad/Nazi says, "is tell them to get a job, and then encourage them with lines like:

"You can do it, Suzie. You have the strength to make it. You have character you've forgotten about. Your common sense has atrophied. When the day comes and you run out of people to make feel sorry for you, I mean, if you ever really got your back against the wall, you'd come around. I remember when Suzie had complete control of herself. I remember when she knew who she was and what she wanted. She has gotten into a bad habit of relying on someone else. That habit must be broken. The umbilical cord must be severed. She must be forced to forget about her family and do what's right for her survival. She must do as the government pleases."

That was the wall of taunts Suzie had been fighting against and now she finds it crushing against her back. She's got it coming and going.

There was nobody as close to Suzie as I. When we were growing up, being four years older than me, I looked up to her and admired her opinion the way young brothers sometimes do. I'd lay on her bed, as she sat at her desk, and we'd talk for hours about school and social activities. I'm here to tell you, that wall Suzan had against her back was made of steel, and she pounded and pounded on it until her fist turned bloody, and still nothing happened. She did not miraculously become the person we all wanted her to be. She became another person, a distant, far away stranger. Where did my big sister go?

As Mick Jagger of the *Rolling Stones* sang in their No. 1 hit song *Far Away Eyes* a decade later:

"I was driving home
Early Sunday morning through Bakersfield
Much to my surprise, there she was
Sitting in the corner
A little bleary, the worse from wear and tear

Was the girl with far away eyes."

I'm sure Mick saw my sister walking the streets Bakersfield that Sunday morning, and it made me feel lonely and afraid for her. *"I know you can all sympathize."*

Finally, Suzan's fifteen days of forced observation and psychiatric examinations at Suffolk County Mental Ward came to an end. In the opinion of Dr. Siebert, the consensus of all three psychiatrists involved in Suzan's treatment was that she was unresponsive, uncooperative, and hostile towards their treatment. A change of scenery from New York to California was exactly what might cause the patient to "snap out of it" – a technical term, no doubt.

The doctor told my aunt that Suzan, being a Californian, felt herself to be in a strange and hostile environment there in New York. The doctor felt that Suzie's antagonism might fade in her own environment. So go ahead, send her to her starving artist brother, who can barely feed himself.

Or as Uncle George wrote, the psychiatrist said, *"She'll need the care a parent would devote to a 16-year-old emerging from an adolescent crisis. Who is going to devote the time? That is the question. Sending her out to California on her own, whether it be to her brother's or to friends...might also be disastrous. And California has plenty of institutions should a relapse occur." Cold hearted bastards, these psychiatrists. "Why should you cry?" the doctor asked Betty. "She's not your responsibility. Let her go to California where her father pays taxes. They'll take care of her just as well as here."*

I can't tell if it was that psychiatrist, or George, or some other bastard talking, but Suzie getting the same care out in California as she got in New York ain't nothing to brag about – it was, oh boy, none! But for those in charge of Suzan's mental health, her care was dictated by the taxpayers, who were only interested in maintaining massive snake pits. And anti-psychotic medicine for paranoid schizophrenics were unforeseen in 1969; comeback in fifty years. But whether my parents were right or wrong regarding Suzan's care didn't matter in the end. They both died soon thereafter.

III

THIS IS TOD

11. Tod Says This is Art!

This is Tod here: In the summer of 1969, I received letters from both Betty and George stating they were doing everything they could to keep Suzan from going round the bend. Since I was the eldest son, they wanted me on board to write to our father on Suzie's behalf – a job I did not relish.

I immediately wrote to Suzan to find out what was going on. I hadn't seen her since my divorce in 1968, and she sounded perfectly sane to me. I wasn't writing this letter of concern to act as Suzie's "Cool Bro" that could tell her *like it is,* but I admit it sounds like it. It's no wonder she didn't answer it.

"Dear Suzan,

I'm writing this letter to you because I must find out what's really happening. I've heard all kinds of reports from different people, but I want you to write and tell me yourself. Why didn't you answer my last letter? I sent one to the Washington Hotel and I thought you were getting along OK. Now Betty tells me you need psychiatric help!

Are you going to go for that bullshit? Susie, what is the matter – I really can't figure it out. You know we all have our problems, and we all have dreams that dissolve, man, I ought to know that, but we can make it, can't we?

I mean, what kind of fucking trip are you on? Are you going to tell me you don't have the brains to get yourself together – I don't even want to hear that shit. Susie, Susie, Susie, when are you going to come down? I don't know who you think you are, or what you think life owes you, but I can lay a few facts on you:

You are not an actress or a model, or clothes designers, ballet dancer, paperback writer, or pop music star. In order to be any of these, you would have had to start early and practice every day for six years at least, and most of those who ever made it there did it like that –on their own – like nobody gave them a God damn thing! I hope I don't have to remind you that neither are you Snow White, Guinevere or an Indian Princess. You are a very lucky girl, though, to be free, white, and 23 years of living in America, the land of opportunity. You're nice looking, you speak well, and you could charm anybody into giving you a good job. Notice I said charm; that means not being defensive. Don't be afraid of it (working) after you do it and get into it for a week or so you'll find it's a snap. It will just be part of your routine and you will have lots of time left over to do whatever you want.

Susie, you must do this – please, baby, save yourself, it's the only way. You can't keep going around making people feel sorry for you. I mean, wow, now you've got some folks believing that you're such a pitiful mess you need psychiatric care. Come on, Susie, get yourself together and make them change their minds. Have some self-respect and others will respect you too.

You aren't going to accomplish anything by forcing daddy to take you over to Germany. Get a job and save some dough so you can go over there and visit them on your own. It can be done, and you can do it!

Write me immediately.

Love, Tod

P.S. If you do not want to stay in New York you can come back to California on the bus. It takes 3 days and costs $60 or $70. Did you ever hear The Beatles sing Get Back?

Get back Loretta..."

That sounds so harsh in hindsight, so patronizing, mean, condescending, authoritative, snotty, small minded and despicably vengeful against a person in dire need of psychiatric help.

I'm the guy that wrote that letter and it sounds ruthless. But I was trying to have her see that no matter how much at fault, or how many mistakes Dad made during Suzie's crucial adolescence, there was nothing we could do to change it. That's just the way it is. If I couldn't guilt shame Suzie out of insanity by calling her a pitiful mess then there was no hope for her. She'd be right back in the Snake Pit.

I was 27 years old at the time of my divorce. I was married to the most beautiful twenty-year-old model in the world, no kidding. Her name was Lisa. She moved on from me after a couple of years. After I took her to Hollywood and found her a gig on *Hee Haw.* I had an Honorable Discharge from the Navy, and a degree in Fine Arts from UCSB. My attempt to fit into the corporate world was dashed at the Decal Company: but you should have seen me in my suit, driving a brand-new beige Dodge Dart in 1966. The company took it back, and that was the only good thing about the job anyway. I hated it. I hated the corporate mentality, the dress code, the short hair, the work ethic, I hated everything about it.

I moved back to Santa Barbara from LA where I found Lisa going to UCSB, and it was only a few months before we were married in Ventura. Lisa was from nearby Ojai. In the photos of the wedding my whole family was there. My parents were there with Suzie, all looking happy and smiling. Suzie, looking sweet and demur – especially when compared to Lisa, who could barely whisper her name without showing her boobs. My brother Mark was there in his suit and tie looking like he might leap from the photograph and kick your ass; with his hair cut high and tight.

Lisa and I moved to Hollywood after our marriage to exploit her beauty any way we could and called 909 ½ Westbourne Ave. our home – two blocks from the famed Whiskey-a-Go-Go. At night, I got a job bartending at the Seventh Vail Lounge. Lisa joined a cult of Buddhist who believed you can "chant" for anything you want. She set up a prayer station in our living room where she knelt and chanted the following verse twice a day, for at least three hours each session. Starting at six in the morning, and again at night, it was most powerful when chanted as fast as humanly possible.

Nam Myoho Renge Kyo
Nam Myoho Renge Kyo
Nam Myoho Renge Kyo
Nam Myoho Renge Kyo

That was a crazy routine looking at it from the outside in, but I was working at night, so I missed the evening chant. But as it turned out, it worked. Lisa chanted herself into becoming Lisa Todd, (using my first name as her last) on the country and western TV comedy show *Hee Haw,* starring Buck Owens and Merle Haggard, a couple more country boys that made it big from Bakersfield. Their show ran for twenty years, or longer.

I always liked Mark's story about how stingy Lisa was. The three of us were sitting around the house on Westbourne, getting high and watching TV. Lisa was eating chocolate wafers from a pack of 26 cookies, lying in rows of two, in a long box revealing their chocolate goodness on the outside.

"Hey, Lisa, mind if I try a cookie?" he asked, motioning towards her stash.

"Yes, I would mind," she responded.

Thinking he hadn't heard her right he asked again, "No, I meant, may I have one of your cookies. They look so good."

"Well, you see Mark, these are my cookies. If you want some of these cookies, you can go to the store and get your own."

"But I'm just asking you for one. You've got a whole box full. I'd like to try one, please."

"Yes, but you see, these are my cookies. You can go to the store and get some if you want one like these," said Lisa.

"I'm going to have to buy a box of cookies in order to try one?"

"These are my cookies. Mine. You don't get any of these!" she responded in the softest, almost baby-like voice, "If you want some cookies, you can go to the store and buy some."

"All I wanted was one."

"No."

"The stupidest, most fucked up, selfish cunt, I'd ever met, in my entire life," my brother called her, not to her face. Just kind of "wow!" I feel sorry for you. You can really pick 'em. But think what that was like to live with, plus the chanting. It was humiliating to cater to her, especially when the director of the TV show would send me for coffee on the set. Sometimes I just wouldn't return.

But she was so seductive, so enticing in a Playboy kind of way, with great big tits, and streaming black hair. She was Amazonian in nature. Really, I loved it. But I determined soon enough that she was saving her cookies for Buck and Merle after the show and decided not to return with the hot coffee, ever.

I quit my job in 1969 so I could finish my painting masterpiece. It was a 4' X 4' multi-colored, yellow, orange, blue, green, purple, and red rendition named the *Fucking Flowers* – a brilliant depiction of two flowers exchanging pollen. This painting came a year before, "*Christ on the Cross with Dog Shit*," so you can get a feel for my timeline. The fact is, I never sold a painting to anybody in my entire life, so there was another dream down the toilet.

But in 1969 I was 27 years old and felt I was teetering on becoming a star myself. Not because there were people interested in my paintings, but because it was happening all around me. And what's the first thing a budding star should do when he feels that way? Go to Hawaii, of course, and paint. If it was good enough for Cezanne, it should be good enough for me. All I had to do was paint, and my fortune would be fantastic in the future.

So, when I went to Hawaii I decided to take my brother with me. You never knew when a young guy like that would come in handy. It didn't take long to find out.

12. Maui WowWee

The first night we arrived in Honolulu we made our way to the harbor to find a certain boat. I had this friend, Wally Zane, who knew this guy who owned a large cabin cruiser we were looking for. We could stay there for the first few nights, so said Wally. This is where you recognize the convenience of cell phones, but there was nothing like that, so you had to rely on fate. What were the odds we could stay on the boat without talking to somebody first?

It was fate that after scouring the backs of boats for names in the growing darkness, lugging our luggage, and after we had scanned the backside of the entire Hawaiian fleet of cabin cruisers docked in the harbor, that we found the one we're looking for: *The Candy Man*.

"Who the hell would name his boat the candy man?" said Tod.

"What's a candy man?" Mark asked.

"That's a man who deals drugs. I wouldn't advertise it," said Tod.

"Nah, a candy man' s a sweet guy, you know, a queer or something," said Mark.

"It's a guy who sells candy...aka drugs, you know..." said Tod.

"It's a guy that gives out candy to little kids…a fucking pervert."

"No, I'm pretty sure it's a drug dealer."

"Why doesn't he scribble that across his stern, 'I'm a Drug Dealer?'"

"Well, if he was here, we could ask him."

"What time is it? After midnight? Seems like everybody's sleeping. Think he'd mind if we snuck aboard and waited for him?" said Mark.

"Wally said he owned half interest in the boat. Let's go ahead and make ourselves comfortable. Doesn't seem like he's coming home tonight."

"I'm climbing up here to the captain's deck to grab some z's. I've got an uncomfortable feeling in my gut. It's not good." Mark said.

"I'm staying down here to sleep. I'll talk to him if he shows up. See you in the morning."

I no sooner had spread my things out, slid my shoes off, and stretched out on the seat cushion when I heard footsteps walking up the gangplank to an area immediately above my head on the main deck. If the person took one more step he would step on my face, so I shot up in front of him. You'd have thought I shot him at point blank range the way he screamed. And that wasn't the end of it either. It was followed by a stream of seaman's epithets so nasty it would make a sailor blush. This Captain was livid over our being on his boat uninvited.

I made the mistake of trying to smooth things over with the salty dog by mentioning my friend Wally Zane. The guy who gave me and my brother permission to sleep on board. This sent the sea captain into a conniption. He was choking on his words; they came so quickly, he didn't know which one to say first. He began to stutter, yelling incomprehensible phrases until I heard him call Wally a "Candyman." What the hell's going on with this candy bullshit?

Lights flickered on from portals around us, making it time to abandon ship. I called out to Mark to come down. He must have heard the old fart yelling. Finally, I see a long leg come over the railing, followed very slowly by a matching one to stand with it. He was moving the pace of a starfish. I thought he was trying to be funny, because the salty lieutenant was really barking for us to get the fuck off his boat, and the slow movement wasn't getting it.

But Mark didn't even look at the captain as he passed by. I helped him as best I could but I was pissed off about getting our sleeping arrangements interfered with. Mark stopped me in mid-sentence, eyes wide he says: "We gotta get to a toilet quick, or I'll shit my pants."

I didn't know it could be so easy to go from one crisis to another, so now I got to save my kid brother. "Oh, man, I gotta go bad."

I remembered the bathrooms outside the gate to the boats. "Use the shitter where the showers are, outside the gates. I'll bring our stuff," I said.

Mark managed to find another gear and zoomed ahead, happy to be reminded about the restrooms. They were separated by gender of course, and I could see him go briskly to the building on the left, then immediately walked gingerly over to the one on his right, just before he threw his hands in the air – a sure sign both bathrooms were locked, and the crisis moved on to the next level.

When I got to him, after struggling with the equipment to the gate, he was nervous and fidgety. He was both angry and uncomfortable with no end in sight –like his eyes were being pushed out the top of a rotten melon. Who knew what was going on below the belt in gastrologic terms, but he looked aching. He spotted a midnight diner on the corner, almost two blocks away, and decided to make a run for it,

I followed along dragging my old Navy bag, a suitcase, and my paint set. Mark was at the door of the *Jolly Rodger Cafe,* but the man he was talking to with the apron on wasn't letting him in. In fact, he was locking him out. By the time I came up to the locked glass door, Mark was exasperated and had decided to take care of the problem his own way.

"The sonofabitch wouldn't let me in," said Mark.

"You think it has anything to do with the way we look?" I said, "Or the time of night?"

We both had hair past our shoulders, along with other standard hippie gear, except patchouli oil, that was really for hippies, believing in unbounded love and complete diversity. I wore a colorful tie-die T-shirt, white bell-bottoms and thongs on my feet, and my brother had longer hair and was wearing moccasins.

"I don't give a fuck about the time. I've got to shit now, I can't wait. Haven't you ever had to shit so bad you can taste it. I see customers in there, and there's cars out here in their lot."

Mark took a good look around before he said, "Move towards the exit, I'm gonna use that car for cover."

The car he was talking about was a good choice. It was a blue Chrysler positioned to cut off the view from the *Jolly Rodger* customers and parked near a bush that cut off the view of him from the street. I was pretty sure he was planning on taking a shit in the *Jolly Rodger* parking lot. I couldn't help but ponder how big it would be, Mark being a commensurate carnivore. It was right then that I saw two gentlemen coming out of the restaurant without a care in the world. They must have closed the place down with their coffees or cocktails because they were jolly and chatting up a storm, trading jabs back and forth good naturedly. But why did they have to head towards the Chrysler? And why does there have to be two of them? Mark was doing his business on the passengers' side. That passenger is going to have a hell of a surprise.

The two men were talking as they approached the vehicle from the left rear. They'd made the natural division between driver and passenger approaching their respective doors, when suddenly Mark's head popped up from the passenger's side, buckling his pants with his hands. This stopped the gentleman passenger in his tracks. Mark didn't stop to chat. He cut a hasty retreat, hoping to get the fuck away from the burden of explaining what he had left behind.

Neither of us looked at the passenger, but we could hear him. He obviously was pained by his surprise. He approached his side with caution. Dumbfounded, at first, all he could think to scream at us was, "Animal!"

13. The Pill Box

He was right about one thing. We lived like animals. That was both good and bad. The bad parts included our reception from the locals. During our short walk from the airport to the bus stop we were greeted by Hawaiian people shouting from passing cars, "Get a haircut," "Fucking hippie," "Hippies go home." That's three taunts while walking to the bus stop.

But the good far outweighed the bad by the government providing the cement pill box to live in on Makena Beach, on the island of Maui. The beach had the best body surfing on earth, and the most magical sunsets in heaven. It was located down a long dirt road, thirteen miles from the nearest mailbox at the general store in Kihei.

It was a time and place that can never be gone back to, because it's just not there anymore. The island paradise Mark and I chose to live in as Americans, on U.S. property for free, got wiped out by entrepreneurs. My brother and I were the only ones to enjoy it during the summer of '69. That's where we chose to be and we didn't give much thought to Suzie's adventure, traveling across the United States to be a model in New York City. All three of us kids were living on our own. There was nothing to it.

Makena Beach was replaced by the Hawaiians. They built condos, golf courses, and Hotels fit for the Prince of Siam. They did this to themselves so they could work for the big resort corporations in their future – that tells you their foresight went no further than the all-mighty dollar.

They steamrolled resorts to the edge of the island of Maui and used it as a cutting board to build more hotels like the Maui Prince, constructed directly behind Makena Beach, where the ocean crashes and claps like lightning over the white sand. Sitting beyond the reach of those thunderous waves was the pill box – a sleek, low to the ground, cement refuge, camouflaged, dark and cool within, with a foot thick cement top to lay your gear out and feel secure.

A pill box is a concrete artillery defensive unit, 12 feet square, established after the Japanese attacked Pearl Harbor in 1941. It's as close to war as you want to get. Made of cement and rebar, it had steps dug in back for an entrance. These "dug-in guard post" at the beach, could hold a squad of men under its foot-thick cement roof that protected the defenders from small arms and grenades. Although I can't imagine anyone on the southwest corner of the island staying there if Maui was being attacked by sea.

From this view, under the cement roof of the pillbox, it seemed like you could see straight to Japan with binoculars (if you were really high). There are no other islands obstructing the view. I wondered what it was like for the soldiers never to see the Imperial Navy advancing toward the island over four years of war. Disappointing? The pillboxes were never put to the test. Lucky soldiers.

The point is it was there for our shelter, kind of like a hotel that wasn't going to blow away in the wind. Arnold Schwarzenegger made his Olympian camp on Venice Beach in '69, and we made ours on Makena. The difference was, there was nobody else on our beach, except the occasionally struggling wanderer who wants to eat dinner. Your dinner. Or a herpetologist studying lizards. Being on the leeward side of the island made it hot and dry – as opposed to lush and wet.

Makena Beach was on the other side of the island from Joe's Banana Patch. That was the local hippie hangout where they had busty women with tattoos on their foreheads, cooking meals gleaned from the root plants in the area and slept in wooded tree forts. Talk about crazy, these gals were really friendly though.

Maui is known for its Eden of exotic green plants and jungle trees, along with scented blooms and lush juicy fruits – that's all on the other side of the island from Makena. The natural foliage in the southwest side, around Makena, is scrub brush and long-thorn Kiawe trees. I'm talking about thorns the size of your fist - four inches across your palm. They grow in dense thickets, crowding out coastal plants that render large areas of the forest impassable, preventing beach access. Stepping on one of those thorns could prove to be amputation time. But they're not hard to miss, and if that was what kept tourists away, it was worth it.

The first thing I did when we hit Maui was buy a 1950 Mercury Coupe from an ex-Marine headed to Micronesia. It was a cool car, still had its side skirts intact. Leroy, the vehicle's seller, had been the local pot dealer and turned us on to ganja weed from Vietnam. I bought some and saw him around a couple of times. Once we went over to his house to enjoy his company and shoot the shit. That's when we found out his personality could change. He could get downright nasty.

He started telling us stories about herding Viet Cong prisoners into helicopters, taking them up about a thousand feet and kicking them out one by one. If they didn't give the right answers to their questions they were asked - out, they go.

It didn't bother me if the story was true or not, but the way it was told seemed like braggadocio that said, "Look at me, I'm bad." But when he told us how he cut off their ears with his bayonet, it made me sick; but for Mark, Leroy lost all credibility. I began to see him as Leroy as he really was — a killer. But Mark didn't have any empathy for that.

I suggested we leave. But Mark whispered for me to hold back a bit as we were walking to the car. I watched him circle back and sneak around the outside of the house which opened into Leroy's back yard.

There was Leroy, sitting on his deck in a lounge chair with his back to Mark, taking in the sun.

Two feet behind Leroy's chair was his cherished Marine bayonet. The one he liked to carry around stuck in front of his pants, intimidating people. That same bayonet was hanging in its sheath from the railing of the porch, right behind Leroy's head.

Why would Mark want to steal the one prized possession of a known killer, a Vietnam Vet, freshly back to planet earth? Leroy had a girlfriend lurking somewhere inside the house, probably watching Mark. But it didn't bother him that Leroy could see, hear, or perhaps even feel his presence, 24 inches away from his head. I witnessed Mark approaching the knife like a cat, then undoing the knot that held the sheath, and last, slipping away like an Arabian Knight.

I don't know how many Viet Cong Leroy killed with that battle knife, but I feared it was plenty. I asked Mark, "Why'd you steal a Marine's bayonet from right under his nose?" And he said, "Because... I didn't believe a word he said about torturing the Viet Cong...and I always wanted one of these."

14. Tod Saves Mark in High School

We got high and drove all over the island of Maui several times, from Lahaina across to Hana, before settling outside Kihei (for post office purposes) and making our home on Makena Beach.

There was no civilization south of Kihei. It was like a desert island. There was not a single building on the southwest side of the island. It was like the world got turned off once you reached Kihei in 1969, and no further services were provided. There were barely any services provided before you reached Kihei, anyway.

The land that came before Kihei had water and was made up of rolling pineapple fields. This was back when Kihei *was* the little general store at the end of the electrical line, in the middle of nowhere. It was little, as in 18' X 20', with no other buildings around it, but big enough to have air conditioning. It sold cold soda and ran the U.S. Postal Delivery System for the area. There might be a crowd of two or three people standing outside in their bathing suits and sandals conversing, waiting to pick up packages or get some news from stateside. Or there could be nobody.

This postal delivery allowed us to receive a package from Wally – the original *Candyman* – filled with pleasantries, such as a couple of tabs of LSD. That drug proved to get us high, then higher, until Mark started to think about his girlfriend from high school and it was "Katie, bar the door" after that. He started crying his eyes out, like he was having a psychedelic freakout. He'd cry, gulp for a breath, and start laughing. It's funny, those hallucinogens. LSD can reach out and twist your mind, so the drugs in control and your mind just follows along.

We arrived in April and by May had settled into Makena Beach for the rest of our lives. Why would we want to be anywhere else? Our struggle to survive was over. We were living at the highest stage in societal history, where man has time to be creative because he doesn't have to pay the rent, or taxes, or insurance, or damn near anything else.

I remember lying on our bunks, which consisted of an air mattress laying on a mat; and a blanket, and pillows, on top of the concrete pillbox, or sometimes in the sand – ruminating over our blessings while staring at *Orion's Belt* and not caring what happened in the outside world.

You may be wondering, how we'd got those air mattresses, blankets, pillows, the huge trash can for water, the big pot and fry pan, forks, plates, and snorkeling gear. Well, I stole them. Not to make you think we were a couple of thieves roaming the countryside. I've been silent on this subject and stealing got me in a lot of trouble later, that included jail time, before I learned my lesson. But I clearly had no respect for the large CBX Corporation's profit margin. It was just a remarkable store that carried everything we needed.

So I drove into their parking lot in Wailuku in my 1950 Mercury and told Mark to wait in the car. "I'll be back." When I did, my cart was full of practical items for survival. I walked into the store, loaded up my cart, and walked out. Thank you CBX.

The beauty of CBX is that it has everything, including large canvases to paint on, and I had the paint. I started my art project with the most ubiquitous and conventional theme that surrounded our daily lives and demanded I paint "Sunset on Makena Beach." This quickly turned into a kaleidoscopic depiction of the ocean and mountains under a sea of fire. The subject of the sun setting prayed for me to capture its golden image every evening.

It was a four-hour event that's worth the wait. It comes around dusk, trying to outdo what it did the night before. Like a hail of speeding comets bursting through the sky. What I tried to recreate were the colors generated by the sun setting below the horizon. That's when the show started up. We'd sit out on the rocks so there were no obstructions in our view and count down the seconds until the last bit of the sun's yellow dipped behind the ocean and disappeared.

I also tried to paint a portrait of Mark. Never has an art object carried as much hate and love as that portrait represented. It expressed the confrontational relationship between the two of us. The painting got torn up and ripped, then put back together, fixed, at least twice over the years. It was a stylized depiction of Mark from his chest up, with the island fauna stirring behind him. It was a glamourized shot; either that, or my brother looked like Jim Morrison with those brown curls draped down over his shoulders.

He was an okay-looking guy, I'll give him that, and the Makena Beach portrait captured the moment he started his journey as a budding superstar – a lot like Suzie going to New York. Where Mark was going was anybody's guess. Perhaps to prison. But he was on the path, even if he didn't know it. He was still young and being nine years his elder put me in the position of trying to guide him in the right direction. Hell, he wouldn't have graduated from high school if it wasn't for me.

I came home once, while Mark was taking a civil law class in high school summer school while he also worked the graveyard shift at Hank Washburn's Richfield gas station. He went to class from work every morning between 8:00 a.m. and noon. He had a paper due on a book written by J. Edgar Hoover called *The Masters of Deceit.* It was standard fare for a senior in high school and had to be done to get a grade in the class so he could graduate. He had eight weeks, but he refused to read the book. In fact, on the night before the report was due, he had the night off at the gas station and chose to go to the drive-in with his girlfriend rather than bother with the one report that would hang up his graduation.

I had read the book in college, so I was aware of its phobic anti-communist message. Sensing Mark was headed for a head-on collision with Mr. Hoover, I spent a couple of hours writing a thoughtful review of his book. Mark then took the report with him to class the next morning, copied it into his own handwriting and handed it in on time.

Mr. Smith, Mark's instructor in the class, would sit behind Mark and Darryl Chapman, the other night-time worker when they watched films in class of Fidel Castro, having people dig their graves before they were shot into them. As the two students began to doze off because they were sitting in the darkness of the theater, Mr. Smith would flick their earlobes from behind with his finger to ensure their attention towards the screen.

You'd think an instructor like that would be a real hard ass, keeping them awake after they had worked the nightshift in a gas station and then made to watch political dogma movies while sitting in a darkened theater.

But on the last day of class, on the last day of summer school, Mr. Smith pulled Mark and Darryl aside to personally give them their papers back. They were both marked with great big red A's. He told them they got the only A's in the class because he knew they worked all night at different gas stations and that he appreciated their effort in his class. The only two A's in a class of 100 students.

Darryl showed Mark his paper which read: "Dear Mr. Smith, As you know, I've been working nights at the gas station and didn't have the time to read Masters of Deceit. I'm sorry."

I always liked that story because I never had anything like that happen to me. I never got held out as special. The way I saw it, my critique of the book was so powerful that Mr. Smith had to find a way of giving Mark the A — and decided to give one to Darryl also. So I helped them both graduate.

I always wished Mark had stuck with football. I taught him everything he knows about that too. I had him running option plays at quarterback when he was eight years old. He was ambidextrous and could make the throws rolling out right or left. Then I left for the Navy, then for college, and before I knew it I was writing his high school paper.

I suppose that was another benefit of being an elite athlete in high school. The problem was his grades, and that's why he went to Boise State. He wasn't dumb, but he might have gone because it was the only place he could go with his friend Bruce Jones. Whatever the case, that's where Mark and Bruce went to raise hell. They wanted to do everything together. That is until Mark got his knee blown out, and there went another opportunity down the drain.

Now he was on Makena Beach with me. I'm painting his portrait as he's lying on his mat in the sand, half covered in shade from the Kiawe Tree.

"You know, I feel like reading something," he said.

"Yeah, that's what you ought to do," I said.

"But I can't think of anything I want to read; I mean a good book. Maybe something about cowboys, something American."

"There's always Louis Lamour."

"Yeah, but I'm talking about something more *intellectual.* Something everybody raves about. You know...something about fighting, and love; ...and adventure, of course ...as for meaning? I don't even know what that means. The only book I read in high school was *Studs Lonigan,* the story of a young man who got the shit kicked out of him then later died of pneumonia."

"I read one other book during study hall called *The Yearling,* by Pearl S. Buck. It's the story of a hungry little boy that finds the yearling deer, so precious, and raises it with great things to eat out on the farm, including warm cornbread with honey. But when hard times come, the little boy has to grow up fast. It turns out he had to shoot the deer." Mark said.

"You never read any other books?"

"Doesn't mean I can't read. I just never found anything interesting – besides biographies of famous athletes like Floyd Patterson, Eddie Mathews, or Babe Ruth ...which I read in junior high. Plus Lou Gehrig and Hank Arron, Willy Mays. But nothing interests me lately."

"You don't want that bourgeois bullshit their teaching in college," I said, "If you don't need it, you don't want it."

"What I want is a good book."

"Next time we go into town we'll go to the library."

"Really, what do they have in there?" Mark said sarcastically.

"No, really, you can skim through the titles. Hey, I know one you'd like," I said.

"I'm all ears."

"It's a story about where you live."

"What do you mean?"

"Bakersfield, where you were born and raised. In the south-central San Joaquin Valley in California, the destination of every sod busting farmer from Oklahoma during the depression, in the dust bowl days. You remember Mom talking about Oakie's living under the bridge. Bruce's parents were part of that movement."

"What book are you talking about?"

"The author's John Steinbeck, from Salinas. He wrote *Cannery Row* and my favorite, *Of Mice or Men."*

"What's it called?"

"*The Grapes of Wrath*."

"Cool name. What's it mean?"

"Well, you'll have to read it to find out."

We went by the library and damned if they didn't have the hard-back copy of *Grapes of Wrath* – a three-inch thick book, that changed his life. It took him most of the summer to read the damn thing. He let the story grow with him, cradled it in his arms and made himself comfortable with the characters.

Mark was in no rush. He read it between fighting the twelve-foot waves for the body surf contest, which was never to be. He'd been slightly aware there was a migration from Oklahoma in the 1930's and took to heart the stories of condemnation they suffered as second-class citizens. It seemed peculiar to read the Oakie's weren't welcome in Bakersfield. It seemed the whole town of Bakersfield was made up of Oakie's.

It was the first time he heard true stories told in an imaginative way, written with a twist of sympathetic humor. But mainly he learned *Grapes of Wrath* was used for social commentary, which was why it was a great book. In the end, he learned the meaning of the title.

It wasn't like I was an English major or something, but I'd been through a rigorous course of study at the university and was alive with the arts. I could carry on a conversation. If you were from Bakersfield, you had a chip on your shoulder about the arts, somebody may think you're gay, and you'd get beat up.

You weren't supposed to know anything about them because you were the river rats that needed to be exterminated – no shit. So you'd have to go heavy on the, "I'll kick your ass, motherfucker!" persona and the whole discussion about the arts would come to a predictable end.

15. Tod Plays Football

I was born in Santa Barbara, so I didn't fit into that Bakersfield mold. My father was an excellent artist from Santa Barbara and that was a mecca for retired artist. But I was brought to Bakersfield from Oakland after the war in 1948 when I was seven years old. But as I got older, I shied away from the theater for a chance to make the football team. I wasn't like Mark. I didn't have the coaches following my play, I wasn't a shoo-in to make the team. Bakersfield High was the rat's ass when it came to schools in southern California. It had a student body of over 5,000. If you want to get lost, go to BHS your freshmen year.

There were seven teams I could have played on. There were the Drillers, the mighty, mighty, Drillers; and the A-reserve team or Junior Varsity. There were the Sanddabs, and their B-reserve team; then there were the Bits, and their C-reserve team, and the D-team, reserved for the smallest freshmen. The D-team didn't have a name, and nobody knew anybody that played on the team, but they must have gotten kudos from somewhere. Football meant everything in high school, and there were no less than a hundred players trying out per team.

That's why I felt sorry for all the young men when Mark started his sophomore year, and the school system took the drastic measure of cutting sports funding. That meant all the teams were eliminated but one, the mighty, mighty Drillers.

As if it wasn't hard enough to play football at BHS. The teams before Mark's sophomore year were divided according to age and weight and ideally, if you were C-class as a freshman, you'd be A-class as a senior. For me, that formula didn't work out. I was 5 feet, 10 inches my senior year but only weighed 145 pounds, which was way too light to play center for BHS, which was the only position I knew. But because I entered elementary school a year early, and was sixteen years old, instead of seventeen years old going into my senior year, I remained in B-class and was made captain of my Sanddab football team.

The Sanddabs always played before the Driller games, and I was the highlight at "center" position. I even got a trophy on banquet night for being "The Most Enthusiastic" player on the team –, the person players looked to for support. I got a lot of fine accolades; they just happened to be on a B-level. It wasn't like the real cheerleaders knew my name, but captain of the team was nothing to sneeze about.

That's why I spent so much time working with Mark in the backyard, teaching him the holes in the line, or how to grip a football like a quarterback, with either hand. He was a born footballer, loved pounding his head against the wall in his sleep as a little kid. He nearly tore his crib apart. That's why getting his knee blown out was such a bummer, but I think his interest in football was waning.

I was more into cars. That was because my real grandfather, Adolph Kraft owned a small lot in L.A. next to his auto-repair shop. He had an eye for cool cars. Besides that, I was his first grandchild, and for my sixteenth birthday he gave me a 1953 Bel Air Sport Coupe and when I graduated from high school, he gave me a 1956 Bel Air Sport Coup. So I was a Chevy man, which was perfectly cool in the late fifties in Southern California.

My best friend Don Caetano built a roadster, cut low from a '32 Coupe. It spun heads when it roared down Chester Avenue. Out of high school, we both joined the service, he was in the army, me in the Navy, just like my dad and his brother Bob did before the War. After our service, we roomed together in Isla Vista at UCSB.

What caught a lot of people off guard about Don, and how smart he was. He proved it by getting his Philosophical Doctorate in Sociology, not bad for a boy from Bakersfield. You'd have to look far and wide for anybody from Bakersfield that earned their PhD. He was an inspiration to all of us, although he didn't give a fuck. But his achievement became my measurement for success, and I had plans that excelled far beyond Don's.

"Hey Tod, I see Don got his PhD. in sociology, what have you been doing besides getting married and divorced?"

"That's a full-time job." I would answer.

16. Sand Skunks Go Home

One day Mark and I decided to take the LSD Wally sent us. It's the type of event you want to prepare for. You never know what to prepare for, but it's always best to prepare for a good time. A time of revelations and getting to know yourself for the first time. You can watch your friends in space and listen to yellow flowers grow from dirt, as you capture moments and rejuvenate and find peace in namaste.

But an acid trip can fool you, and that's what is scary about it. That your mind led you into a trap where you felt secure, in the most vulnerable position of your life, and the guillotine drops and don't be surprised if it misses your head and cuts off your ball sack. Surprise! Your mind has betrayed you. But you won't know that, as the guillotine goes up again, and chop, chop, chop.

It was a fine day to take acid though. If you were a torpedo skimming across the Pacific Ocean from Japan and aimed straight for the pillbox on Makena Beach in 1969, you'd be in for a rude awakening – because the pillbox was inhabited by two American Sand Skunks, or ASS.

You'd know why they called themselves sand skunks as soon as you arrived. The moment you got a whiff of their under-arm. The term "sand skunk" was derived from and created on the shores of Makena Beach, where Tod and Mark got their 1950 Mercury stuck in the sand.

They weren't aware that meant it was stuck in a never-ending trap of sand. That this trap could replace the volume of sand Tod and Mark removed from around the tires, with more sand sliding down into the hole it was dug from. This caused the boys to dig an even bigger hole. It was a trap for idiots. Never had two American boys made a stupider mistake then when they realized this one, after three days of digging.

No, no... their stupidest mistake was driving the car out on the sand in the first place, while high on acid.

The true lesson learned from this sinking car scenario was not only had we lowered the tail end of the car three feet deeper into the pit, but there was no way to get the car out of the pit. We also managed to generate a smell from our sweaty armpits after five days that was so toxic to smell, so ghastly appalling, that we synergistically created and branded our *Keep the Fuck Away* stench, as part of our Sand Skunk Collection, not to be duplicated anywhere.

It was the sand and sweat mixed with the flesh of despair and disappointment, flecked with anger, metal and tires. We couldn't believe how bad we smelled. It was like aliens infected us. We laughed and guffawed about being sand skunks, with the ability to spray a long and odiferous scent from our armpits that could peel the nose hair off your nostrils. We kept on digging until it got so desperately hopeless that we quit.

On the seventh day, our attempt to build a new coastal highway from the rear end of the Mercury to the dirt road had failed horribly. But we were saved by a man in a jeep that had a winch – a native Hawaiian with a bad back. "Doc said no lifting," said the Hawaiian. Who could blame him? Being caught under the Mercury with either one of us would be torture, near fatal.

Can you believe a native Hawaiian showed up with a winch mounted on the front of his four-wheel drive jeep, out of the blue. It was like we called triple A and asked for a tow truck.

It was going into August and Mark finished his book, and I finished painting two canvases. We were restless to get back. To what? What for? I don't know. There was no one waiting to buy my paintings. The thrill of living like Robinson Crusoe was gone after 90 days, replaced by the yearning for female companionship. I sure wasn't going to get any female attention smelling like a sand skunk.

The island life wasn't working for me. This may sound trite, but if I wanted to see a play, I like the idea of being able to drive to L.A. and see one, which is impossible from Makena Beach. Living on an island is like standing on the corner of

Time Square watching the girls walk by but being restrained from saying hello. If I stayed on the corner of this island the whole world could walk by and I would lose my chance at giving the American Dream a try.

I know, I'm already living the American dream, but what about my sister? She deserves to give it a try too. But will she? Does she have a chance? And if not, whose fault is it? Should she file a lawsuit against her parents for being born? Have you heard of that? You could put it on the docket behind Mark's lawsuit for practicing cosmetology without a license.

17. Tod Plays His Hand

I couldn't have been more wrong about coming home. It was a bust. There was still no love. Hollywood was just a room off Laurel Canyon where I had lost Lisa. I was back in Los Angeles, then all the way back to Bakersfield. A heck of a place to call home in 1969.

That's when I received Aunt Betty's letter, five days after Neil Armstrong landed on the moon, outlining the journey Suzan had taken to the Suffolk County Mental Ward. Was it the fault of my parents, more specifically, my father, who abandoned Suzie in her time of need? As Betty wrote in the opening paragraph of her letter, "Your father is either the most stupid man in the world or the most selfish, or both, because he refuses to face up to the problem." The "problem" being Suzie.

Man, that was a huge issue when we got back from Hawaii. Did Dad abandon Suzie – leaving her in outer space? Who was right and who was wrong? Did my sister not deserve to be helped because she was 23 years old? Is there a time limit on love? When is not helping your mentally ill child acceptable? She had 22 years of sanity before she turned 23, how'd that happen?

Let's face it, the insanity came from my parents, Jack and Mary Cornwall. Suzie inherited her schizophrenia, although be careful who you say that to. But if your parent or close relative has schizophrenia, like an uncle or an aunt, you have a 1 in 10 chance of developing the disorder. Without the genetic link, your chances are 1 in 100 of developing the disorder.

Call it what you will, but schizophrenia is a complex genetic disorder that runs in the family. At the time, unfortunately, we didn't have access to this kind of information and were still operating in the dark ages in psychiatric medicine as recently as 1969.

Below is the letter I sent in response to Betty's letter which portends a certain pragmaticism towards life. Suzan has got to save her own ass, because if it's left to me, I can't do anything for her. Like Mom said, "No one can lead your life for you!" I've already heard how the letter I wrote to her is bombastic and not caring about the status of Suzie's true mental health. Well, to that I say...

"It's all a bunch of bickering."

Here is my response, which Mark, although amiable as a young man, became very despotic as he got older, and insisted he add in his bracketed edits for the purpose of publishing this book.

Sept. 4, 1969

"Dear Betty,

"Everybody has their character flaws, weaknesses, and personal shortcomings to cope with. Some have enormous traumas and serious personality deficiencies, but, believe me, drugs do not cause these afflictions. These things might lead a person to drug abuse which will in turn compound one's problems. Too many kids put themselves on! And a lot of sympathetic, but inexperienced, and innocent people go for their story when kids blame all their problems on an LSD trip, or meth, or marijuana. [That's ridiculous!].

I know how much Suzan has taken and the amount of pot she smoked. She may have taken a few methedrine pills, but really? Don't let yourself get sucked into believing that her light experience with all these drugs could possibly have played any more than a very minor part of putting her "where she's at" right now. [How do you know that? You haven't seen her for a year.] The minor part I refer to is, the fact my parents had such a fear, and absolute ignorance (along with a lot of people like them) that they completely overreacted to Suzan's experimentation, alienating themselves from her that much more. [True that!]

Anybody tells you that a brush with drugs ruined their life is feeding you shit (if you'll pardon the expression) and you better tell them where to get off. [What?...there's more!!]

Drug abuse is a reality – just like alcoholism, but this is going into a new form of prohibition, right now, because our law makers, or keepers won't recognize that drugs, and marijuana especially, are here to stay. They are now a deeply imbedded part of our culture. Granted – Suzan is insecure and unstable due to all the things I just hashed out and she can't "hold her mud" [a little hippie vernacular for you]. I told her that before and suggested that she lay off so she wouldn't get confused about what drugs do. She could keep it separate from life's own bum trip. No sense going on with this topic – I'm sure you get my point, Suzan's drug scene is minute.

Now, let's look at where "we" are at the present: [Oh, boy, listen up!] Suzan has seen her chances for a modeling career go down the drain. The fact is, she's too old now to break in – it's too bad, it's mean, it's terrible, and my parents are partly to blame – she can blame it all on them if she wants to, but if she can accept this as her reality, great. She has taken a big step in the right direction. [But she didn't accept this.] If she can't, then she is still in trouble. But, sending her to Germany isn't going to do her any good unless there's a total understanding, or the other end [our parents?] are going to have to accept the responsibility for the "sick kid." And to tell you the truth, I don't think you or we could convince them that such was the case."

In this tit for tat exchange, on September 9, 1969, Betty wrote Tod back with the news that Suzie had voluntarily committed herself to Suffolk County Mental Hospital. She told the psychiatrist she was voluntarily signing herself into the hospital for fifteen days because "my aunt practices witchcraft."

So much for any more home cooking at the Scullin's. In the end, Betty offered me this observation as a good-bye:

"I don't know what you want to do from now on in, but your-onward-and-upward-Suzie-you-can-do-it-theory will have to join Jack's fatuous "the gold will show through sooner or later – just work" theory."

IV

SUZIE'S IN THE HOUSE

18. Suzan A. Cornwall Talking

Let me tell you something, Daddy was pulling on the wrong end of morality. I was 23 years old and had been abandoned in an insane asylum, as my parents made their new home in Berchtesgaden, Germany. I was left alone in the mental ward to stew over my parents' love for their daughter. Is there a time limit set by the State, after which the parent has the legal right to disown their child?

Yes, and it's 18 years old. But what was the moral obligation for Jack and Mary, the two "loving" Headmasters of Berchtesgaden's American Elementary School? Should they have done something, anything at all? I'm sure they would have, if they cared. But my father showed nothing but indifference. It would have cost him money, and he was staunchly committed to not giving a dime. Jack had no spare change in his pocket, even for his daughter. I saw him once pull his hand out of his pocket filled with nickels, dimes and quarters and literally say to the needy, "No spare change."

I think the reason Daddy didn't care what happened to me was that he looked at me as his enemy. He never loved me from the start. He thought my purpose since birth was to take his money. I was the one person who could see behind the curtain and knew he was a fraud. That he was acting like the loving father, always available for other children, but never his own. Except for discipline, he was always there for that. He put all his energy into teaching eighth grade and had none to spare for his own kids at home. Daddy tolerated us if we did exactly what he said. But when we strayed, or desired something else, he would show us the same tolerance Hitler showed the Jews. If he said, be home at 11:00, don't be a minute late, or you may have committed a life altering offense. Breaking a rule was an offense against Jack's authority, and nobody in his household was allowed to challenge his power. He was never physically abusive to me, but somehow his mental brutishness always made me feel like I was getting the brunt end of a power play by my father.

"You'll have no dates, no going to the library, or to the movies with your friends, you'll come straight home from school and study, no after school events or Lambda Kai Tri-Hi-Y. You'll come home and clean the house, wash and iron our clothes, and these shoes you're wearing, God-damn "Capizios" (he starts throwing my Capizios from the shelf of my closet down on the floor) "you're not getting another pair of these God-damn shoes, do you even know how much they cost?"

And there you have it. For Daddy, everything had a price tag.

He didn't care what happened to me at age 23 because he had no financial obligation to me under State or Federal law. My request for financial aid from him came from outside the law, under the morality clause found in society's unprinted parenting rules and family doctrines. Jack wasn't doing anything illegal by depriving me of money, it was more like he was filing for an offshore corporation to save money on taxes. He even wrote me out of his will, like I was chattel that never existed.

I saw through his façade when I was 16 years old. His façade of being a family man, happily raising three children, while creating a lucrative family business and building character amongst the young Yokuts Club members. Now came the final award for achieving his pre-eminent position in education as a high school counselor, with his wife, Mary, who taught first through fourth grade. They were rewarded the honor of Headmaster and Assistant, teaching the children in an American school located in Germany. They were the only two teachers on site, located on the outskirts of this tiny village high in the Bavarian Alps. "*To the victor go the spoils.*" My Daddy won the war as a Naval mail-clerk in San Francisco.

I wanted to blow that fucking place up. I never wanted to hurt anybody though, and the Alps sounded so cute with its little churches in the mountains. But I never got any further than New York City with my modeling career, and now I'm stuck in Suffolk County Mental Hospital. I'd rather be with the fluttering butterflies, painting the sky orange with their black framed wings.

Schizophrenic is a funny word. It means nuttier than a scoop of Skippy Super Chunk. Cute, huh? I can say that because I'm schizophrenic. What is schizophrenic? It means every time you hear the word "schizophrenic," you should replace it with the word "fractured," like a mirror. That's where schizophrenics dwell. They're living their fractured lives in the black fissures of a broken society. The schizophrenics fell into cracks because there's no way to reconcile their delusions of life with the real world. For the schizoids, it is all one big mistake.

Fractured means living in that dark space between reality and illusion. When nobody understands your illusion, it becomes a delusion, and that's bad. Believe me, it's in those fractured cracks we live, trying to make sense of it all. It tends to make you mad and resentful when people think you're crazy just because you don't share the same *weltanschauung,* or world outlook.

I like the term *fractured* because it doesn't carry the implication of something gone crazy, like schizophrenia. Fractured is a gender-neutral term, like leg. My leg just gets fractured. It implies there were times before when I had something to break, and now I'm left *fractured.*

Anyway, the result is the same. I'm locked up. So, you can call me a paranoid schizophrenic, but I wish you would change it to a "fractured fissure." As opposed to the Greek *schizo*, which means split, and *phrene* meaning mind. *Fractured* means 'to live', and *fissure* means 'in a crack'.

Yes, I'm one of "those people". There's no place for us to fit in, except the insane asylum. It seems bizarre that society has built huge hospitals to house us all together. We have nothing in common. We're all delusional, doing the Thorazine shuffle to the game room in a daze. But what can you do when there's no family? There's no one to guide the fractured fissure toward security.

When the family is the cause of the fracture, what's the State going to do about it? What's the implied social contract with a citizen when it becomes necessary to house them? You don't want your kid turning your aunt and uncle in for witchcraft, do you?

Why did I call the police about the witchcraft business at the Scullin's? Because I was sick of it and they had hodgepodge written on their souls – as illustrated by Betty Wont in *The Satanic Bible*. But that's a bunch of gobbledygook and poppycock. The real reason I called the police was because my father was not responding to me.

He knew I was broke. He knew I was sleeping in Central Park. He knew I was thousands of miles from home with no transportation, few clothes, and unable to work. He knew all about this dreadful situation and refused to help me.

To add insult to injury, Daddy sent me fifty dollars to add to my "nest egg." What nest egg? I'm out here with nothing to my name, and my father refused to help because it would have killed him to send a thousand dollars. "Just be throwing good money after bad," I can hear him say.

I know he could afford it because he was a wealthy man. He was notorious for his penny-pinching ways, never giving an inch. But as soon as Mark left for college and our parents were empty nesters, Daddy went out and paid cash for a brand new 1969 Pontiac GTO. Where'd you get the money, Daddy?

19. Yokuts Ruled the Plunge

I'm not a bad person. I wasn't asking for money just to prove my father was a bastard. Or was I? It would have been nice to have a sign he loved me. My parents were moving to Europe forever, for Christ's sake, there was no more "Cornwall family home" to go back to in the States.

What was Mother talking about when she said I should clean my room because Aunt Betty's house is not my home. Where the hell was my home, Mother? The tribe's disbanded and nobody told me. At any rate, I called the police on *him,* my father, not my aunt, so the authorities could see how horribly I was being treated. It was all I could do. Well, the authorities didn't care about that one iota.

I was raised to think I had some privilege for being brought into the world. At a minimum I thought I had a family to rely on. Not all of us can be great or strong from the start. I was medium. I wasn't the brightest or most popular girl in class. I had a droopy eye that required I wear glasses, so I wasn't the cutest either. But I was there, on the playground playing four square and hopscotch, jumping rope, maybe secretary of the class. Not a straight A student, except I always got an A in 'Conduct.' Hear that, Daddy, always an A in conduct.

I don't think I came into my own until I turned sixteen. I became a camp counselor at Yokuts Club for my parents, and it was like earning money for nothing. They were just giving it to me. I was the counselor of my own tribe of Yokuts, the nine and ten-year-old Apache, who were all adorable. And the greatest thing about Yokuts was our swimming program. Bakersfield got toasty during the summer, to say the least, and the Yokuts taught swimming lessons at the Union Avenue Plunge. We accessed the pool before it opened to the public, every morning at 9:30.

It took three station wagons and the Yokuts Club bus to shuffle the whole crew back and forth between the pool and Jastro Park, our shady home base. I drove the brown station wagon with three on the column to pick up the youngsters at home, starting at eight, and dropped them off at their home after arts and crafts in late afternoon.

It made me feel good to have a grown-up job. I felt good about being alive, about my future, and the future of my family. Why not? Nobody said anything about the family breaking up, and that the love and support system wouldn't be available for my future. That I would be orphaned wasn't conceivable.

The Union Avenue Plunge was a site to behold. The customer received exactly what they paid for when they plunged into the pool's cool refreshment. It was a temple to the

Gods of Swimming — a mecca for those seeking relief from Bakersfield's heat. Built like a giant cement reservoir, it was 100 x 300 feet long, with a bathhouse to accommodate 300 patrons. Below grade, the pool sloped from four to twelve feet and was filled by a ten-horsepower motor pumping water from a 145 foot well.

The pool had a constant stream of fresh clean water running through it. And there was a twenty-foot tower at the deep end, above the diving boards and slides to get your kicks through the air. Magically, there were no liability problems back then.

It was an oasis in this desert of petroleum, surrounded by palm trees. Donkey pumps stood outside the entry door to the bath house, reminding you where you were. The donkeys were camouflaged along old Highway 99 by a line of palm trees. Man, that was some heavenly body of water.

I loved teaching the Yokuts how to swim, or rather, helping them improve their swimming techniques because they already knew how to swim once they made it to the Sharks – my group. We were close contenders to the Whales, Daddy's team. We had swimming meets once every four-week session, to exhibit competitiveness within the different age groups. I handed out awards to the campers with their parents present at the pool.

The Sharks were my minions, second only to the Whales in terms of excellence, but far from the Minnows, who were beginners and taught by my mother. It was a hundred feet across the pool, and I was teaching them the strokes: breaststroke, backstroke, Australian crawl, the butterfly, even side stroke. They were all lined up before me in the pool, with my whistle around my neck, and *"Can't Get No Satisfaction"* playing on the speakers. The Sharks would be hanging on the side of the pool, one eye watching me, the other on the giant flow of water billowing into the pool from an underwater pump. I'd have to blow my whistle to keep their attention.

It was a lot of work after dropping the Yokuts off and coming home to prepare for tomorrow's arts and crafts. I earned respect that summer amongst the Yokuts' parents also. That was an additional selling point for the next summer, and you know how Daddy loved those selling points.

20. *Tess of the D'Urbervilles*

It was the following semester after a summer of Yokuts that I was introduced through the English literature class to *Tess of the D'Urbervilles, A Pure Woman*, by Thomas Hardy. After I read it, or maybe it was before I read it, I became Tess, and Tess became me. It made a huge impression on me and I carried that book with me until I left high school. If you don't know the story, don't worry. I'll tell you the same story about *Tess,* using myself as an example. I call it:

Suzan, A Fragmented Woman, by Suzan A. Cornwall. A true short story:

I'm not beautiful. But I'd make a good runner up for style. I've got that sweet, flat hairdo, with straight blond hair almost to my shoulders, but it flips up on the ends because I sleep with curlers in my hair. I know how to dress my figure demurely enough to show it off. Cheaply. No choice. Except for the shoes, they've got to be Capezios! I was sixteen years old, starting my junior year and only had eyes for one guy: Dick Owens.

Dick was a big boy. He was a junior, like me, only man size, six feet tall, weighing 200 pounds. He played tackle on the Drillers Football team, but was second string, due, I thought, to his gentle nature. I watched him for a long time, just saying hi.

He had blue eyes. I couldn't see him ripping off some player's head to get to the quarterback, but he said that's exactly what he did.

We met socially after the game at Steve Eudy's house, the original party pad, and Dick was so funny. He made fun of everything. (How many paranoids does it take to screw in a light bulb? Who's asking?) He had me laughing with his puns, too, which he assured me were the lowest form of humor, but I loved it. (You say your dad pinches pennies, maybe he's lost his cents?)

I lived only a few blocks from Steve's and since I had to be home by 11:00, Dick offered me a ride. He had a '57 Chevy Bell Air that was silver, on a rake with slicks on the rear end, and four on the floor, adding another element of surprise. He walked me around the car to open the door like a perfect gentleman, then left twenty feet of scratch on the roadway to impress me. I was impressed.

So there I was, at the "momentary threshold of womanhood," and with the man of my dreams, riding shotgun in his 327 Chevy. I could feel it in my body all the way to my soul. Lightning bolts down my arms and legs to my feet, pressed against the metal floor, vibrating. I was almost panting. I smiled at the excitement because it made me feel free – like a burst of air when you're swimming. I decided why not go for it. This was Dick.

"Hey, I got an idea. Let's go park at the beach and watch the river flow. It's right over that away," I said, pointing my thumb in the opposite direction.

"You said you had to get home."

"It's a quarter till, we'll make it. Let's go look at the river, it'll be shimmering...help me sleep."

"Let's do it."

Dick turned his rumbling Chevy around, trying to keep his pipes to a low roar after his exhibition of speed in this otherwise sleepy neighborhood. That's before he turned right and opened it up again on Oak Ave., flying to 24th St., where he turned west toward the river. There was a bridge spanning the river, but Dick turned before the bridge onto a dirt road that led to the beach – which was an opening to the riverbank between the tule reeds growing along the shore.

He parked next to a lonely oak tree where it was peaceful and solitary. He turned off the engine to listen to the silence. The crickets resumed their chatting, and the frogs began barking from their pads in the river, hidden in the dark of night. This was the powerful Kern River. The harvest moon shimmered off the ripples. The river had taken nine lives as of

September of that year and everyone in Bakersfield was aware of its danger.

There was a light breeze that felt good after another sweltering fall day. It felt cool in our short sleeves, and made the river look inviting. Light was glistening off the tiny waves.

"Let's take our shoes off so we can feel the water," I said.

"You sure you don't want to go skinny dipping?" he said, smiling.

"We don't have time for that. I just want to touch it. I used to swim in this river all the time as a kid."

"Wow, you're brave. Did you swim in it naked?"

"Boy, you got a one-track mind," I threw back at him.

"No, I don't, because you got five minutes to have your fun then you're going home. We've just met...don't make your Daddy mad at me."

"Oh, pasha on him," I said.

We were out of the car with our shoes off. I stripped down to my blouse and jeans and stood in the water up to my ankles. We started a competition to see who could find the best rock to skip across the river's veneer. We were counting how many bounces. The most I could muster was three.

"Okay. I bet I can make this stone skip five times. If I do it, you're gonna have to remove your blouse," said Dick.

"And what happens if you don't skip five skips?"

“Well, fairs fair, I’ll remove my shirt.”

“You’re never going to skip it five times, so I bet.”

“Oh, don’t underestimate me.”

Dick picked his stone and gave it his best shot. The stone skipped one, two, three, four…times.

“Ah-hah, sorry Charlie, only four hops, you failed! Take your shirt off.”

Now I saw Dick, for the first time, be the humble teenager he was. He really wanted that fifth skip, and damnit, it didn’t happen. Dick sheepishly took off his wine colored button-down, to reveal how hard he’d been working in the weight room. His muscles were taught, but his core was taughtier. My mouth almost fell open, he looked so *gallant*, so ready for …sex. I was feeling at the threshold of womanhood alright, and here was the door.

“Give me another chance, Suzie.”

“No, no. You had your chance.”

“This time I bet I can skip this rock… that I’m looking for right now … six times, and if I don’t make it, I’ll take my pants off, and you win. But if I do make it skip six times, you only have to take your blouse off.”

“Only, you say? Well then, I say, you only have to skip the rock eight times to get me to take my blouse off. How do you like that deal?”

"Alright, you're on."

"Yeah, and your pants are going off."

Dick got serious about it. He didn't want to get pantsed by a girl, I suppose. There was his false pride to protect. But it was weird watching him comb the beach half naked looking for the perfectly round, flat rock to use for his final throw. There was carnal stimulation in watching his long arms search through the tule vines, pushing and shoving to find the right stone.

"Here it is." he said, tossing it in the palm of his hand, admiring it. "This baby's taking me to the promised land."

"Don't throw it too hard," I giggled.

Dick wound up, not like a pitcher, but like a guy that knew what he was doing and shot that rock with the rifle arm, that went 1, 2, 3, 4, 5,.6,..7,...8 plops. He did it!

My jaw really did drop and stayed that way until Dick grabbed me around the waist and started dancing in the shallow water like we were part of a giant hoopla having a square dance. "Take your partner round and round kiss 'em on the lips and set them down," sang Dick, and that's what he did, and I can't say it wasn't divine. When his lips met mine, the world winked at us caught in mid twirl, then kept on rolling as we were stuck in the kiss. Was this love at first sight? I thought to myself.

It was a marvelous event that ended most abruptly. Our feet got tangled and we lost balance, splashing down in the water of the moonlit river. It made us look like river rats for sure, our clothes hanging sloppily from our bodies. My hair, blouse, and jeans were drenched. But as awful as that was, it was also comical. And it hit our funny bone in some strange way and we couldn't stop laughing and giggling. I mean we were sopping wet and hissing and poking each other, and continuously tittering, we probably sounded like a couple of schoolgirls.

I knocked him over as we floundered in knee deep water, then landed on him. We were lying on the sand of the river, our lower bodies beneath the water's edge. I straddled his leg, climbing on his torso so I could whisper in his ear, "I don't want to go home." I knew as soon as I said that I shouldn't have. But I meant it.

I squeezed his bicep as we laid in silence for a moment. Dick didn't want to say a word for fear of spoiling the moment. I felt powerful. He felt confused. My lips were nestled under his earlobe, pressed against his neck. Moving my lips up to his inner ear, I blew in it softly and breathed, "Dick, Dick, Dick... Dick...is there something you can do?" Dick was on the spot. "Well, I'm a little confused, are we coming or goin?"

"Don't you know where the party is?" I asked him straight faced.

"No, I don't."

"It's in your mouth, and everybody's coming! So come on." I jumped up and gave him a hand to get his lazy ass up. "I'll race you to the other side," I said, making a break for it.

"No, wait. You gotta be careful about swimming at night out here. There's giant mud suckers and water moccasin that come out at night."

"Don't be silly. There's no such thing. What's the matter, are you chicken?

"I'm not chicken, I'm just saying. There's a lot of shit out there."

"I know all about the Kern River and the people it's killed, from Yokuts Club. 'The current underneath is three time faster than on the surface.' Right?"

"Be careful is all I'm saying. I'm not that good a swimmer. In fact, I can't swim."

"Why not, couldn't your parents afford to send you to a private club to learn?" I said teasingly.

"I never heard of Yokuts."

"You don't have to worry about me, I'm a good swimmer," That was me bragging a little, drunk with the power of a wood nymph luring a man to me.

"I'm not kidding, up to your waist is too far. You're too far out tight now."

"I'm not going beyond my head" I teased. I could feel the current pushing me on my hips. It made me stumble once from a gust of wind striking me in the back, but I liked it, so I wasn't scared. I was walking backwards, looking at Dick near the shore, beckoning him not to be a chicken.

I was losing ground to him as the current pushed me down stream, so I had to turn and walk up stream, against the current to make up that ground. That's when I realized I'd made a stupid mistake because the current felt three times stronger trying to walk against it. I couldn't do it. The water kept pushing me out of balance.

It was like a giant squid snared me, pulling my feet to make me stumble. I stopped and leaned into the current. My ankles were caught in tule weeds growing out of the riverbed, wrapping my feet in the vines. My pant legs were hooked on the roots, so I was stuck in the mud, not going anywhere.

Suddenly, I was in a precarious situation. A torrent of water was streaming past my belly button, splashing up to my breast. Using my arms for balance, I pulled my legs hard to free myself but lost balance and almost fell. I was like a kite tied to an anchor and thrown in the river.

Dick sensed something was wrong. He was maybe thirty feet from me at the shoreline when he began sloshing through the water towards me.

"Wait there Suzie, I'll come help you. Just stay steady," said Dick, replacing the tone of our friendly repartee from fun to fear. "I'm coming," and he was coming, not timidly, but with purpose, kicking his knees high to slog his way through the shallow water, until he too was waist high in the river, about fifteen feet from me.

"I'm okay, I guess I'm the one who can't tell if she's coming or goin'. I'm sorry. You were right. You can't tell shit about this current till you're in it."

"Are you caught on something?"

"My feet are caught in the weeds. I can't use my hands to free myself ...the current will take me down. It's the current. It's strong, right here, be careful Dick, be real careful."

"You think I can dive down and pull them off?"

"No, don't do that, the current will take you. I need you to hold me...from behind... get behind me and hold me here so I can use my hands and arms to get out of this mess."

"I can do that."

"And watch out for holes, because they're out here — and the current..."

"Look whose giving warnings about—"

That was the last thing he said. He stepped into a hole, his weight shifted and he lost balance for a second. That was time enough for the current to sweep him away, and he was gone, just like that. The current sent him tumbling, rolling and thrashing his arms, unable to right his body. The water turned into a turbulent brown funnel taking Dick Owens with it.

Shot with adrenaline, I immediately stuck my head under water, using my hands to free myself from the rooted mass, after which I too was released into the current. But instantly I squeezed my head above water to ride the flow of the river as any swimmer was trained to do. I rode that current using my breaststroke for half a mile downstream before it beached me on an island of rocks and trees.

But I never saw Dick again. His body was dredged up much further downstream the next day.

21. Daddy Makes It About Him

That night will never be over for me. Not just because Dick drowned, but what happened afterward with my father. I was crushed by Dick's death and couldn't believe it happened. We had finally met and he, the object of my pubescent desires, was ripped from me and killed by the river. Worst of all, it was all my fault.

You might think, "Ooh, poor girl, no wonder she went crazy." But no, that was just a horrible accident that people, with support from their family, are expected to get over. It was a tragedy, but I didn't do anything intentional to drown Dick. His death was a result of him being too good a guy.

What Daddy did was intentional. The police brought me home at about two in the morning draped in a grey police blanket. The Sergeant laid out the facts for my parents, just as I laid them out here. He then had the courtesy to take his leave so we could begin the healing process, beginning with some well-deserved sleep.

But that wasn't my father's plan. His plan was to get to the bottom of my story, and to root out the evil participation by his daughter. That way, he could understand the devastating morbidity she cast upon his reputation. It was all about him. He never cared about what shocking trigger mechanism this trauma developed for my future psyche. It was always, how's this going to affect the reputation of Jack?

He needed protection from people whose opinion he held in high regard. When his own father died and was buried in the family plot in Santa Barbara, he refused to pay for a headstone to mark his father's grave over an inheritance dispute.! Tsk, tsk, such disrespect.

"Well, you've really done it this time, haven't you," said my father. "What the hell did you think was going to happen to you, swimming in the Kern River past your curfew with a strange boy. That screams out, "slut". 'Hey Jack, I hear your slutty daughter drowned her boyfriend!' How does that sound?"

"How can you say that, Daddy? That's not how it was."

"It doesn't make any difference, it's what people think. You realize what you've done, don't you? We've worked twenty years building our reputation through Yokuts Club and education. We are pillars in this community and people look to us to obey the rules and expect us to be leaders. You're leading us down the toilet, like one turd leads another. Get your head out of your ass and look what you've done. You led a young boy to his death."

"How are people going to feel about sending their children to camp now – being counseled by a boy killer. Your actions have consequences, and oh my, you know all about that now. You've got to think *before* you act, use your brain, not whatever else is guiding you. Instead of going out and screwing some kid you didn't even know."

"I didn't screw him Daddy. And you didn't know him at all. He was a nice boy, and I loved him."

"Oh, you loved him, did you? Is that what love is? You find the guy with the fanciest car and you're in love. You're not in love, you're in lust. I'm so disgusted with you. And now he's nothing because he's dead. All because of you. You did it, right Suzan? You had him come save you from being caught in the weeds - that's such a load of crap. What were you doing swimming in the river with your clothes on in the first place?"

"We were just fooling around."

"Fooling around after curfew. You were supposed to be home at 11. That's why we have curfews. So things like this don't happen. But you can't follow the rules. What am I going to do with you, besides throw your privileges in the trash? No more meetings, or talking on the phone, no more Y, or Job's Daughters, or library, or doing anything. It'll be a long time before you ever have another date."

"What's the proper punishment for branding our family with a foul name? You know I'm president of Planned Parenthood here in Bakersfield. I have responsibilities to this community. People look to me as an example of how to raise a girl that's not promiscuous. We have meetings every week and how do you think this looks? It looks like I don't have control over my own daughter, who's acting like a ... You should know better. I've taught you better, God-damn it, and now it's on me. All your actions are a reflection on me. You know that don't you?"

"I know they shouldn't be. You didn't do anything."

"Well, that's the point. They'll think I've taught you nothing. That your value system is...you must not have one. And it reflects on your mother too. She doesn't deserve a daughter that detours from the norm. That's all we've ever asked of you. That you walk the line, stay out of trouble and make your parents proud. But no! You couldn't do that. You think this makes us proud?"

"But I didn't do anything."

"Yes, you did. Weren't you the one who wanted to go see the river. He didn't kidnap you, did he? You were just having fun. Well, how'd that work out for you? If you had him bring you home, Dick Owens would be alive now, instead of dead."

"Daddy, you're being mean."

"Mean? I haven't even started to be mean. This whole incident is you being mean to us. It's not fair that we give you food and clothes, and care for you and give you money; and you turn around and shit on me, by acting totally irresponsible. Are you trying to ruin my life? That's what you're doing by casting doubt on my character. We are the Cornwall's, and that means we have a perfect family that can work and play together. That's how we make money. You create trust, not destroy it."

"So, what did you do to him? What got this Dick so excited he risked his life for you. Were you drinking, smoking marijuana, goddamn it, Suzan, if you were high. Yeah, I thought so."

"No, I wasn't. I've never even seen marijuana."

"You better not have, but you got the same result – a young man is drowned, and a 16-year-old girl has a scarlet letter wrapped around her neck."

"Why, I didn't do anything!"

"You keep saying that, but you're wrong. I know what you were doing out there, everybody knows. You were flaunting your body at him, teasing him, flirting with him like a tramp, trying to sexually arouse him until he...he had blue balls, or in your case, killed himself. You teased him and made him follow you into the river, why else would he be out there if he couldn't swim. It was because his girlfriend used him to satisfy her own libido."

"Why would you say that, Daddy?"

"Where'd you think Tod came from when I was only twenty years old."

"We didn't have sex, I told you that."

"You're a liar. I don't believe you. You did it, and it's best that Dick drowned to avoid unwanted pregnancy issues. We'll have to take care of this at Planned Parenthood."

"There's nothing to take care of Daddy. You're being a fascist... I don't need this."

And that's why I carried *Tess of the D'Urbervilles* with me every place I went.

The End

22. Paranoia Strikes Deep

Hmmm...so now I am stuck in Suffolk County Mental Ward without my clothes, or toothbrush, or hairbrush for that matter. I have nothing to make me look pretty. So I'll sit here like a bump on a log. Sounds like a verse to my new song. It could follow, I don't know why I'm here, I should be moving on.

It's not funny. Nothing is. How would you like it if everybody wanted you to be incarcerated for doing nothing. Everybody wants me here, there's no escape. They do. You may have had a bout of paranoia before, but it was nothing like this. This is psychotic paranoia, and it's in addition to schizophrenia. I've got that too. It's like paranoia, but much worse because nobody knows how deep schizophrenia goes. The thing about it is, you can't see the wound because it's all in the brain. I'm injured, but nobody can see how bad it is.

"You're talking paranoid." You're darn tootin' I am. I'm delusional too. I see and hear people talking about me on T.V., sometimes on the news. But other times they have entire dramas devoted to me, sometimes sitcoms. You'd think I was narcissistic, but I'm not. I'm a schizophrenic, that's paranoid. That makes it tougher for diagnosis and treatment. It's why they thought I was hostile towards them. Sometimes I think if you give the orderlies and nurses a hard time, they just dope you up and call you a schizophrenic. It's insidious how paranoia works. I instinctively sense fear and mistrust in everybody, and it makes me angry, and deeply afraid.

Psychiatric doctors have told me that as far as inheriting paranoia, "it's unclear whether a genetic predisposition to paranoia – if such a thing exists at all – is inherited or not."

Hah. Isn't that definitive? It's like saying if we had some ham, we could have ham and eggs, if we had some eggs. My point is that psychiatry has gotten nowhere in its research on paranoia since the dark ages of '69. There's no new treatment for me now than there was fifty-five years ago, which was nothing.

"Isolation" is the number one factor causing paranoia. Well, I'd like to know how I could be more isolated. I'm stuck in a mental hospital with a bunch of people like me, three thousand miles from home, and left here to die by my parents. They've abandoned me here, thrilled at the prospect of me being incarcerated.

"Fate does work in very strange ways. It's as if our prayers for two years have been answered," wrote my mother to Aunt Betty and Uncle George upon hearing I had been incarcerated at Suffolk while they vacationed in Bavaria.

And having access to all that free psychiatry at Suffolk? What a deal. "This should surely teach her a lesson about the values she was brought up with," I can hear my Daddy saying. "This incarceration should be good for Suzan, apply a little tough love to the tarnish, and the gold starts shining through. Watch for it, any day now."

V

WRANGLING OVER HAIR

23. The Apocalyptic Hermaphrodite

By 1969, the Vietnam War loomed over every aspect of life carrying a bloody sign that read, "Hell no, we won't go." The draft was scouring the Nation for young men to serve in the armed forces by giving them all a physical exam and the young men were doing everything they could to flunk it. If you were nineteen in '69, you were raw meat.

In response to the draft, violence popped up in colleges everywhere. The National Guard was called in to quelch the violence, culminating in the burning of Bank of America in Santa Barbara, and four dead and nine wounded, at Ohio's Kent State, both in early 1970.

The lottery for the draft was set up in 1968, and it was no small feat to get out of the draft in 1969. You had to be clever, and lucky, and care enough to get yourself classified 4-F. Being 4-F meant: "I'm sorry, but you are ineligible for the draft." That was the exact language used by the military officer with whom I conferred at the end of the physical exam. I took the exam in Fresno, along with a couple hundred other draftees.

These great United States began picking draftees by lottery in the summer of 1968, according to an inductee's birthday. I wasn't too concerned about it because I was going to Idaho to play football for Boise State. I had a scholarship for the next four years and they were still giving deferments for being in college. There would be no draft notices for me.

When I blew my knee out the second game of the season, I remember standing in the shower by myself, the game still going on, thinking how these torn ligaments were going to change my life. Football has been my identity since I was born. It made me whole, and I loved playing it. Getting that scholarship was a goal I worked on for eighteen years, and now it was gone, the result of a player on my own team missing his block and taking out my knee. I could have rehabilitated it to play the next year, but I had little interest in sticking around a hick-town like Boise. My friend and I had plans on being stars in Hollywood.

Nevertheless, it was a shock to me when it happened. The "football life" was all I'd known, and it hit me hard, as tears began to swell in my eyes. The only thing that consoled me was the thought the injury may help me out of the draft. That was the issue on the mind of every 18-year-old male in the country, right next to having sex. A deferment was a great consolation for having my identity stolen at such a young age.

Bruce and I moved to Hollywood in January of '69 and did have a lot of fun growing our hair out and living the hippy life on Sunset Strip. Our apartment was a couple of blocks from the *Whiskey,* and we had enough free love to feel good being on our own for the first time. We had an apartment with no furniture, no time to be anywhere, scraping by...I can remember at least one activist anti-war rally or Black power movement or free concert or whatever it was we attended in Griffith Park, but we weren't too invested. We chalked it up to good times for all.

I became concerned about military service when my number was picked for the draft. My parents received a notice that I was to appear for an exam to determine my physical fitness as a potential inductee. These exams were happening everywhere in the state of California and across the nation for all men of draft age. Its purpose was to weed out those not suited for the job. There weren't many.

These exams were extremely unpopular among the inductees and there was no limitation on their imagination on how to flunk it. It was an accepted practice, and a widely discussed topic, whether jokingly or not amongst the contenders for Vietnam, to at least try to flunk the exam. My own cousin, Laurie Scullin who is 6'2" tall, although naturally thin, fasted for twenty days to get down to 125 pounds and didn't bathe over the same period either, or change his pants.

He thought his "freak" appearance would make him unsuitable for fitness. He was wrong.

The problem was nobody knew what they were fighting for over there. Even the good old-fashioned red-blooded Americans that normally bust ass to go to war, didn't want to go. By 1969 everyone was confused. We were getting mixed messages from every walk of life.

Some of the older football players would come back to watch our practices in high school and they would have their legs blown off. From what I could see, they got no glory. Nobody could explain why they lost their leg. Was the fight against communism? Our own fathers of World War II didn't think to ask for an explanation. "Yes, it's about the threat of communism!" they said. It was just another thing you were expected to do.

This hard-core issue about the draft was only raised once in our household. That was after our family friend's son got shipped back from Nam in a box. That was a horrible event because this young man was not supposed to die. He was extraordinary in everything he did. He was smart, handsome, popular, a leader by natural selection. If anybody was going to be a hero, it was him. But one month in Vietnam and he was dead. I remember feeling so sorry for his father. One month.

There was never any answer as to why this happened to 11,780 other soldiers in 1969. Only tolerance by our parents, implying that it was a necessary evil to eradicate communism? I believe our parents would have done anything the Fuhrer asked of them, which was an ironic twist to winning the war.

In rebellion to this, young men started growing their hair out like women. This was in stark contrast to getting the normal haircut every two weeks. Every man was getting his hair trimmed every two weeks and intended on doing that forever. Growing your hair long was a statement! What it stood for and how it was used was hard to say. But it put society on notice that something was changing, even if you couldn't say what it was. That's cool. Long hair said it all. It didn't just draw a line between those for, and those against the war. It drew world-wide attention to the hostility between the "long hairs" and everybody else in America.

I recall ranchers in Bakersfield threatening to hold me down to shear my woolly head. Little things like refusing service and dirty looks, and the multitude of times I got flipped off by passengers in cars, yelled at to get fucked, "get a haircut" was a constant cry, by those that hated long hair. There was a gap. They really did not understand why a man would grow out his hair like a woman unless he was a "freak." They didn't understand there was a revolution going on.

I trimmed my hair before going to my physical exam in Fresno. But I didn't just go take the physical. I learned you could put it off for a few months if you changed addresses. So I changed my address from Bakersfield to Hollywood, until I received another notice, then changed it back to Bakersfield, then back to Hollywood, but then I received my last notice, so I switched it back to Bakersfield and boarded the bus from Bakersfield to Fresno at five in the morning with a busload full of other disgruntled grunts.

Everyone slept on the way to the exam, but once we were there it was lively. Everyone put on their game faces, but when it came down to it, we all played it straight as to whether we were fit or not. The wiseacres that tried cheating on the colorblind test were guilty of nothing more than tomfoolery.

The physical exam takes a couple of hours of getting poked and prodded and asked questions to a group of five at a time. Near the end they have you pull your pants down and look up your butt hole and in the crack of your ass for something they don't explain. It was after that exam that the doctor told me I had a condition where I was growing another asshole above the one I have, and that condition would make me ineligible for the draft.

So now he tells me. I knew vaguely what he was talking about, but it caught me by surprise. What was I supposed to do about that? Hey, I got deferred from the draft because I've got two ass holes. That's all I needed, another asshole. I put that idea on hold. They also told us if we had any documents or doctor's opinions now would be the time to present them to an officer. I went with that one.

My documents were in order. In the nine months I was delaying the exam, I sought out, or I should say my girlfriend Page, had enough sense to seek out the help of a sympathetic orthopedic surgeon in Beverly Hills. She got the name from a bulletin board at UCLA. There was no doubt I had the injury from football, but was it bad enough to prohibit me from withstanding the rigors of basic training? That was the question, and the doctor being a sympathetic American, stated it was his opinion it did.

The doctor's name was something like "Goldstein" and buck for buck my investment in him was many times his weight in gold. Being 19, I was very impressed with his letter of twelve pages. What could he possibly have said about my knee that would take twelve pages of type? I never read it, but I realized what it did for me. One visit to his office, to which I was reluctant to go; not a single question about my politics, and $50.00 later, I received this twelve-page letter. On page twelve, under the heading of Doctor's Opinion, it read:

"It is my professional opinion that Mr. Cornwall will not be able to withstand the rigors of basic training."

The officer to whom I spoke with that day in Fresno, in the privacy of his steel gray table draped on both sides by green linen, did not read the letter either. He went directly to page twelve to read the doctors opinion, after which he remarked, "I am sorry to inform you Mr. Cornwall that you are ineligible for the draft."

Ineligible for the draft? Are you kidding?

I was the happiest 19-year-old in the world. It was a defining moment when the army officer confirmed I would not be going to Vietnam. If nothing else, I wouldn't die there, and I didn't have to get a haircut, and dress up in a very uncool uniform.

You may think this is shallow thinking but there was no need to think deeper. Death was lurking on the other side of that green linen. Actual death, and this was the draftees first chance to even think about it. There were three people out of the busload full that didn't pass the physical. We kept that to ourselves. The rest of the bus remained eligible for the draft, would be drafted, and would be sent to Vietnam.

24. The Sympathetic Bus Driver

Back on the bus, the aggregate state of mind grew into a melancholy death ride.

"What the hell's in Vietnam anyway, besides goochie girls?"

"Who cares?"

"You heard Country Joe, 'ain't no time to wonder why, whoopie we're all goin' to die," sang a guy from in back.

"Fuck you, man. Where is Vietnam?" asked one man.

"Somewhere a long place from here, I'll tell you that," said another.

"It's a giant jungle divided by mountains and surrounded with rice paddies and has signs with letters you can't read. And oh yeah, all the people wear the same thing, round straw hats and pants below the knee so they can slog through their rice farm in their bare feet. The problem is you can't tell the enemy from the folks you're there to…protect? Protect them from who? Or are we there to take? What do you do with the people that work there?"

Whatever the U.S. Military's mission was over there, they were doing it wrong, and everybody on the bus knew it. This wasn't a busload of sissies, or inductees' fathers going off to fight Hitler. All these draftees had to do was look around and breathe —the evidence was in the air.

This was the first time any of us were forced to ponder what it meant to go to war. We had all seen the vets come back amputated and shot up, but that's not what put doubt in our minds. What put doubt in our minds was the lack of gratitude the vets endured when they got home. There wasn't the slightest "Hurrah" waiting for them. No stretched butcher paper reading, "Welcome Home Johnny."

Us bus riders represented the members of society chosen to go fight communism. A fair swipe of youth across the nation. We were in our soldiering prime and ready for action, but not this action. The only thing us young, single, uneducated men had on our minds was pussy. Everybody knew how fast the returning soldier got out of his uniform so he couldn't be identified. He tried to blend back into society, but his haircut was a dead giveaway.

The result was: no respect. Imagine, if you can, you went to Vietnam to fight for your country, but you never got any recognition for your service from your friends or family. It was the wrong time to apply for West Point. If their football team was an example of their leadership, it was at the bottom of their league during the entire Vietnam era.

Your average soldier wanted to get back his life, but the girls back home weren't willing to accept "baby killers" into their bed. That's how they were portrayed in the media.

I met this one dude at a party who had spent his last eleven months in a service hospital after being shot in the stomach. War was written on the lines of his face. But as an American I didn't feel sympathy for him, nor did I feel any notion of bravery or honor on his part. The Vietnam vets' persona shaped up to be a question mark as to how he ever got in this situation in the first place. How he became an outcast in the community he fought for. It was the question everyone was sick of thinking about.

And here's the answer: The soldier fighting in Vietnam did not make his sacrifice for our freedom back home. It had nothing to do with our freedom. That was a lie from our government to keep the military machine well-greased. In fact, nothing the soldier did in Vietnam was related to our personal rights enjoyed daily, such as reading the newspaper. By nature we should be thankful to this soldier for risking his life for us, but what he fought for wasn't for us.

It was not America's war. We weren't fighting for anything. We had nothing hanging in the balance. And damned if America didn't do it again thirty years later when they went to war in Afghanistan – only there wasn't a draft at that time, or you'd have heard about it.

Be that as it may, the humble bus driver bringing us back from Fresno sensed the ineffable contempt for the U.S. government perpetuating this myth. He decided to risk his job on behalf of the young lions and do something about it. I guess he couldn't take the melancholy silence coming from his busload of bridled men.

So the driver, who looked a lot like Steve McQueen, pulls the bus off old Highway 99 into the little dirt town of Pixley and stops at the liquor store. None of us were legal drinking age, but that didn't stop the liquor store from selling us whatever spirits we could afford. It was the exact tonic to cure the illness of silence. We proceeded to get drunk and by the time we got to Bakersfield we were all a bunch of good ol' boys that didn't give a fuck.

After we arrived at Bakersfield's terminal, the bus driver told us to just walk off the bus and he'd take care of the mess. Now that's what America is all about.

Ten months later I found myself trying to get into the military. Go figure.

25. I Needed Dope!

It seemed everything had gotten much worse by the end of the first quarter of 1969. Life hadn't turned out the way I planned. I had my reasons for being an angry nineteen-year-old. My parents moved to Germany; my sister was put in an insane asylum; my brother beat me over the head with a bat; I was fired from my job at the lumberyard for having long hair; my friends had become riff-raff; and I had no place to stay. Life hasn't been kind to me so far.

1969 was the year of "sex, drugs, and rock and roll" all over again. If the moral of Vietnam was, "It don't mean nothing," the antidote back home was "Turn on, tune in and drop out."

There ought to be a study of how much drug use was caused in response to the daily litany of the following questions:

1) Why can't I get a job with long hair?
2) Why is my father so uptight?
3) Why is Reagan calling for a blood bath?
4) Why can't we smoke dope?
5) Who says it leads to harder drugs?
6) Where are the drugs?

Wherever they were, that's where I wanted to be. My brother and sister too. Does that seem odd? Why?

From both ends on the spectrum of society, the massive concerts from New York to Altamont, California, all came to a head in 1969. It was the greatest concert of all time being celebrated in Woodstock, on Yasgur's farm in New York. 400,000 people partying and the worse injury was a drug overdose while Jimi Hendrix played the *Star Spangle Banner.*

Then on the West Coast they had the Hell's Angels killing at Altamont, California, with 500,000 people watching while the *Rolling Stones* sang *Sympathy for the Devil.* With those kinds of polarities swirling around in the magnetic fields of decision making that year, it's no wonder my sister went crazy.

What price do we pay our government to protect our Constitutional rights? Blind obedience to the commander? That sounds like fascism, in a cruel and oppressive way. Hoping the people above us in authoritative positions will act in our best interest seems laughable considering Vietnam.

I feel sorry for anyone who lost a loved one in Vietnam, because they were fraudulently led into battle by jingoisms and used as cannon fodder by the same scoundrels who sent them there.

We citizens back home, during that same thirteen-month tour of duty in Vietnam, were also subjected to random violence. In Bakersfield, fighting was something of a ritual. Fighting, fighting, and fighting some more. One time there were six of us sitting around the living room of my brother's apartment and all six of us had a black eye.

And when there wasn't someone else to fight, we'd fight amongst ourselves. That's what led to me getting clubbed over the head by my own brother, and me putting my gun to his face in response.

26. Cruising to Nowhere

It was a warm spring night, perfect for driving with the windows down. Julio and I were cruising in my '56 Chevy, and we were feeling no pain. In fact, we felt great. We cruised by a house we knew had a bevy of girls in the prime of their life, coming and going at all hours. It was a party house. On any given night there'd be a party of males getting entertained, and the next night it would be someone else's party. This inevitably led to rivalry between sharing partners. Julio's brother had gotten beaten up there the night before. We thought we'd check it out.

When Julio and I showed up it looked peaceful. There were no cars to put us on notice, so I parked across the street and got out. As I neared the other side of the street toward the house, the front door screen slammed open and out stormed four Oakie's from Lamont. They were looking for a fight, and they found one whether we liked it or not.

Fight or Flight. Without skipping a beat, no hello, nothing, the first one marched up and kicked me right in the balls. He missed though and caught my inner thigh. I always thanked God for that. Two others ran after Julio who hightailed it back to the car and locked the doors.

So now I've got two shit-kickers from Lamont in front of me, punching and kicking from right to left. I'm fending them both off, keeping them at a distance and keeping my balance, stepping back from the curb to keep my feet. Mother fuckers!

Then this fifth shit-kicker comes out the door screaming, "Back off, he's mine! Oh yeah, I want this one. He's all mine!" He comes strutting down the stairs of the porch, shoulders humped through his white t-shirt, flashing his fresh out of prison biceps. The two nitwits kicking at me dropped back with grins on their faces, like they were about to witness a royal ass kicking. One of them announced this was Larry Shaddon, four years in San Quinton and the prison's middleweight boxing champion. I guess I was lucky I never heard of him.

He comes at me with a look so confident you'd thought he already knocked me out. I had no intention of getting hit by one of those ham hock fists he was swinging. He's punching and jabbing at me. I step back across the street guarding them off. Then he did something that happened to me once before.

He's moving in on me closer, then he lunges and wraps his arms around my neck to squeeze my head like a pimple. He grabs me tight, pulls my head down to his waist level, his head banging mine, his face right over my left shoulder. He grabs my neck and twists with both arms, pulling me tight against him to gain control, pulling me down; but I'm not going.

He doesn't give any thought about my free arm; he figures he's got me. But with his face locked next to mine with both arms, I had a perfect shot for a right uppercut. I could see his nose bulging there like a goose egg. BAM! He goes flying back, arms waving to keep balance, his nose so bloody and broken, the front of his white t-shirt looks painted like the flag of the Samurai.

His buddies immediately jumped on me, hitting and kicking me again; all the while Julio is still locked safely in the car. But big, bad Larry Shaddon called his goons off because he was too proud not to continue the fight – he couldn't see himself or he might have felt different. But something had happened. He was still caging me with fists clinched but his self-image was shattered, now he didn't know what to expect. He was scared. Not of getting hurt, but of things getting worse, right there in front of his hooligan friends.

This gave me the first opportunity to talk my way out. I was surrounded by five thugs and their ringleader's nose was swelling and beginning to turn purple. He looked frightening with blood spattered over his face and running down his shirt.

It wouldn't be long before a police car came. I had a gun in the trunk of my car, so I suggested Shaddon and one other guy, follow us to the railroad yard where we could settle this undisturbed. I knew they would all follow us, but I needed to get in my car.

He agreed. I go to my car where the fifth member of their gang named "Bear" was still growling at Julio through the locked window on the driver's side. Turns out Julio had fucked his sister or something. Bear was standing in front of the driver's door with both paws on the car. When I reached for the handle, he turned and punched me square in the chin. He was fuming mad. He also had a big ugly ring on his finger that tore off a big ugly chunk of skin on my chin. I still have a scar from the gash. But somehow it didn't bleed.

I acted like it didn't faze me. "Oh yeah, you just jacked my jawbone loose, but I've got to get in my car now, so we can go down to the tracks and fight some more, you big fucking idiot."

Bear stepped away from the door and I slid in happily to escape the scene. We took off in the car. What else could I do? I was surrounded by self-proclaimed hoods that really wanted to put me in the hospital and brag about it. All I had on my side was a speed freak Julio. My opinion of Julio changed dramatically.

I never planned on going to the railroad yard. I was going to get far enough away so I could stop, open the trunk, and diffuse any more violence from these cowboys with my gun. That's assuming they didn't have a gun. But his posse kept close on my tail. I'm sure their suspicions arose when I missed the turn to the freight yard. I was heading in the direction of my brother's apartment a few blocks away.

There was one thing I really hoped wasn't going to happen, when it happened. I pulled to a stop sign in a residential area next to Franklin Elementary School, and my engine died. Not now! Not Now! I'd been having problems with it, but why now? The engine wouldn't turn over, and Larry and his band of ignorant sluts were stopped right behind us in two cars.

We were trapped. No lights, no cars, no probing police. I didn't know what to do other than take a moment to think. It was evident my back was against the wall. I had no desire to pull that gun from the trunk and brandish it. Getting the gun now would be a deliberate escalation. That means deadly trouble. Too much trouble.

I suppose if we were in Vietnam, Julio would be sufficiently trained to access our fire power from the back seat. We could have fired enough weaponry against our foes to blow their arms and legs away and leave them dangling from the telephone wires. Maybe Julio could get off his ass and start firing rounds from an M-60. We'd have a grenade launcher, and at least 30 fragmentation grenades and 40 magazines of ammo for my M-16. Heck, I'd take the M-60 and give Julio the M-16. We could have jumped out of the car from both sides and caught them in a crossfire. We'd blow them to bits.

What was the difference between killing five of these hoodlums, as opposed to killing five Viet Cong? There was nothing about these troublemakers that I admired or wanted to be a part of. They talked differently too, like they'd been raised on *Wonder Bread* in the back of a packing shed listening to steel guitar music all day.

Since that night I've traveled from the Amazon, to Tibet, to Kilimanjaro, and have found local people raised on dirt floors to be much more intriguing characters than these five brutes. What would be wrong with placing a couple of claymores under their cars? So what if they were unarmed. I don't know them any better than I know Viet Cong.

But, alas, I wasn't in Vietnam.

I got out of the car and leaned against the door waiting to see what they would do. But when Larry Shaddon approached me there on the street, there were no more looks of anger and hostility. In fact, Larry wanted to be friends.

The entire escapade turned into a weird male bonding experience provoked, no doubt, by the five-minute drive that gave Larry time to think and lose his adrenaline. His nose started hurting badly, throbbing, feeling it with every breath. He was wearing a pool of his own blood, his shirt was drenched in sticky red, and it coagulated in the pores of his face. That couldn't have felt good.

What if, in the off chance, I got him down and pummeled the shit out of him again, how would that feel? Larry wasn't afraid of me, or anyone else, but he was deftly afraid of suffering any further indignity in front of his friends. Hell, he kept saying, he'd never had a bloody nose before. Yeah, I'll bet, especially one that spreads your nose all over your face.

I got a windfall of notoriety for kicking Larry Shaddon's ass. The big joke was how I got them to push my car so we could get out of there. One lucky punch and I was the undefeated street hood of Bakersfield. I was riding high for a week. But then I made a couple of bad choices.

27. Bad Choices for 1969

My first bad choice was to join the U.S. Marines Corps.

I walked into a recruiting office in Bakersfield and told them, "I want to start killing gooks as soon as possible. How long, exactly, would it take me to get over there?" The recruiter welcomed my enthusiasm, but when he told me it would take another ten months of training before I got to Vietnam, I was sorely disappointed. Ten months!

The recruiting officer was looking me up and down and having a hard time getting past my physical exterior. I had long hair past my shoulders, which meant marijuana, which meant I could get my hippie ass out of there. He asked me straight:

"You ever smoke marijuana?"

I pretended to be straining my brain, there may have been one time, let's see. "There was this one time, we were at a party in L.A., and there were some guys smoking it there, but we didn't have any," I said. "No sir."

Not completely convinced by this denial, he had me come back the next day to take an intelligence test. That way he could advise me of my future in the Marines.

I went over to my brother's apartment excited after this meeting. We made up for him smacking me over the head with the bat, and I shared with him the pamphlets I got from the recruitment office. I was particularly fond of one showing a muscular soldier lugging an M-60 machine gun while on patrol through the jungle. "That's the guy I want to be," I told him proudly.

My brother had been in the Navy about ten years before, so he had some credibility.

"Are you crazy? Do you have any idea how heavy that gun would get humping an extra fifty pounds around the jungle? That would be the worst grunt job ever. Let me tell you, that machine gun would get real, real heavy. You don't want any part of lugging that machine gun anywhere!"

Good advice? I thought he was being a pansy. I went back the next morning to take the intelligence test. The sergeant set me off in a room beside his office. There was a glass window and door so he could see exactly what I was doing. I finished the test within the hour and gave it back to him at his desk to check the results. He had nothing else to do. People weren't lining up outside for their chance to join the Marines in 1969.

I watched him tally up the score, looking down, then looking up at me, wincing, as though there was something wrong with the test booklet. He checked it and re-checked it.

As he finishes this chore, he looks me straight in the eye and asked, "Did you cheat?" I thought he was joking. But he wasn't. I laughed and motioned my incredulity at his accusation. I mean, how could I? He saw me, I was right there in front of him. He wasn't smiling and appeared to be using his best intimidation routine to cut through the bullshit.

He got up and walked around the desk. "According to this score you would qualify for helicopter school down in Texas."

"But how much longer would that take?"

"We're talking about flying helicopters so it would take a while. You'd still have to go through basic training, but that's not the point."

"What do you mean?"

"I'm talking about your score being in the 90 percentile and I want to know how you did it."

It began to get through that he honestly didn't believe a long-haired hippy could do well on the test. I didn't know whether to be insulted or flattered.

I let it go and changed the conversation back to the enlistment. But it wasn't the same. He warmed up once it got through to him that I couldn't have cheated. It was logistically impossible. He was sitting there watching me through the window. But this fact broke the sergeant's image of what pigeonhole I belonged in, and it sure as hell put me on notice of what to expect from my future officers in the field.

I gave those officers the benefit of the doubt because they'd never know I had long hair. But for whatever reason, I decided to get a haircut and go back to being the clean-cut American boy I always was. The next morning, I went to the mall and cut off all my hair. Not severe like a crew cut or a buzz, but neat and clean.

It didn't look so bad at first, obviously because I was still in the barbershop. But as I walked out into the mall and sat on a bench in the middle of the courtyard, I experienced the most significant epiphany about myself. It was like sitting there naked.

It had started before I got to the bench. I saw an acquaintance of mine with long free flowing hair, and when he said hello, his look, from this nobody I even cared about, shot a glance of contempt and ridicule. He commented on my getting a haircut. I was hoping he wouldn't tell anybody about what I'd done. What was this feeling I had? I never felt this way with long hair. Even when I fell victim to mockery, or hatred for long hair, which was often back in those days, I still felt proud. I never had this feeling of being ...ashamed. I was ashamed of cutting my hair.

As I sat there, all I could think of was getting off the bus at Camp Pendleton, a fresh recruit arriving at the training base. The Vietnam war had been happening for years and I heard stories of impossible drill instructors. I met Marines on the run, AWOL from the tyranny, had them in my apartment, bore witness to their running from the cops with fake IDs. Peter Inkpen? I always thought less of these AWOL suspects. I thought I would never do that; I'd be better. I would be tough, and I would like it, and endure.

I realized I could never get on that bus to Camp Pendleton. I couldn't withstand the rigors of my identity being stripped away and being reshaped into a 'jarhead'– whose only purpose was to be ordered around by a military superior. Fuck that!

Sitting on the bench with a shaved head in the middle of the mall with the freedom to get up and walk away was bad enough. If I was confined to a barracks, I'd go AWOL. I would be one of those guys that couldn't take it. I'd lose both ways. First, by giving up my identity to the Marines, and second, by having to assume a false identity to survive being AWOL.

That wasn't right. Nothing felt right.

I was sick of this shit. I walked to my '56 Chevy, and drove to Jastro Park, a small park in my old neighborhood where my mother and father had lived, and the family was raised. The 9mm Berretta I had in the trunk of my car was now in my hands, sitting on my lap, as I sat in the driver's seat of my car.

I sat for some time watching the children in the jungle gym. Nineteen years old and nothing to live for. Nobody cared. There was no place for me, either in the war or out of it. No loved ones, no job, no friends, and it was hotter than hell this March afternoon in Bakersfield. Suzan had found her place at Patton State Mental Hospital. Where was I finding mine?

It was then that I made my second bad choice. If you have ever put a loaded gun to your temple, hammer cocked with your finger on the trigger, you know it makes you think extremely fast and precisely.

I suppose the ones that go ahead and pull the trigger are the ones that let their emotions get in the way. For me, I was never deterred by my tears from thinking through the prospects.

I recalled a time in my life when I was happy. It didn't matter how long ago it was. It could have been my birthday when I was ten years old. But then I was very happy about ...everything.

Then I thought, what if I could be that happy again? Maybe not tomorrow, or next month, or next year for that matter; but it's possible to be happy. The point is, I don't have to miss it. I can save myself for it right now.

The very worst that can happen is I'd feel horrible and want to kill myself. But I already feel that way. How much worse can it get than the absolute depths of despair? Nothing. And who knows, in a few months something good might happen. There's no way of knowing without living.

I put the gun down and thought over my next move.

Fuck it. I'm going to Grandma's house in Paso Robles, my mother's mother. I'll get a job on a ranch. And that was the best decision I ever made.

VI

LOVE: THE ULTIMATE HIGH

28. Suzie Finds Asylum

I wrote to my little brother often after I moved away from home. I transferred to San Diego State from Bakersfield Junior College my junior year and never went to class again. It was freedom at last. Nobody to tell me where to go or how to do it. It was all my choice, and because it was 1967, there was no place I'd rather go than San Francisco with flowers in my hair. The question was, "How are you going to get there?"

"Hey Johnny, you wanna go to San Francisco?"

"Sure, I hear Hendrix 's at the Fillmore."

Nobody ever asked, "Who's paying for this?" That's very uncool, man.

Suffice it to say, "I made it, just like I made it to New York, ya dig."

Anyhow, I made it to 812 Guerrero St. in the City, and that was where some real weird shit went down. Remember the letter I sent you July 1, 1968? It was sent a couple of weeks after you graduated from high school.

July 1, 1968

Dear Mark,

I guess summer brings not only warm weather but also itchy feet. At least it seems to have burdened John to a point of departure, among other reasons, I'm sure. I'm moving someplace cheaper so I can have time to sew the dress I designed and only have to work part time to put myself through school. The sorrow I've gone through is never worth telling, not because it's not a beautiful part of a relationship, but because it hurts the ones you tell. I will always love him as I love Johnny or even Gregg, but perhaps more because of its completeness. If a relationship must "end," or shall I say change to a point of separation, may the two involved back off gracefully like ladies and gentlemen. That probably sounds corny, but it's the way I feel. His eyes were so kind and gentle, and I don't want to forget that image.

Thought you might like to send some postcards for brochures to photography schools. If I had the cards, it would be faster than copying them here but -----

(Suzan copied the names and addresses by hand of twelve schools of photography)

These are the only accredited schools in California for photography.

Want you to know I really enjoyed my stay at home – it all proved to be rather touching. I'm just listening to music from

"The Graduate" and it reminded me of you. Good luck Mark – I love you. Your gentleness is the most beautiful part of you. Please take care of yourself.

Tell mother and daddy I may not make it this weekend but will write soon. My mail will be forwarded.

Love

Suzie

As I reread this letter, it sounds like my swan song. Every time the topic of drugs and how they might have influenced my going insane arises, I have to laugh. Drugs weren't the problem. They were the vehicle that transported me to the problem, e.g. Patton State Mental Hospital.

Between'68 and '69 I began to study the world on drugs. I wanted to discover everything about it: from popping veins to going insane and I saw it all. I had my reasons, but why was everybody else doing it? It seemed the whole world was geezing up. Drug use and abuse in this golden era of rock-n-roll was society's child. It appeared to be here for good, or until you couldn't take it anymore, or it killed you.

"Tie me off Rick," I said.

"What'd I tell you about that?" said Rick.

"Please."

"You're in the City now. Learn to tie yourself off... needing help to get off is like asking somebody to wipe your ass."

"Next time... just tie me off."

Rick Hale, wearing a long blue wool trench coat, and a shaved head, reached over and tied me off as I stood in the kitchen of the musky San Francisco apartment, next to the gas stove. I squeezed my fist to pump more blood into my veins, pooling it in the crescent of my arm.

I cooked the powder in a spoon with a couple of drops of water, then drew it through cotton into a syringe. It's best to put a plastic grape on the end of the syringe so you can draw up the hit and squeeze it into your vein. When you release the tie around your arm, you feel the power of the ocean breaking around you, until the rush engulfs your brain, and the tide rushes over your head.

"Oh my God, I feel it going up my spine ...my hair's standing on end. God, that feels good!"

"You like it, baby?"

"God, I love it. And I love you. I love everybody!" I said.

"Yeah, it's exciting. It's got that ether wash on it," smiled Rick.

"They should use this drug for making friends," I said. "The rush up the back of my neck, raising those little hairs, is real friendly."

"You feeling friendly," Rick said, "like you've become the nicest person anyone ever met?"

"That's it."

"Feel like you could be the life of the party, with your good humor and wit?"

"That would be me," said I.

"Or maybe obnoxious as hell because you can't shut up."

"Only because it's a good cause," I laughed.

"We'll see. You're in the safest place in the world now, let's see how you feel when you're coming down. A room full of speed freaks getting off may be the friendliest place in the world, but the same room coming down is ...well, the crankiest place in the world."

"Yeah, that's understandable. Like I get it. It's groovy man." I stammered to say, accentuating my words and trying to exercise my jaw.

"You don't have to worry about coming down for days, baby. I'm taking you on a trip to 'never, neverland,' said Rick.

"Wow, that sounds cool. I love it. Gives me tingles across my shoulders, sort of lifts me on my toes."

"Outta sight baby," said Rick, "This high 'll last four, maybe eight hours, then we'll geez some more."

"That's great, love it, so listen...oh, let me take your coat."

Rick removed his great coat to reveal his pudgy build sticking out of his t-shirt. He tied himself off, holding the belt in his mouth. He touched the cushy area of his elbow pit to examine the damage to his skin. His veins had healed. Rick had just spent nine months at Patton State Mental Hospital. He wasn't committed there because he was crazy. He was ordered to the *snake pit* because that's where they sent drug addicts, if you played your cards right. Rick spent nine months in the pit and was now slithering back into society with fresh new arms.

He found where he wanted to go with the needle, amidst the scars and signs of discoloration. He slid the needle under the skin and watched the blood swirl up into the cannister of the syringe. The magic was squeezed into his arm, which pumped it to his head, where it exploded in his brain.

Rick dropped the fit and slid like a bag of potatoes to the floor, his eyes rolling back in his head. That's where he sat, momentarily knocked out by the dose with his eyes looking comatose red.

That's the way we started up. Rick was an addict and could not restrain himself. He was like me only he wasn't paranoid or delusional. He was an addict that loved the high from methedrine which would end up making him paranoid and delusional. I loved the high from methedrine too. This race we were on called "speed" could only last four or five days, I mean, the human body can only take so much abuse before it shuts down. Staying up for five days without eating is a feat. Let me assure you, it can't be done without drugs.

As each day went by, we'd become more disassociated with reality. The connections in our brains between memories and thoughts became blurred. The reality between actions and feelings got mixed up, making it necessary to do more drugs to keep our world in check. That sense of disassociation got so comfortable we thought you could make a life of it.

The needle was instant Zen. It makes you feel better about being a woman than ever before. Call it cockiness— with the nimbus of your soul surrounding your ass in hot pants, and black net stockings. Parting the seas with a single hit of meth. If you keep pricking yourself, you'll turn into the ancient monk in the *Tibetan Book of the Dead*, spending hours staring at the Paisley print on the living room carpet.

Did you get that? I just said it all, man. That's cool.

Unfortunately, you must come down because you can't keep going up. Your sense of identity as Suzan Cornwall gets erased, and your companions become depression, anxiety, and suicidal thoughts

After you've been up for five days and five nights, you'll know when you can't go any further. So much shit had come down over those five days. Rick and I ran around the Haight, visiting everyone we knew, telling them how we're going to New York City, how I'm going to be a model, how I'm getting a diploma in modeling, and how we'll make serious money on the runway, like Twiggy, and I'd remember them all. My Daddy was supposed to send me money any day now.

On the fifth day, I entered the realm of the never, neverland, or the ultimate mind-altered state. It's like passing through a painful death experience of an old friend. I wanted to bust through the death scene to get to the other side and see what's there. Rick told me the best way to get to the other side was to take a tab of acid to scrub your brain free of methedrine. And then you take a shot of heroin. That's how you ease back into the theater. That was the answer for a tired, worn-out brain.

No doubt I would need help with the shot of heroin, because as soon as that coolant hit my burning brain it would either kill me, or knock me to the kitchen floor, and I'd have to be carried to the couch. That's when your mind is most vulnerable and could start freaking you out in ways I don't want to know about. Some people end up getting dumped on the hospital lawn where hopefully the staff finds them. Fortunately, that wasn't my case.

For those of us who are hard core, and that includes sweet little me, heroin tranquilizes the roar of the beast burning inside you. Everything you ever knew is as forgotten. LSD is washing my brain. Heroin makes the roars fall silent. Staring, staring...until hours later...you can move a muscle on your face and begin to wonder what you can do next, if anything. People were walking by, kicking my chair, with me staring into the Paisely carpet. It was the absolute best way of coming off a five-day run. By the time I came down off the shot of heroin, I'd avoided the pain of coming down on speed.

But I had had enough. I wasn't an addict, I was schizophrenic. So I was able to decide for myself if I ever wanted to poke my body with a needle again. I did not. How I wish it was that easy to quit schizophrenia. Try just saying no to that. But my saying no to schizophrenia —which was what my parents wanted me to do — was like telling Rick to just say no to geezing up. He had nine months to get it out of his system. But he was a hop head, and it wasn't in his DNA to just say no. Two weeks later, Rick killed himself using the grape on his little fit.

Now Daddy wants me to sell shoes – Capizios I bet...

No, he's gone too far. I'm worth more than that. All those things I loved like shoes and perfumes I want to drag across his grave, because I know how much it torments his cheap-ass soul.

VII

JACK AND MARY vs. THE DEVIL

29. Your Boys Did Not Exist

Jack was two years younger than Mary when they met at California State Teachers College in Santa Barbara. It was before the roots were joined with the University of California making it the third oldest University behind Berkeley and UCLA. Santa Barbara was a romantic setting to fall in love with the man of your dreams. Its eucalyptus canopy shaded the red tile campus, looking over the breakwater built by Jack's father, Robert Cornwall, among others. Mary was a bronze skinned 21-year-old from Paso Robles, and her father was City Manager of that small city, last name of Tucker. Jack was spawned locally by a one-legged sea captain and was 19 when he met Mary. The same age as his son Mark, only thirty years earlier.

Jack and Mary made a carnal mistake. They had a shotgun wedding in Las Vegas, so they could squeeze Tod's birthday under the penumbra of the nine-month rule granted newlyweds after wedlock. If your child's birth was less than nine months from wedlock, it better be pre-mature, or eyebrows were raised. Morality becomes a factor; as it did when Tod was born prematurely by C-section on February 1, 1941. He claimed he had suffered from the effects of being born a preemie his entire life. But that was just being Tod. It was his reason why he never matured beyond his teenage years, so he said. But what he should have been ecstatic about was that he wasn't born a bastard.

There was a problem after they got married. It seems Jack had some hesitancy with commitment in the beginning, so Mary moved with baby Tod to Buttonwillow to teach, as Jack remained in Santa Barbara for about a year. But when war broke out on December 7, 1941, with the attack on Pearl Harbor, Jack joined the Navy and the family moved to Oakland for the duration of the war – adding Suzan to the clan four years later.

Jack worked in the Naval mail room to keep the letters flowing to and from the fighting men in the Pacific, to their folks, girlfriends, and wives back home. When the children sat around the dinner table at night and asked what their dad did to help win the war, Mary always told them the reason their father saw no action was because he was married and had a child. That made sense. I didn't know the military could be that sensible.

What would Jack have chosen, if he could choose anything he wanted to be during the war? He would have chosen to be a naval aviator. That always sounded a bit precocious, or a little ironic – compared to sorting mail for four years. He always expected so much from his own children, it was disappointing to think of him in the mailroom for four years. He had a real war injury though. It was a scar on his upper lip from where he always had a cigarette hanging down as he sorted mail. It created a cyst under his lip which had to be cut out.

There is a photograph of the young Cornwall family taken on November 26, 1950, on the back porch of Grandpa Cornwall's house in Santa Barbara. It captures the first Thanksgiving Mark was alive. Huddled together on the narrow backsteps of the house, with eight-month-old Mark sitting on Tod's lap, Suzie's face is the only one that can't be seen because she's turned back to question her parents that are looking down at her. The family dog, "Slippers" has his butt tucked under Tod's legs and sits alert, looking happy with Tod's arm around him.

It's the perfect picture telling the tale of our dysfunctional family. Mark at eight months, Suzie at five years, Tod at nine, Jack at thirty, and Mary at age thirty-two. It all began with our ages, starting with Jack's age of nineteen years old when he got married – still a teenager. That mixed Dad's life up from being what he really wanted to be, which was a faraway sojourner. Perhaps exploring Polynesia with his princess bride. He never forgave us for holding him back.

"I can't believe that George, who the hell does he think he is, talking to me like I'm a child," said Jack.

"Oh, that was the wine talking. He's so full of himself, threatening to charge you for his professional letter writing, that's a joke. He hasn't published anything in years," said Mary.

"Suggesting we take Suzan with us? Oh, I can see that, 'Isn't that marijuana in your luggage?'" said Jack, acting like a border guard.

"You know it would happen, just like when she left the baggy of marijuana under the porch," said Mary.

"Right after I found it the first time," said Jack. "The girl just doesn't think."

"Bringing marijuana into our house is unforgivable," said my mother. "It's so disrespectful."

"She realizes it's against the law, doesn't she? I can hear it now, 'The Cornwall's got another felon on their hands'. That's all we need with us in Berchtesgaden," said Jack. "We'd be held hostage by her."

"How are we going to handle this with Betty and George? They sound so desperate. You'd think Suzan was *their* daughter; and to call us negligent in her care...that's so unfair. That's the alcohol talking, because nobody who knows what we've been through with her 'spoiled little girl act' would say that."

"Hold on there! Let me get this straight," said the Devil's Advocate, "You write in your first letter responding to the Scullin's plea that you help Suzan find a home in California, that you have "written Suzan at *the boys* since that is where we thought she was."

But that's not true, is it? At the time you wrote that letter, "the boys" were living on Makena Beach in Hawaii, nowhere near Suzan who had taken off for New York City and spent the summer of '69 in Stony Brook, NY. at her aunt and uncle's. If you thought she was living with "the boys" before that, you obviously weren't talking to her at all. You write that Suzan agreed with you to stay with Tod, "That was what she agreed to do the last time we talked."

When was the last time you talked with Suzan? Everything you say about where she was to go in California is premised on your understanding that Suzan was "in perfect agreement to be with the boys." That would be Mark, the 19-year-old fool, and Tod, the 27-year-old artist, barely able to feed himself. This is where you expected Suzan to go for help?

Then you write, "So you see we have made an attempt to get in touch with Suzan." Is that true? It appears you were packing up and leaving in the middle of the night. You had not contacted her, nor made it easy to contact you. You were evasive about your whereabouts. You didn't even contact your sister-in-law about her concerns for Suzie when you were two hours from her door in Philadelphia, on your way to Germany. You didn't know where she was for the last six months and didn't want her to be near you at Maquire Air Force Base.

But you write, "We have tried to help this girl for the last three years, but she will not do anything we have advised her to do. She is an adult, and we have no jurisdiction over her."

I can feel you pulling away, distancing yourself from Suzan, as though she has some cooties that might spread onto you. As though she is an alien and you want no part of her, the same as she wants no part of you. And yet, she cries for help.

But you write, "Tod is capable of taking Suzan in hand and he has better communication with her than anyone else."

Are you kidding me? She won't even return Tod's letters to her. Tod is no more capable of taking "Suzan in hand" then he would be taking her by the leg and swinging her around his head. Tod takes his welfare stamps and drives out to the fairgrounds to get a block of cheese and butter. He's dirt poor. It doesn't matter his intent, which is always dubious, or his obvious lack of financial wherewithal to assume the role of conservator over his sister; that's not the problem. The problem is Suzan is mentally ill and looking at a long and expensive road to rehabilitation with many psychiatrists and hours of care. That's the problem.

Beyond all those preliminary considerations, did you actually believe you could turn your responsibility for Suzan over to your eldest child, just because he was the oldest? Older doesn't mean wiser. Have you talked to Tod? Did you know he's getting divorced? That he doesn't live at 909 ½ Westbourne, in Hollywood anymore? That he was living the life of Gauguin over in Hawaii until September.

When you write the absurd line, "If you wish to send Suzie on her way, just let the boys know that she is coming," you know that's rock-solid bullshit. "The boys" as you call them, don't exist. They're getting in fist fights with each other, rolling on the floor, biting and clubbing each other – sticking a loaded gun in the other's face. Those boys don't play nice. Yet, that's where you decided it is best to send Suzan?

When you wrote, "The instructions to Suzan when we left, were that she was to stay with you only until she got the money to get back to California. We think this is the best place for her until she decides as an individual what direction she wants to go," were you high on drugs?

Listen to what you're saying. Your instructions to Suzan before you left for Germany were that "she only stay at Betty and George's until she got enough money to get back to California". Oh, geez, can't she stay longer? Please. She's such a perfect house guest. Maybe she can call the police again to check the hodge podge on their souls. Then, she can go back to Tod's non-existent pad in L.A., until sometime in the future, when she gets good and ready, and then she can make an "individual decision" as to which direction she wants to go. Good idea! Tod and Mark can look after her and support her individualism, whatever that means.

Can't you understand Jack and Mary? Your daughter is insane.

30. Suzan Capitulates

Jack and Mary. Your family dynamic is built on the school system type of love. That's where the parents are the masters, and the children are the students. The students desire the headmaster's love, so they follow their instructions. If they stop following instructions, the love stops. End of story. It's so simple and demands only that parents do not actually love their children. They treat them like cattle. Do as they say and become happier, with more productive lives. Because if they don't do as instructed, they become an outcast and will be forced to live outside the limits with no home.

Because when your parents write in all caps: "PLEASE REMEMBER THAT IT IS NOT YOUR PLACE NOR IS IT OUR PLACE TO DICTATE TO SUZAN CORNWALL WHAT SHE IS TO DO", you know you've been disowned.

That means their hands are not only washed of Suzan, but they're not touching her at all. Yet, on top of this threat you have the gall to write, "Has anyone asked Suzan what she would like to do? It is her life, you know."

What do you think this crisis is all about? You? It's all about what Suzie wants to do. And she's confused over whether she is the suspect in this scenario, or the judge, jury, and executioner.

You, Jack and Mary, offer an apology for Suzan's behavior, still not able to understand she can't be blamed for the way she acts. You write: "She is like so many young people these days who look down on the standards of behavior and social functions that their parents have tried to set."

Suzan was not like the many young people who found fault with the system in the '60's. She was different. She was an adventurer. Perhaps that was the catalyst that drove her to be a delusional schizophrenic – the ultimate altered state. She knew it, and that's why she voluntarily committed herself to the mental ward. It was her only way to escape being crucified by her delusional thinking. She was forced to join the foreign legion of outcast patients.

After you got the news that Suzan had decided on incarceration, you praised "fate for working in strange ways, and that your prayers for two years had been answered." But it had nothing to do with either Fate or God. You forced her hand and celebrated your victory by declaring, "I am sure Suzan made the best choice for herself."

What are you talking about? It was her only choice. I'm sure your supporters are saying, "Thank God! Now they can tranquilize the girl." But you're talking like Suzan acted like any other reasonable outcast would act — choosing from various life plans, like searching for colleges. It was nothing like that.

And you "knew she'd make the best choice for herself," did you? That means Suzan chose to live her life in the Snake Pit rather than in society. After she chose the pit, the onus of making that decision was lifted entirely off Mary and Jack, and rested on Suzan, even though her parents made that decision for her by leaving her with no other option but to join the Snake Pit.

It was Suzan's fault; she deserved the Snake Pit. It was Suzie's decision, individually, solo, on her own, it's her life, no one can live it for her, her parents did not dictate anything to Suzan. They simply abandoned her by leaving the country and flying 8,000 miles away without a peep, so Suzie could make her decision on her own, all alone, isolated. That would have been a clever move by Mary and Jack, but for the Scullin's interfering. Clever or cruel? Whatever way you look at it, it was done. Mary, did you think of that yourself?

Trust me, no one saw that coming at the time.

How far down in the sand can you stick your head, Jack and Mary? You didn't even try to help her. Didn't even throw her a grand. You were too busy trying to escape. Uncle George was right. You were headstrong on going to Germany and didn't need your mentally handicap daughter hanging around for fear of being exposed as the neglectful father you are.

Your prayers had been answered. Finally, somebody would take responsibility for Suzan and do it for free. "Free" was key, because no psychiatrist was getting their fingers on a single red cent of Jack's money. The parents had already given up on Suzan and now she was incarcerated. Hallelujah! Now they would be safe from her craziness.

In your formal letter to "Betty and George" from "Jack and Mary", in fact, your last letter to the Scullin household ever, you use the term "regret" five times, each time regretting Betty and George's involvement in the Suzan debacle. But what would have happened if they had not become involved?

What if they had never opened their door for Suzan to come vexing, drumming her fingers on the wall and washing her hair incessantly? What if they hadn't been willing to share their love and concern over her demanding and selfish ways? What if they slammed the door shut the very day she appeared on the doorstep of the 62-year-old writer's cottage? What would have happened to Suzan then?

No, she needed George and Betty to go to war with her father. His lack of action was appalling. Susie kept poking and prodding them to act, often out of pure frustration. The walls kept coming closer and closer, moving in on her until she was finally surrounded. Do you think that her decision to go to the Snake Pit was a capitulation?

Hah! That'll be the day.

Jack and Mary never did thank the Scullin's for helping Suzan. Instead, they regretted they ever got involved in the Cornwall family affairs. But how else could Suzan have ever gotten to the airport with a TWA ticket to California.

I guess that's what families are for.

31. Mary's Wedding Dress

But alas, in the end there's truth.

The final letter from the Cornwall's to the Scullin's reads, *"You surely know how we regret this – we know everything you have gone through for we have been through it over and over again and it hurt much deeper because she was our daughter – she was a lovely daughter too and I have many happy memories but she wanted no part of Jack and I, and has fought us and put us through a great deal.*

You have been very angry with us, and this too is regrettable. But you have not had a thorough understanding of our situation. When we applied for this job, it was because our children let us know in no uncertain terms that they were on their own and that they did not need us for anything. We were proud of the fact and felt that now we had a chance to do something we had wanted to do – is that really so selfish?"

Yes Mary, it was. And it's sad to hear you talk in past tense about your lovely daughter who is not dead yet. We know it hurts you the most, not because you loved your daughter more, but because you had more false pride invested in what she should be. Look at the cost to your family for abandoning Suzie; you don't have one anymore.

Perhaps you never did have a family. Every child, aged 19, 23, and 27, told you that they were not just on their own, but they didn't need you for anything? That sounds like the boasting of young adults whose brains are still growing, young adults who are unaware of their need for family as they get older.

Perhaps you never taught them that "family" is an asset. It's not something you can make disposable when it doesn't suit you. You don't rip it off and throw it away like old gloves, just when the work gets tough. How can a child know if they will need their parents in the future?

There is a moral bond between parents and their children, isn't there? One that extends beyond the age of twenty-three. But in our situation, it sounds more like the parents wanted to dissolve that moral bond. Or they would like the State to step into their shoes and do something with the poor girl. Feed her, house her. That way, Jack and Mary can go on their merry way to Berchtesgaden thinking "Our work with Suzan is done!" I can see them brushing off their hands. Or perhaps they never even cared.

But now, here you are. Your daughter's incarcerated in Suffolk County Mental Hospital, your eldest boy is divorced with no job, and your youngest is unemployed with no place to live either. And you decided to pull up roots and leave the country.

You're never going to accept the fact you were wrong to believe your children wouldn't need you. Or is this punishment for Suzie treating both of you so unfairly? And now, you're escaping to the Alps to fulfill your dreams of a lifetime together. Good for you!

But when you write, "We were proud of the fact" that our children made us feel they didn't need us, that is a lie. You're not calling the kettle black; you're calling the kettle gold. You're not looking at your family as it is, you're looking at what you wanted it to be; exactly how it fits into your plan.

"The gold will show through" Jack claimed. Let me help you folks. Your family is dysfunctional. You prove this when you write, "You have had plenty of counseling and guidance all of which you disregarded because it wasn't your way – *that is as it should be,* you know yourself and what you want to do. No one can live your life for you."

What? That's not as it should be. A daughter isn't supposed to disregard the counseling given to her because it's not her way. What does "her way" even mean, anyway? The *paranoid schizophrenic's* way? You can hear the irony and disrespect gargling in your voice, *that is as it should be.* The gears are grinding to make sense of how that possibly means you, "know what you want to do." It doesn't make sense.

Then comes the undeniable superlative of meaningless phrases. I can't argue with that. "Can't have teats on a boar," and "Nobody can live your life for you." That's all a bunch of bologna, and I can't help but feel that you're doing it on purpose. Your proclamation "so be it", doesn't make it so.

You write, "The fact that you didn't want to see the doctors should have shown Betty you have faith in yourself. We know you are capable – all that is lacking is your will to do it – no one can create that for you."

Words to live by? I'm going to be sick.

Yes, Mother, it's all a question of will power, and *paranoid schizophrenia* are just letters that make-up words. But tell me something Mother, how much of that power did you use when you got pregnant out of wedlock with Daddy? Those youthful indiscretions ruined any hopes of seeing Mary in a wedding gown, radiating the purity of woman. No wedding pictures for you.

Sometimes you need a little help and understanding from your parents – is that really so selfish?

VIII

THE GREAT ESCAPE

32. Mark's Got a Plan

How many times have I written, "What do I know?" when talking about what was expected of me when it came to Suzan going crazy. But here's an example of what I didn't know, and why that got me in deep doo-doo. "Aiding and abetting an escapee from a Mental Institution in the State of California is a Felony."

Suzan returned to Bakersfield from Suffolk County Mental Health Hospital in October 1969 and found herself reincarcerated the next day in Ward 3B of the Kern County Mental Health Hospital. It had been Suzan against the world ever since then. Now it is Christmas.

It's black, real black. A pitch black pupil of an eye is looking out. From somewhere deep within the pupil you see a light shining, a spotlight trying to escape. Shapes begin fluttering from behind the spotlight. Shiny colors, an old movie, a slot machine maybe?

The rolling images are coming from a T.V. screen. The pupil is watching local newscasters saying something. There's the green and blue iris, with two men in suits pulsating in the eye's reflection. They sit behind a large desk, talking, but background noises drown their voices out.

The ambient noise grows louder. The clunking of the tables, the scraping of chairs on the linoleum, even shuffling feet, help create a gentle moan that echoes down the halls. And now comes the eyebrow; a sandy blond shade; with her nose, cute and angular, slim nostrils, meant for the face of a young woman indulged in certifiable delusions of grandeur. She is not disturbed by her surroundings. Her focus is on the newscasters. She hears fragments of their voices through the din of background noise. The T.V. image is swallowed up in the texture of her flesh, her hair, and a black mole on the upper lip of Suzan Cornwall.

Welcome to Suzie's world. *Caveat Emptor.* Here's what's on her mind:

Newsperson No.1: ... "New York fashion model...everyone is watching and knows...from the president..."

Newsperson No. 2 ... "it was by Greyhound...twisted her Mind...hodge podge..."

Newsperson No. 1 ... "attention getting behavior...get a job..."

Newsperson No.2 ... "witchcraft...no, hodge podge...on their souls..."

Suzan, now approaching twenty-four, had almost blossomed into the beauty she hoped to be but didn't quite make it. The proverbial "also ran." She'd been to modeling school, so she had the right moves. She knew what to do, that wasn't the problem. She tried to keep the charm alive, but it got pushed down by defiance and resentment. Two defense mechanisms used religiously by paranoid schizophrenics.

She had to defend herself against her older brother and parents, her worse critics, for being the most pitiful person in the world because she was getting psychiatric care from those fine government doctors. This meant, according to Dad, that she was the laziest, good for nothing scammer on the planet, all at the cost of the poor taxpayer. She better get a job.

Suzan was a single woman that needed a parent at home that loved her. A place where she could feel safe. That's the way she was raised. No one ever told her, "Enjoy your family while you can. We're not going to be here for you later." Or did they?

She wears an unapproachable veneer so nobody can talk to her. She had it all, at one time, except for her sanity. Something wasn't quite right, got misplaced, or lost.

The view is reversed now and focuses on the television screen. You can see the newscasters debating:

Newsperson No. 1 says, "It's something we've seen over and over again; the homeless, the cursing, the talking heads...Who cares?"

From somewhere in back, she could hear the deep thuggish sound of the orderly, Ramon's voice saying, "Suzan Cornwall!"

Newsperson No. 1. says, "Oh boy, it looks like a visitor. Think it's Johnny? Hey, let's call the sheriff. ...the mother's turning her in...more later."

Suzie doesn't react to Ramon calling her name. She can hear the huge Hispanic bellowing her name throughout the hall, but she chooses to ignore him. She enjoys ignoring him and is smiling.

"Suzan, your brother's here," says Ramon, standing right in front of her.

Susie doesn't move a muscle; well, maybe a shiver from her lips.

Newsperson No. 2. "Did you hear that? I wonder if she will continue to pretend not to hear him?'

Newsperson No. 1., "I doubt it."

Newsperson No. 2., "It's her little brother. I wouldn't think that long."

Suzie snaps out of it. She's sitting in the T.V. room at the Visitors Center in the Mental Ward 3B in Bakersfield. This is where you go before being sent to the big house at Patton's Snake Pit. It was like starting over again at Suffolk County for a fifteen-day non-voluntary observation. It's a large area on the top floor above the criminally insane located on the second floor. This is where Suzan was taken for observation after breaking a window while visiting Johnny Burnette's home. It was her welcome to California's looney bin. The patients were not free to leave.

The patient was transferred to the Visitor Center from the dorm if they were lucky enough to have a visitor. The Center was on the third floor. The entrance to the Visitors' Center was through a locked white door guarded by orderlies and nurses. The Center itself is a high-ceilinged cluster of rooms, with threadbare sofas, and chairs with saggy seats.

The rooms were fluorescently lit to show the crevassed faces of the patients. Some of them looked odd, some were addicts, all are in dull gray uniforms putting up red and green decorations for Christmas. It was that time of year again and I had the Christmas spirit in my heart. There was a big Santa Clause cut-out on the locked door leading to freedom.

I finally found something I could do for Suzan. I could break her out of the mental ward. That's what she wanted; she told me so many times. That's what she was begging for. She was still in the fucking mental hospital and all she wanted was out and everything would be okay. I knew she had been wrongly accused. Why doesn't the government just let her go? Whatever happened to *habeas corpus?* Try to explain that to a nineteen-year-old.

Well, this was something I personally understood and could properly respond to. It was something I had to do to live with myself. I wasn't trying to be rebellious or some kind of hero. I was trying to give my sister her God given right to live her life as she wanted – free from captivity. That's all there was to it.

My parents would not have liked the plan to upset the will of the government but fuck my parents. They were the ones that dumped this whole problem regarding Suzan on me in the first place. They're the ones who refused to take care of the problem they created, that they brought into the world – Suzie.

They gave their child to the State of California. That's when my parents said she was old enough to know she had to work. It never entered their minds that they, as parents, could have raised a child that turned out to be a paranoid schizophrenic. Nobody knew it could happen. After living twenty-two years of vitality, it seemed unfathomable she would go crazy. This wasn't my parents' fault, was it? It was hidden in the genes.

It was all Suzie's fault. She trapped her parents into thinking she had a promising future. She'd have no problem wrangling a husband from her many suitors. But it was equally disappointing to watch Suzie's dating life falter.

All I could think of was freedom for my sister. When I was 13 years old, I would lie on Suzie's bed, and she would regale me with tales of what it was like in high school, while I lingered in junior high.

I was the Emerson Junior High School President, the Junior Optimist President, Captain of the basketball team, winner of the O.D. Williams Award, even winner of the Bakersfield Talent Show, playing the *Hungarian Rhapsody* on the piano, an all-around good guy – except for the week I sat on restriction bench for pounding on Mrs. Beason's music room door. That random act of junior high stupidity I am guilty of. I did learn to play the spoons while on restriction. Nevertheless, I longed to be just like my sister.

33. Suzan Shows Grit

Suzie let me come along one night when she snuck out the station wagon with her girlfriends and we'd run a "Chinese fire drill." That's where you get to a corner, and everybody jumps out of the station wagon and runs around the vehicle waving your hands in the air yelling. I only did that once and it was a blast.

Suzie got the car back without getting caught also. That's the Suzie I was following anywhere that night. Now I'm 19 and going to extend the Christmas spirit to Suzan. Not taking her with me from Ward 3B would have been like leaving her at the orphanage.

With that as my inspiration, I enlisted Tod to drive the get-away car. It wasn't hard, I offered him dope. I visited Suzan several times earlier in my own '56 Bel Aire Coupe, observing the lay of the land around the Hospital. My plan was simple. We'd drive to the Hospital for an evening visitation. I'd go up and get Suzie out. Tod would park where I told him, so when he saw us burst through the double doors running towards him, he would know to "get his motor running."

It's a long haul running from the hospital to the pick-up spot, where Tod would swoop us up. But for sure there would be no shooting. It would be a matter of intimidation for the extraction.

Here's how that plan worked out:

It took fifteen minutes to drive up to the mental ward from Tod's apartment. I went over the plan one last time. Tod would park on the utility road in the back. It had a clear view of the exit doors at the bottom of the building that were about a hundred yards away. He'd start watching the doors at 7:00 pm. And when he sees us bolt out the glass doors, he'll start the engine and we'll be running down the sidewalk, directly along the grass to the parking spot. We'll jump in and be gone. A smash and grab type of deal.

I checked into the nurses' station and was received in the visiting room by the hefty orderly, Ramon. I was asked to wait there, which I did. And soon I saw Suzan walking behind Ramon, looking like she knows something nobody else does. Her features soften when she sees me. I know she loves to see her little brother, not so little anymore. My eyes get wet from tears just from the sight of her. She sees I'm distressed and tries to console me.

"Did you hear them talking about me on the news?" she said.

"What'd they say," I said.

"They said the President is sending troops into this hospital. So don't even think about breaking me out because we don't have a chance. But if you do, will you take me up to Cannery Row, because that's really where I want to be."

"Do you really think they were talking about you on the news?"

"It's a conspiracy...and thanks for not being part of it. But I *know* they were talking about me. Just don't let them know I know. Otherwise, I'll never get out of here," she said, giving me an assured nod.

"Whatever you say."

"Have you seen Johnny Burnette? Did he contact you?" she asked me anxiously.

"Don't ever mention that name to me again. Not ever. Do you understand?

"Geez," she said under her breath, "Don't you understand, I have to talk to him."

"He doesn't want to talk to you."

"That's not true. Why do you think I went to his house? Not to visit his mother. If she tells me one more time he's not there..."

"Let me guess. You'll call the police?" I said.

"You know, with all these medications they give me, there's a lot I don't remember. But I think she called the police."

The incident to which Suzan was referring happened in the gap between the time she left Suffolk County Mental Ward, and the time it took for her to arrive at Patton State Mental Hospital. She was given a "get-out-of-jail-free" card by Suffolk County and released to her aunt and uncle who immediately raced her to the airport to put her on a plane to Los Angeles.

Unfortunately, nobody was notified she was coming to L.A. from New York City. My brother had left Hollywood. I was somewhere in Bakersfield. My girlfriend, Page Forsythe, who assumed the lease on Tod's and Lisa's bungalow in Hollywood, answered the phone when my uncle called, but she couldn't pick Suzie up either, because she had a class, and couldn't recognize her anyway.

So there was my deranged sister, one step away from being homeless, unwanted and forsaken at Los Angeles Airport. Bakersfield is 110 miles north of the airport. My aunt and uncle were mortified. Then my aunt remembered Mrs. Bovard in Bakersfield, whose daughter Bonnie was a friend of Suzie's. Bonnie was now married with two kids and living elsewhere. It was Mrs. Helen Bovard who came to my sister's rescue.

Helen Bovard was a saint of a woman. The type of woman who could take control of the situation immediately upon being contacted. After Aunt Betty telephoned her in Bakersfield, out of the blue, not knowing her personally at all, and pleading who knows what about Suzan, Mrs. Bovard had it in her heart to drive the 110 miles to the airport in L.A. to try and find Suzie from amongst the thousands of travelers at TWA. And she succeeded.

She found Suzie wandering through the TWA terminal and brought her back to her home in Bakersfield. This was no easy task and demanded extra-ordinary patience given Suzie's bouts of "excitement." I didn't have a car at that time, but when I finally got over to the Bovard's, who I didn't know either, I saw crazy in Suzie's eyes for the first time.

I saw it immediately in her twitching eye. As we sat out on the grass, talking in the front yard, it became glaring. I began to wonder if it had always been there, and I organically accepted it as part of Suzie's personality. But no, she had lots of friends growing up. No one ever mentioned "crazy" and "Suzie" in the same sentence. But she had no friends now, because she was crazy, and you could see it. She'd gone so far around the bend I barely recognized her anymore.

34. With a Cherry on Top

I never saw Suzie as an insane person until I sat with her on Bovard's lawn and got smacked by the fact she'd gone nuts – just by looking at her. It didn't matter what she said, although I'm sure that was crazy also.

She looked different, like my mother did at her funeral when I finally realized she was dead, with her black-eyed Halloween mask on, her red lips still tied with twine, and a tuff of black hair on top of her head. A horrible looking doll no one wanted to play with. That's how sure I was that Suzan was mentally ill.

It was emblazoned across her face and replaced with two sorrowful, nutty eyes. She had one eye on me and the other in a faraway place. I hated that look, because it left no room for hope.

The next day, she wandered off to Johnny Burnette's house. Who is Johnny Burnette? Well, he could be Dick Evans, Elvis Chavez, or some other boy she thought deserted her in the past few years. It didn't matter. Suzie had it in her head that Johnny Burnette owed her something, and she was going to plead her case or shake it out of him. Good luck with that.

Johnny wasn't home, but his mother was. She wasted no time having Suzan arrested. Or I should say, Suzan wasted no time in having herself arrested. There was no doubt the arrest came because of the planter Suzie threw through their kitchen window, not believing his mom when she said Johnny wasn't home.

It was apparent she was begging for government intervention, and that's what she got. For the price of a broken window Suzan was punished with a life sentence in the Snake Pit. It's not like she ran from the police; she welcomed them. And just like that, Suzie's observation period was over – it was straight to Ward 3B. When Mrs. Bovard heard the news about Suzie getting picked up at Johnny's house she said, "All I can say now is, "keep the faith" and hope God or somebody will be good to this girl. I'll do what I can."

But she had done everything she could.

It was now my turn.

I was trying to do something good for Suzan. To show her there was still a person that loved her, even though she couldn't recognize it. To let the world know she was loved and not abandoned by her brother who wouldn't let her go to the Snake Pit; surrounded by perverts and other demons lurking about, preying on her, sharing her torture.

I was Suzie's last chance for romance. Her last chance for hope. I was the last person who cared enough to do something about her incarceration – even if it was wrong. I saw nothing wrong with busting my sister out of a Mental Hospital for which she was unjustly committed. You shouldn't get a lifetime of incarceration in the Snake Pit for breaking a window.

The word "unjust" was the controlling factor. We had taken a seat on the couch of the near empty visiting center.

That's how I saw it. The whole world was against my sister after she was nothing but sweet to me. While my parents discarded her for her antics, that was their business, but I was not letting go of Suzie's hand.

I was old enough to have a beef with society myself. My life was upended by my football injury. Without football I had little to go on. I didn't have the intellectual capacity to make something bright out of such a bleak tragedy that befell our family. We had a misfit in the clan, a potential leader who turned out lame. It happens.

Who cares whose fault it was or where the umbilical cord ends, or when parental advice is sought and listened to. Would Suzie and I have fared better if our parents had decided to stay in Bakersfield?

Hah! That would have been hell!

35. Free at Last

I was looking around the Visitor Center, acting like we were having an interesting conversation as I scouted things out. There was a clock on the wall that read a quarter till seven. That gave me fifteen minutes to put the plan into action. I noticed another orderly in the Hall, a skinny Caucasian with tattoos. Why do all the orderlies look like they come from an underprivileged socio-economic background that likes to fight?

I sized him up. An old habit from Bakersfield. He didn't look too tough.

"I'm taking you out of here right now," I told Suzan.

"Are you crazy? That big Spaniard will break you like a pencil. They keep those doors locked you know. It's not like anybody wants to be here. We could all walk out, we'd run out if the doors weren't locked. We're "crazy" you know? Not crippled. You don't see anybody in wheelchairs here, do you? You know why? Because people aren't scared of wheelchairs, but they sure as hell are scared of crazy people."

"I'm not interested in that now. I don't know when I'll get a second chance. Maybe they'll move you tomorrow. That's what I'm afraid of."

"Well, you've got a point. But we're three floors up. How are you going to get Ramon to unlock the door? He is not going to be happy about this. It's his job and...no, no, he's not going to let us out of here..."

"I know that. ... It's his choice if he wants to get physical. ...But you're goin' out tonight."

We both got up to peer around the corner to see where Ramon was standing. He was next to the front door with Santa on it, swinging a ring of keys on his finger. There's nothing friendly about him. I admit to being demoralized by his presence – but I'm nothing, if not an optimist.

"Ah, he's probably too fat to be able to do anything about it." I muttered, hoping that was true.

We returned to our seats.

"Tod's waiting in the car. We'll have to run a couple of blocks, then jump in and go. It'll be a clean getaway."

"Sure. If you say so."

There's one thing a getaway man should be when behind the wheel, and that is cool. Tod was anything but that. The last time he looked at his watch it was seven till seven. It was everything Tod could do to get his roach lit. A little-o-bitty butt of a joint he kept trying to light with a match. He was burning his fingers out of nervousness. "Come on man, one more try."

The roach, the time, the car, its gears were all coming together in his mind at once. But first, the joint. There was nothing cool going on with Tod. He was the opposite of cool in anticipation of the breakout. Very excited. In retrospect, I can understand why.

"Suzie, all you have to do is follow me up to the front door. We'll act like you're saying good-bye, and blah, blah, blah. Then, when Ramon opens the door for me, we'll both run like hell down the hall."

"That's your plan? Well, I don't see how that can work. I mean, they'll stop us. There's sheriffs on the second floor, the criminally insane are down there. They'll chase us like criminals and the worse thing I've ever done is smoke too many cigarettes. I..."

"Stop," I said, "You want out of here, right? This is the only way I can think of. Don't worry, Tod's waiting for us in the car. We'll just jump in and ride away. You can outrun this fat loaf, can't you?"

"Oh, I hope so."

"Are you ready??"

Suzie and I got up and inched our way into the front hallway. It was about twenty yards from there. The clock struck seven o'clock as we exited the visitor's center and headed down the hall to the only door guarded by Ramon. We paid him no mind because we were so engrossed in our conversation, saying our goodbyes and making plans for future visits.

We were half-way down the hall. They weren't on to us. A cadre of orderlies didn't suddenly emerge from the walls. There was that skinny orderly somewhere on the premises, but nobody else was leaving. It was just me, and my nemesis there to stop me. He was standing in my way with the keys to the door in his hand. I straightened myself up and tried to act as nonchalantly as I could. I smiled at Ramon, and this act of sanguinity cracked my sister up. We continued sauntering down the hall. Timing is everything in these matters.

"Thanks for coming. Say hi to Dad. Say, would you mind if I came with you?" said Suzan.

"I'll be back on Sunday," I almost shouted this at Ramon.

"That's fine," said Suzie, "but I won't be here cause they're shipping me to the Snake Pit tomorrow. Remember, paranoid schizophrenic? Dwells in the Snake Pit."

"Oh, that's right. That's the big pit in the middle of Berdoo where they drug you and keep you for the rest of your life."

I was on the edge of making myself mad and completely blowing it. I stole a glimpse of Ramon waiting at the front door, listening.

"Don't forget the shock therapy."

"Yeah, mom and dad will be happy about that. Okay, take care of yourself."

"Say hi to them for me," she managed to say in finality.

"I will, and of course, Tod sends his love. ...hopes to see you soon."

Tod, having smoked his way through the roach, is now trying to light an even smaller roach, the size of his fingertip. He was ready at seven o'clock, ready to drive, engine running, staring at the doors at the end of the grass, but where were they? He waited and wondered, but he wasn't going to waste the gas, so he turned the engine off at 7:05.

He then searched the ashtray for the biggest roach not yet smoked. He burned his fingers while lighting it and sucked the flaming roach down his throat in the process. Spitting ashes, he jumps out of the car and brushes the embers off his shirt.

"God-damn rag weed," cursed Tod.

Meanwhile, Suzie and I were at the door with the big Santa on the front of it.

"How's Tod doing anyway? I wish I could see him," pleaded Suzie.

"Doing great. He's got about ten weeks of unemployment left," I said.

We were at the door watching Ramon turn the key. He gave a snort at this last comment. He doesn't like unemployment, he doesn't like crazy people, and he's the one with the keys.

All three of them are closing in on the front door.

"Well, give me a hug," and I gestured toward Suzie, as Ramon opened the door wide for me to leave. When he did, I made a move on him that took him by surprise. I turned on him quickly, forcefully shoving him a few steps back with my left hand, pinning him against the wall. It wasn't a violent shove, it was a matter-of-fact type of shove, that made my point clear. "I'm taking her out of here," I said, looking right in his face.

I left my right hand free in case I had to enforce my command. Ramon read me loud and clear, and stepped back to clear the way. But the threat to Ramon's authority had been a surprise and was quickly replaced by anger, and fear of losing his job. "Help, they're escaping. Stop them. Stop them!" he called out to the other orderly, yelling as loud as he could.

Ramon grabbed the desk phone by the door, "They're escaping. Stop them...Police!

The chase was on. I didn't waste any more time with Ramon. I grabbed Suzie's hand and tore off down the hallway like an escaped ape from the zoo. Suzie hung on like a little monkey. We got to the stairs and hurled ourselves down the steps.

Ramon ran into the hallway and caught a glimpse of us turning down the stairwell corner. He stopped and yelled at us. "You can't get out of here, you're caught!"

Ramon continued to chase, lumbering after us, but by the time he got to the stairs he was already out of gas. He was tired, feeling all 325 pounds of himself. You could hear him breathing like he had glass packs in his lung's – rumbling deep inside.

But here came his colleague, the skinny white kid with tatts, a tall drink of water that could fly. He pulled up next to Ramon on the stairs:

"Go get 'em Vernon. God-dammit, get those motherfuckers, or it will be our asses. My Momma gonna kill me I lose this job."

"Don't worry Ramon. I got those crazy bastards."

I was more worried about the sheriffs myself. I'd seen them on my way up. The two of them were posted in front of the second floor to guard those visiting the "delusional criminally insane". But the way we were taking the stairs, we passed right by them before they could get up. The sheriffs watched us circle around the linoleum and charge down the next flight of stairs as they rose out of their seats to see what the ruckus was about. They probably got the idea when they saw Vernon following in hot pursuit, and finally Ramon, but it was too late by then.

We blasted out the double glass doors and ran into people coming in. This slowed our escape dramatically. People were making their way in, a whole mob of them, and I began to shout..."excuse me, sorry, pardon me"...

"Run faster, run faster!"

"Who do you think I am, Wilma Rudolph?"

We were running between the building and the wide-open lawn. It was the last fifty yards to the Chevy — the only car at the end of the sidewalk. Vernon was gaining on us, in fact, he was right behind me. Ramon had just left the glass doors. I had to do something. I let go of Suzie's hand and told her to keep running to the car. Then I turned to face my foes.

Vernon stopped in his tracks at the threat of violence and backed off.

"What the fuck are you doing?" I asked Vernon, "Stop right there."

"You're in a lot of trouble. We got the police coming right now," he said in a jittery voice.

I turned to make certain Suzie was still running. She was almost there. Then Ramon finally showed up. He was panting, angry, and generally fed up with this whole escape business.

"I ain't taking this shit from you," he said, "you white-paddy motherfucker...I'm getting your crazy ass sister back here, and making damn sure both you get locked up in the Snake Pit." Ramon approached me with anger in his eyes. I took one step forward and kicked him squarely in the nuts. I could hear 'em crack, folding Ramon over in two, immediately dropping him onto the sidewalk. He was crawling on his hands and knees to get away, moaning like a little bitch.

"Those are the only nuts you'll be taking with you to the Snake Pit. Don't forget the strait jackets and looney bins."

I looked at Vernon and could tell that was the first time he saw a tough guy get kicked properly in the balls. It hurts everyone the same. With mouth agape, he watched his boss crawling on the pavement, balls in hand, his mouth drooling on the walkway. Vernon said, "I still got to chase you, man. It's my job."

"Well, chase all you want. Just don't catch us."

I took off running after Suzan, and Vernon dutifully lagged behind like a puppy dog. He stayed close enough to get my license number though. I remember seeing him out of my peripheral vision as I jumped in the car and Tod floor-boarded the engine — only to find he accidentally shoved it in reverse. How did that happen? It's an automatic. I heard the evil sound of gears grinding wildly before the car stopped. I glared at Tod like he'd just dropped the engine.

"What have you done?" I glared at him.

"This car is fucked up man," said Tod.

"What imbecile can't put the car in drive and drive."

"It's not my fault," said Tod.

"You put it in reverse!"

"Reverse osmosis man," said Tod, shaking his head.

"Motherfucker."

We sat there, stranded. Tod struggling to get the car started, turning the keys over and over. It sounded like the starter was going next. Vernon was standing around the back of the car awkwardly because he could have grabbed the door and opened it if he wanted to. But the engine grabbed first and suddenly we were screeching tires to get out of there, leaving a cloud of rubber on the road.

Suzie had the last laugh on that one. I celebrated setting myself free of any further moral obligation to my sister. I was young and felt good about freeing her. Things were made slightly more right with the world. Suzie was given back her life, her right to privacy, and Constitutional right to pursue happiness.

Tod knew all along how it was going to end and just came along for the ride.

36. Justice is Done

Four years later, I was picked up by the Sheriff's Department in Santa Barbara with a warrant out for my arrest. I was a passenger during a routine traffic stop, where my brother was driving, of course. We were just leaving FUBAR's, a local drinking hole, when were followed by two sheriff's cars out of the lot. Tod, being the idiot he was, made a right-hand turn without using his blinker, giving the police officer probable cause to pull us over for the traffic violation. And having our licenses checked for warrants.

"Grab him, he's a felon!" said the sheriff after being informed by the officer on the radio that sure enough, he came up with a fellow who committed a felon. He couldn't tell me what the crime I violated was, just that it was a violation of a felony. I'm not sure I knew the difference between a misdemeanor and a felony at the time, but I knew enough to know I didn't commit any felony.

It was very much like a page out of Franz Kafka's *The Trial.* They couldn't tell me what I was accused of, only that it was a felony, and that I committed it. It seemed impossible none of the four officers present knew what the crime was I was being arrested for. It was so strange: they didn't even want to give it a guess. I was going to have to wait until I'd been fingerprinted and shuffled through the system before I found out the true nature of the charges against me.

"You're accused of 'practicing cosmetology without a license,' which is a felony according to the California Criminal Code," said the police captain who knew everything, but wasn't sharing it with me. I was thrown into complete befuddlement. "Practicing cosmetology?" It made me think, "Who's hair did I cut?" And then I thought, "Does this have to do with reading Tarot Cards?" Of which I was guilty. But no, I had not committed a felony against the cosmos, or have I? But it's not astrology. It's cosmetology, "dumb ass."

When I went to my arraignment in Bakersfield a month later, I wasn't worried because I was obviously the butt of a big mistake by the police. I didn't get scared until I was sitting in the court room in Bakersfield with a cranky old judge handing out sentences of five years, ten years, twenty years to the young fellows in the jury box wearing orange jumpsuits and looking like me.

They were accepting their plea agreements and there must have been twenty of them. It amazed me the State of California could so easily be willing to house and feed these men for years of incarceration. What the hell did they do? What's one more? It seemed uncanny the way society was so willing to incarcerate its population, and the next one may be me.

After the judge finished with them, he turned to me.

"Okay," said the Judge, "you're here for a failure to appear on charges of Aiding and Abetting an Escapee from a Mental Institution; how do you plea?"

I almost fell to the floor. Talk about a shocker. That was the first time I had heard those words "aiding and abetting" since I was in the fifth grade. That's when I learned of the assassination of Abraham Lincoln, and the doctor that helped care for the broken leg of his assassin, John Wilkes Booth, was found guilty of 'aiding and abetting' the assassin of Lincoln. Remember that? So I knew anything that had to do with aid and abet was bad. But I hadn't assassinated anyone.

When you hear it in a courtroom in connection with the charges brought against you, you feel a blow to your gut. But when it's followed by "an escapee of a mental Institution" it brings down the house. The jury of orange jumpsuits cooed at the sound of it, they were immediately drawn into my case and impressed by its stature. That's a felon, baby. The words "escapee" and "Mental Institution" made it sound as though I'd done something crazy.

I stood there, not knowing what to say, so I said, "They told me at the time of my arrest it was for "practicing cosmetology without a license..."

"It doesn't matter what you were told, the charges are 'aiding and abetting an escapee from a mental institution.' How do you plea?"

"Ahh..." I stammered.

"Perhaps you should consult with an attorney."

The only attorney in court at the time was the Assistant D.A., Rock Tanner. He turned out to be a reasonable prosecutor, if there was such a thing. Anybody that listens to your story is reasonable if they believe you. For me, this escapee bullshit was old news. Now I was 23 years old, and the confusion over the sanity of my sister was resolved back in 1969. It was now 1973.

1969 was the year Suzie demonstratively proved she was loco, and nothing could be done about it. Except, institutionalize her – she was a *paranoid schizophrenic* and that was hopeless. She thought there was a conspiracy to put her in a mental institution. Hey, no shit! As my mother said, "No one can live your life for you."

This whole imbroglio had killed my mother with an aneurysm in 1972. After that, my father remarried a *frauline* in Germany, then died ten years later, a painful death from melanoma cancer. He'd been fighting it for years. It was his gift for teaching kids to swim at the Union Avenue Plunge in Bakersfield.

I told the attorney Suzie's misfortune was my parents' fault for leaving her in Bakersfield. There was no need to punish me now. I showed my redemption to society by continuing my education and became a student of philosophy at UCSB with only one quarter left to graduate. I wanted to go to law school.

Otherwise known as Mad Dog Tanner, the Assistant District Attorney listened to my plea and allowed me to talk him into dismissing my case in the interest of justice. Perhaps he had a sister languishing in a snake pit somewhere. I doubt it. But he did find a soft spot for a kid that broke his sister out of an insane asylum, only to have her return the next day on her own accord. Or perhaps he simply had an affinity for the absurd.

The naming of my crime got mixed up when the police officer in Santa Barbara read the Code Section from the California Criminal Code, instead of its proper Code Section which was the Health and Welfare Code. That's why I was arrested for Practicing Cosmetology (not Cosmotology) Without a License, which is a felony, if you can believe that.

In the end, I figured Suzan played a big role in the outcome of my case. Craziness is contagious like that and can affect everything it touches. Suzan stood over the giant cauldron like the witches in MacBeth and decided to stir the judicial pot.

"Still crazy after all these years."

PART TWO

1969

IX

I'M NOT MY SISTER'S KEEPER

37. I Am My Brother's Keeper

(Suzan Speaks)

That break-out of Ward 3B may have been the last good time I had in 1969. I know it was the last good laugh. It's funny how Tod made the car stop right as they were catching us. You could always count on Tod for something like that.

We climbed the staircase of the old McGill Apartment. Mrs. McGill was filling the air of the cockroach infested apartments with the scent of stewed prunes. Tod's apartment was on the second floor of the two-story edifice.

In the corner of the living room stood a small, green, and still cheerful pine, reflecting the spirit of Christmas that only Tod could project. Tod spent hours cutting orange and black swastikas to place around the tree for decorations.

"Hotsy totsy, another little nazi. Where's Mussolini? Weenee problems?" I said, replicating a teacher's harsh voice.

"I stole it from the lot at Safeway. Stayed up all last night trimming it – hanging the swastikas and everything. I wasn't expecting you at that time. Think of it as art," said Tod.

"I'm thinking it's about as much a piece of art as saying a turd's art – man's purest creation," added Mark, trying to be funny.

"It's kinda like anti-Christ, isn't it? That, and anti-semitic, and anti-everything really. I'm not feeling any Christmas love from that tree – let's take it down," I said.

"That's the point. It's anti-Christmas. No gifts, no commercialism, no dogma, no Jewish holiday. It's not antisemitic. Our grandfather was a Jew for God's sake," said Tod.

"Our genetic grandfather was named Adolph Kraft for God's sake," said Mark, sardonically.

"Kraft is Jewish," confirmed Tod.

"How do you know? You're saying that because his first name was Adolph. You're all mixed up. Do you think he would have swastikas hanging on a Christmas tree?" said Mark.

"It's art. It's anti-Christmas art. Can you dig it?"

"Nah. I can't dig it. And they call me crazy," I said.

Tap, tap, tap.

Tap, tap, tap.

"Can you hear that?" I asked.

I thought I could hear tapping, but it wasn't strange for me to hear things.

Tap, tap, tap.

Tap, tap, tap.

"Where's it coming from?" asked Mark, looking around the room, "Is someone at the door?" He jumped up to check the door but there was no peep hole. "Goddamn, man, why don't you invest in a fucking peep hole."

Knock, knock, knock.

Knock, knock, knock.

Mark opened the door, "Marshal, what's happening, man?"

"Hi Mark. I knew it was you."

"It's me, alright. What are you doing here?"

"I'm looking for you and your brother," Marshal had a reticent look on his face, "I need a place to stay for the night."

"Well, I got my sister here..."

"Who is it?" asked Tod, sitting on the couch, across from the door.

Mark let the door swing wide so Tod and Suzie could see the young man. It was Marshal Mezey, a tall, lanky, nineteen-year-old, same age as Mark, only slim and awkward by comparison. But he had a special quality. It was a mixture of friendliness by nature, and just as much a magnet for trouble. If there was a group of young men standing on the corner, he would be the one chosen to fight. Always. And because they like to fight in Bakersfield, he was an easy target because he couldn't fight his way out of a wet paper bag. They must have smelled the loser on him, but he kept on fighting.

Mark allowed Marshal to enter, carrying a large black duffle bag that must have weighed a hundred pounds. He took a seat in the easy chair in the corner of the room, by the stereo. It was opposite the end of the Christmas tree. Marshal lit up a cigarette, opening and closing the top on the Marlboro red box.

I must say, I was surprised. I found Marshal to be a very interesting boy to look at. He had an ugly crimson scar wrapped around his neck like a scarf. Another dazed innocent, with a bandana around his head. I remembered him from when he was in Yokuts Club, when he was just a kid eating an ice cream sandwich. Tod had been his counselor at camp, not that long ago.

"Suzie, you remember Marshal Mezey, don't you?" said Tod. "He graduated a few years after you...from BHS."

"No, I never graduated...joined the Marines my senior year," interrupted Marshal.

"You were in Yokuts Club too. I remember Mark and you playing together as kids...What name you going by now Marshal?" I said.

"Peter Inkpen."

"Peter Inkpen? What kind of name is that?"

Marshal pulls himself out of the cushions to sit on the edge of the easy chair. He looked all arms and legs. The cushions were grey and threadbare, but comfortable. It was tough to get a read on Marshal, smoking and chewing on his bottom lip, he looked like he might be a nervous twit. But he talked quietly, and directly to me.

I was distracted by the tattoo of a saber-tooth tiger rolling dice on his left forearm. It had a muscular, toothy grin, stretching back all fifteen stripes of his blood orange coat, from ass to end, rolling dice. Was it a homage to *Tony the Tiger*?

"It's the kind of name you get stuck with when you're AWOL from the Marines."

"AWOL. What do you mean?"

Tod said, "He means *absent without leave*. He just walked away from Camp Pendleton. Now he's on the run."

"Like me," I said.

"No, not like you. We're only aiding and abetting an escapee from a mental hospital with you. He's way more serious. Marshal's a federal case," said Tod, "He's on his way to Leavenworth."

"And the best name you could come up with is Peter Inkpen?"

"No, I mean, it's on the fake driver's license I bought.." Marshal took out his wallet and showed it to me. I looked at it and passed it to Mark.

"What piss poor imagination," said Mark.

Everyone was comfortable now, situated around the coffee table in the living room. The normal activity was for Tod to roll a joint for them to light up. Tod announced to the gang, while listening to *"Almost Cut My Hair"* that, "Marshal is going to stay with us for a day or two."

"What's the plan Marshal?" I asked.

"I plan on selling some of these claymores," Marshal tugs on the three-foot duffel bag beside his chair. "Nothing easier than stealing weapons from a Marine base. I've got two M-16's left, had an M-60, sold it, C-4 explosives, ten pounds, ten grenades. And, this is the kicker, I've got twenty-four claymores. Do you know what a claymore is, Suzie?"

"What are you doing with claymores in here? You trying to blow us up?"

Marshal was bewildered by the response.

"What do you mean?"

Tod was lighting the joint now and could only speak while inhaling, "Marshal spent a lot of time in the jungle killing gooks. You were there for how long?"

Tod passed the joint to Suzie, who didn't want any, so he passed it to Mark.

"Tell her how you almost got a bronze star, with the V attached for valor. Tell 'em about the intrepidity, that's a good one," said Tod.

"Nah, I ain't into explaining that shit."

"Come on, Marshal. We don't get to hear it from the hero's own mouth. Ever?" said Tod.

"Intrepidity," winced Marshal.

38. Marshal's Main Event

Marshal Mezey may have gotten his ass kicked when he was younger, but practice makes perfect, and after the Marines were done with him, he became a capable fighting man. He came from good stock, that's for sure. His father was part of the ruling elite amongst the large landowning farmers that came to the Southern San Joaquin Valley early in the nineteenth century. His farm was south of town near the Sandrini's and Mettler's homesteads.

These farming families produced for their children all the benefits of rich kids, which included Marshal when he turned sixteen years old. His daddy bought him a new GTX, Chrysler's answer to the GTO. A high performance, 440 cubic inches, was standard in every model. That was the highlight of Marshal's high school career – it took him two weeks before he smashed it up.

Marshal was lucky like that. Walking away from death defying collisions without a scratch became his forte. There was this one catastrophic event in Vietnam when he was lucky enough to get away with only a scratch, *albeit* it was the Grand Canyon of all scratches. Luck played a role in his getting the tattoo of the tiger on his arm; it's called bad luck.

They were on patrol in South Vietnam, all six of them in a line with their nose three inches off the ground. They were deep in enemy jungle, moving slowly and quietly. So quietly you could hear a blade of grass rustling in the wind. A parrot would squawk. Then there was an unidentifiable snap of a twig, or pop, followed by the inverse push of green leaves against the branches.

Marshal was on point, the first soldier walking single file through dense foliage when the corporal gave the signal to get down. Hell, they couldn't get down any further. It was dense and deep. The corporal was six feet behind Marshal and watching him like he was his only child.

From ten feet above Marshal's head, a 900-pound saber-tooth tiger uncoiled its flanks and jumped down on Marshal. Its seven-inch claws grabbed him around the neck and tried to rip his head off. The giant cat twisted and turned to suppress his prey as Marshal fought to protect himself. There was nothing in the fighting man's manual about what to do in defense of a cat attack.

The corporal knew what to do. He couldn't fire his weapon for fear of alerting the enemy and killing Private Mezey in the process. In the alternative, the corporal drew his 13-inch bayonet and jumped on the tiger's back and began stabbing it repeatedly. He stabbed it in and about his great head of wired whiskers. Several times the tiger flung the corporal from its neck, but the corporal kept coming back to finish the job, stabbing it again, and again, until finally, with the help of the startled yet amazed squad, the magnificent tiger succumbed to his wounds. The corporal was put up for a bronze star.

And as for Private Marshal Mezey, he survived too. He was wearing a helmet, which helped. But Marshal's days as a Marine were over.

39. The Bronze Star?

Marshal spent seven months in the hospital, recuperating from his wounds that made the scars on his neck and back look like competing railroad tracks. After the scars' healed Marshal was sent for reassignment to Camp Pendleton, and after that he went AWOL, right before his honorable discharge. The time for him to be a Marine was over – now he was on the run. He wrote the whole experience off as a patriotic duty gone awry. There was nothing else to say, it was a mistake.

"So, you got the bronze star for stabbing a tiger to death?" asked Mark, "I mean, you deserved it, getting ravaged by the gook tiger. You were protecting yourself."

"Nah," said Marshal, "I didn't get anything. Captain said I didn't win the star on the "field of battle." It wasn't against an "opposing force". The corporal did all the stabbing anyway."

"What kind of force was it?" asked Mark.

"Natural force? Maybe he was right."

"You were on the god-damn battlefield, fighting a gook tiger. All of Vietnam is a battlefield," said Mark.

"Not against an enemy force," said Marshal. "A saber-tooth tiger don't equate to an enemy force."

"Not enough "intrepidity," according to government standards," said Tod. "You needed more intrepidity. You needed to be more fearless, and braver than you were, only in the face of an opposing force."

"The same standards they used to determine my sanity. Are you going to be okay, Marshal?" I said and reached over to put my hand on his knee.

Marshal thought about this for a second before he burst out laughing, "Hey, if we couldn't laugh, we'd all go insane."

40. Merry Christmas

It was four in the morning when the darkness of night met the dew of dawn. The tide of light shifted, pivoting the universe from dark to light. The earth keeps rolling after all these years of bringing joy where once there was only sorrow. It exchanged the moon for the sun to spread the warmth. The world came alive and danced toward the end of 1969.

It's Christmas morning.

Mark was sleeping on the couch. Tod rolled out from the back bedroom still rubbing his eyes and said, "Where's Suzie and Marshal?"

"Merry Christmas to you too," answered Mark groggily, "Suzie's in the back bedroom."

"No, she's not."

"Don't say that. And where's Marshal?"

"That's what I'm asking you."

"Maybe they went to get coffee."

"When's the last time anyone went to buy coffee? We got Folger's freeze dried right here," said Tod.

"He left his claymores. Must mean they're coming back," said Mark.

"It's Marshal and Suzan. They could be up to who knows what. They may have gone to the moon."

A terrible clamor rose from the door. Somone was pounding it hard enough to rip it off its hinges.

X

SUZIE'S IN LOVE

41. Her Lips Curled Phallically

Suzan and Marshal took off on his Harley Sportster and headed for blue sky country. It was on the other side of the rainbow. Just beyond the unseen tether, tying them to their hometown of Bakersfield – a town filled with "scummy" people, so said Suzan. But that was after she was incarcerated again. As for now, she was free of delusions, and she felt good enough to love the man she was with.

Marshal was deserving of that love, but he could never grasp it. He acted goofy, but he was sensitive and crazy. That's it. But crazy carries too much baggage, he's more of a 'fractured' type of guy. In fact, he's exactly a fractured type of guy. And we all know how unpredictable they can be. You've got to be ahead of them, or you'll never catch up. They're so smart, don't you know?

"Let's go back," said Suzie, "I'm freezing."

They were both leaning on the bike at Panorama Park. The Park is a memorial to the countryside that made Bakersfield rich. From the vantage point of Panorama Park you can see mile after mile, the oil derricks of Kern County. Thousands of them, pumping up the black goo that comes from beneath the soil, and storing it in huge round industrial tanks painted green to match the colors of the earth.

"Move in here next to me," said Marshal, pulling her tighter as Suzie snuggled in to feel his warmth.

"I'm not so sure this is what I'd call beautiful," she said, panning around the scorched landscape from the cliff above. It was brown dirt with black deadwood, and sage brush everywhere. If you squinted your eyes, you could see cottontails running from bush to bush as the snakes and lizards crept from shade to hole. There were no trees, save those skinny excuses for greenery they planted along the road to Hart Park. If you drove fifteen minutes to the park, you'd be rewarded with the worst rotten egg water in the county as drinking water. But the deceptive Kern River runs through the shady acres of Hart Park. You can float a tire tube all the way to Bakersfield Beach on the swift and smooth current, running downstream.

"You ever do that Suzie? Float a tube down river? I wouldn't want to do it today."

"I did it once We took watermelon and beer. It was so hot in the summer – then so refreshing to slip under the water."

"Yeah, but not so cool if you couldn't swim."

"Don't tell me you can't swim?"

"Well, nobody ever taught me."

"You poor neglected child. Hey, wait a second, you went to Yokuts, right? Didn't you learn there?"

"I guess I wasn't listening. I was young."

"That doesn't matter. I was a swim instructor; I'd teach you to swim perfectly. You'd listen to me, wouldn't you?"

"Probably not, but I'd be watching you. You're fun to watch."

"You think I'm funny to watch?"

"You know what I mean."

"Thanks Marshal, but I'm too old for you."

"You're just right for me."

They took a long pause. Suzie pulled herself a half-inch closer.

"Merry Christmas Marshal, what do you want for Christmas little boy?" said Suzie.

Marshal smiled, "Peace, joy and happiness would be nice. And maybe a kilo of cocaine to make it a white Christmas. How 'bout you?"

"I'd like some vengeance, some retaliation for deeds past done, said Suzie."

"Whoa, what are you talking about, vengeance? Against who?" Said Marshal.

"Against the tiger, that same tiger that got you with its claws, that would have killed you."

"Well, he just about did," said Marshal.

"Don't you want vengeance?"

"On a tiger? Mayhem's all they know, ain't it?"

"What if it was a man?" said Suzan.

"If a man did that to me, the first thing I'd do is get his nails trimmed." Marshal let go with a whooping laugh before he realized it was only immaturely funny.

"But if it was a man, I'd say he deserved a good ass kicking, and I've got the stitches to prove it. They should lock the animal up and throw away the keys – same as they'll do to me for going AWOL."

"It's so unfair. You go to Leavenworth for going AWOL and the man who used a turkey baster to kill my baby goes free – not even an investigation. He said no one would believe me and he was right," said Suzan.

"Back up Suzie, who said that?"

"Johnny Burnette, my old boyfriend," Suzie said.

"Did you have a baby with him?"

"Yes, but he never hatched. Johnny made sure of that," Suzie said.

"What are you telling me Suzie?"

"Something I never told a soul before."

"Let's go someplace where we can warm up first," said Marshal, shivering.

"Let's go to Stan's for coffee," said Suzie, "and maybe a shake."

"Alright. And maybe some shit on a shingle, I love that stuff. But first, we're changing our mode of transportation."

They rode in Marshal's champagne colored GTX — just like the one he totaled when he was sixteen. His father had it rebuilt, and it's been sitting in the garage ever since Marshal enlisted in the Marines. His father saved the GTX for him when he got out. With that plan squashed when Marshal went AWOL, he felt there was no better time to drive the behemoth of a race car than now.

He snuck it out of the garage early that Christmas morning for his new girlfriend, the blond woman with long straight hair, who was not a paranoid schizophrenic, but a sensitive girl fractured by an old boyfriend whose voice continuously replayed in her ears: "I don't want you, leave us alone, forget about it, you're not good enough, I don't need you."

Marshal and Suzie headed to Stan's Drive-in for the warmth they sought. The hostess seated them in a sunny spot, each sitting on their own side of the booth. Marshal ordered some cream chip beef over toast, and Suzie ordered coffee and a chocolate milkshake.

"You ever had a chocolate shake from here? They're so good, you're going to love it."

"I'm okay," said Marshal. "I got what I wanted. They always made fun of it in the Marines, calling it "shit on a shingle", but it's warm in the tummy."

"Well, you're going to want what I'm having."

"So, tell me Suzie, why Johnny Burnette? Can't you just stop thinking about him?"

"No. He stole something from me. All my dreams. I went to see him the morning I got back from Suffolk County last October. I can't be sure why I went to Johnny's house, but I had to. Everybody thinks I'm crazy for going there, and maybe it was – but enough with Johnny Burnette! I had to get something straightened out that only he could understand.

Johnny's house has a swooping driveway. You could get lost standing at the end of it. I don't know what his dad does, but he's never home. He's the owner of some telecom company. The garage is at the rear of the property, like a barn, but it can be accessed by an alley that runs behind it."

The house is the standard one-story ranch style architecture you see everywhere, only bigger. I approached from the garage in back, coming through the carport gate and around by the kitchen. When I got there, I peered into the living room and saw no one. So I advanced to the sliding glass door that entered their den. It was locked.

I looked around the patio for something to throw through the window. I found a potted cactus and heaved it through the plate glass window of the door, shattering chards of glass everywhere." I made the universal sign with my fingers expressing a large explosion.

"Wow. Did that get their attention?" asked Marshal, as he shoveled another bite of shit on a shingle into his mouth.

"I stood there and waited for them to come to me. The first one out of bed was Johnny, the rich kid. He's a big pansy, stands over six foot four, has a big beard and long hair. He's a real freak. He comes out bare foot, hopping from one foot to the other, trying to avoid the glass.

"What the hell are you doing, Suzan," he says.

"We need to talk."

"What the hell, we already talked. I mean there's nothing more to say. My mom's going to be out here in two shakes. They're just going to take you away again, Suzie."

"You could explain everything that happened. You could make it right for me. Can't you just do that?"

"You're the one that could make it right. Just leave us alone and forget about it."

That's when Mrs. Burnette showed up at the den door in her bathrobe and slippers. She's got a cigarette in one hand, a broom in the other, and she's pissed off.

"Goddammit. I warned you Johnny. This mental ward thing is just not enough for her. We're pressing charges this time. I've got the police on the way."

Then she turns towards me and says, "Are you just so crazy you go around breaking everything that's beautiful? I wish my husband was here, he'd take a switch to you and whip you good! There's no use running away, they'll catch you!"

"Running away? I don't have anything to run to."

"Then you got what you deserve. It's not my fault your parents ran away from you, but I can understand why. It's easy to see why they're acting dead."

"Johnny, help me out," I said.

"It's no use Suzie. Go stay at your brothers' place."

"They're no better off than me."

"Then you're all a bunch of losers."

Sirens can be heard in the background. I couldn't care less.

"Oh Johnny, why did you do it?"

Harriot took her broom and began sweeping chards of glass in my direction. Chards strike me as I turn away. Johnny makes a lame attempt to stop his mom.

"Don't touch me," said his mother, "I know what I'm doing."

Marshal had finished his cream chip beef while listening intently, "So you never got to speak to him about what you wanted to talk about?"

"I didn't get to talk to him about squat – that Mrs. Burnette hates me. That's how I got put back in the mental ward again. I explained my position to the police, and they didn't arrest me. They took me straight to Ward 3B."

"What did you want to talk about? I mean with Johnny."

Suzie lowered her voice to a whisper, and when Marshal said he couldn't hear her, she climbed out of the booth and went to sit on his side.

"I said, 'People like to say, poor Suzie, she ran off to Haight-Ashbury and took LSD and went crazy.' But that's only half true."

"What's the other half?"

"His dominance. The way he preyed on me. I never liked drugs, but I obeyed him to make him happy. Then he betrayed me."

Suzan put both her hands between her legs and squeezed hard. Marshal could feel her discomfort and stretched his legs also.

"Sounds like you got your heart broke," said Marshal.

Suzan recoiled from this statement; a crimson wave flushed her cheeks.

"You think I'm sitting here, an escapee from a Mental Hospital because he broke my heart? No, it was much more complicated than that. He broke my mind...confused me into surrender, overpowered my virtues. Johnny Burnette stripped me of everything I called love. And for what?"

"I don't know...?"

"Because he thought me acting against my morals was funny."

Marshal was silent for a long moment.

"Shit, Suzie, what do you want to do about that?"

"I want to kill him."

Marshal blinked twice and swallowed.

"I don't think you should do that. I mean it's so violent, killing someone. It's horribly violent."

"I could do it to him"

"What exactly did he do to you?"

"He didn't let me understand what he said until it was too late."

Marshal stops eating, as though what he's heard will turn the tides, like he's been waiting for the waves in the ocean to stop breaking so he could go swimming, and now's the time.

"Are you kidding me? That's what all the girls say."

"It's the way he made me feel. It's dominance, it's being made to suffer indignity, and it's cruel."

"Cruel? Isn't that love, or the end of love?"

Suzan lowered her voice an octave lower than a whisper.

"I don't want to tell you what he did. I'm ashamed."

Marshal paused.

"You don't have to tell me Suzie, not if it hurts you."

"It hurts me and makes me mad and vindictive because it was out of my control."

"Tell me then, but only if you want."

"I don't want to. Because it can't be undone. It involves a fetus."

"A what?"

"F-E-T-U-S, an unborn baby. Johnny's and my baby."

"You guys had a baby?"

"He killed it. He killed our unborn baby."

Suzie said this as a matter of fact, but her sad eyes told Marshal there was a lot more to the story.

Marshal has never been good at times like this. He didn't know whether to give her a hug or go mad, but he was uncomfortably sad.

He said, "Did you call the pigs on him…I mean…what?"

He tried to be there for her in her moment of pain, but it was awkward. Marshal had a hard enough time talking to himself.

"Johnny had his way with me, doing what his mother said."

"His mother? What's she have to do with anything?"

"I told you she hates me."

Suzan's torment was broken with these revelations, and she sighed with relief. The end of her thin lips curled prior to her laughing, "Haven't you heard? I'm a paranoid schizophrenic."

"Do your brothers know about this?"

"Can you imagine if I told them?"

"What do you think Mark would do?"

"Mark would kill him. But he wouldn't have insanity for a defense."

"What do you think Tod would do?"

"Odd Tod? That dear brother of mine, if given the chance, would fuck it up. But I suspect he'd crawl around in a devil's costume and sneak up from behind to try and scare her to death."

They sat peacefully for a bit, lost in chaotic thought.

"You're a paranoid schizophrenic?"

"Yes, isn't that romantic?"

"It's sexy... 'Noid Zoid'. See what I mean, Noid Zoid?"

"Oh Marshal, I bet you say that to all the girls."

"No. Only one, and that's you."

Suzie suddenly realized she was slouching all over Marshal like two peas smashed together in the green leather seats of the pod.

"Oh, I'm sorry, I'm practically lying on you." She began to sit up. "I'll go back on my side."

"That's okay, I'm comfortable...we're kicking it here, for Christmas if you don't mind," he smiled at Suzie, and she was pleased with the earnest tone of his voice.

"We ought to call Tod and let him know where we snuck out to," said Suzie.

"We will."

42. Marshal's Coalescence

Suzan began to give Marshal some serious thought. She didn't let her schizophrenia get in the way of her libido. But this was bigger than that. Her moments of lucidity had been greatly enhanced since she escaped. The psychiatrist, Dr. Sielbert, from Suffolk County, was right — the sudden change of venue snapped her back into acting quite normally, the same old Suzie Q. – whoever that was. She never had reason to fall in love with a man like Marshal before, but he was like the second coming of Christ for her now.

Her moral integrity both in God and science, mythically and analytically, everyway it could be thought of, that's what Marshal was going to save for Suzan. All he had to be, was himself. She expected nothing else from him, other than money ironically. But if he didn't have it, she'd get the money because what she loved most about him he'd already performed. He proved everything to her by surviving the tiger's attack. "Man must suffer to be wise." Isn't that the way we learn? How many stitches did he suffer?

That act of surviving the tiger attack proved everything she wanted in a protector. And that's what she wanted, to be protected. That carried enough virtuosity for both she and

Marshal to last until the near future. They were in no position to make long-term plans.

But there was nothing wrong with making short-term commitments. It was Suzie's first chance to feel comfortable in a man's arms for years. It felt safe there. The fact that he was AWOL from the Marines, and she was an escapee from a Mental Institution, made their relationship tenuous, yet exciting, if only it lasted until tomorrow. As she laid in his arms that Christmas Day, she felt their bond could last forever. She harbored that thought, loving the very idea of an existence together somewhere, sometime.

But for now, she looked up at him, "Do you think you could love me, Marshal?"

"Why not? I've been looking for love; I'd be yours if you wanted me to be."

And like that, they started to plan their coalescence. They pretended they were on a beach in Hawaii, rather than sitting in a booth at Stan's Drive-In.

"I remember you from Yokuts, Marshal. I was four years older than you so when I was twelve, you were eight. You were kinda cute as a kid, but you sure did some strange things. Like peeing in the girls' tent when we went to Yosemite? I thought that was weird, seeing as though there was a bathroom right there. What's up with that?"

"I don't know. Sometimes I felt lost," Marshal said, "I just got anxious. Funny it was in the girl's dressing tent though; I see what you mean."

"And what about the time we were all playing baseball and you were up to bat? That's when John Plank got a bat and came behind you and swung it as hard as he could, smacking you in the back."

"Yeah, that was surprising. It hurt a lot. Why's everybody always picking on me?" laughed Marshal.

"Well, John Plank was certifiable psycho. I guess every camp has one and he was ours. Kicked out of camp at ten years old because he didn't like your batting stance? Good thing he smacked your back cause lesser backs couldn't take it. May I look at what the tiger left behind."

"Oh, you don't want to see that. The scars are ugly, they're real ugly."

"I'll just peek. I'd like to see your scars. See what you're made of, I guess. Suffer through it with you, if you don't mind. It hasn't been that long since you were in the hospital, has it?"

"About two months."

"Please, with a spoonful of sugar, I'll just glimpse it," said Suzan, tugging softly at his shirt.

"Ah, alright. But just take a little peek because it's still red, and still healing, so just a little peek goes a long way."

Suzie started pulling at the end of Marshal's shirt as he turned his back to her. The plaid cowboy shirt had a long tail that made it hard to untuck, but she was almost there when, she screamed:

"Jesus Christ Marshal you've got to go back to the hospital. My God, it' fire, it's festering or something, it's red as a beet! Oh God. How are we ever going to make love? I don't want to kill you but those scars are wrapped around you like blood sausages."

"Don't worry Suzie, we can use your back if we have to."

"Man, you weren't kidding, a little goes a long way."

"Yeah, that's what she said."

"That's not funny," said Suzie.

"That's always funny."

43. True Romance

"Marshal, we got to get out of here."

"Where to?"

"Someplace on the river, a little cabin where we can have a fire."

"My family's cabin is halfway up to Kernville. There's a great swimming hole up there, not that we're looking for one. But nobody's up there."

"Does it have a telephone?" said Suzan.

"It's a cabin."

"Sounds perfect."

"It's my hideaway. It's where I've been hiding out. I was using my bike to scoot around; you know, no need for creature comforts. Seems all that's changed now. Would you like to run away with me on a magical mystery tour, Suzie?"

"I'd love to."

Suzan took what Marshal just said literally. Marshal may as well have asked her to marry him; she was overjoyed at the prospect and considered herself engaged – all justifiable because that's exactly the way Marshal meant it. Marshal, being a man of few words, would've loved to tell her his feelings, but didn't. He could have told her how he fantasized over her as his counselor, in her lime green two-piece bathing suit, with green stripes, with tiny blond hairs on her thighs, but didn't.

No. This was an amazing twist in Suzan's life. A turn for the good. That she could find a person of the opposite sex under the circumstances was unique, but to have that love going both ways was astounding. It was the love never given by anybody else in their lives. This was requited love. The only kind of true love there is.

As they gathered their things and paid the bill Suzan kept daydreaming of Marshal and her lying before the flames of the hearth. She was dreaming of how they'd be laying on a polar bear skin from Alaska, and long hair sheep skins from New Zealand. They'd lie naked before the fire, its warm glow spreading throughout the cabin. A neat wooden cabin, with Indian blankets accenting the western motif over the furniture, and a large porch with mosquito netting, to protect from bugs in the summer and snow in winter.

There wouldn't be much snow this year, but the river was running at full capacity because of the nasty winter the year before. But this winter was different. It held the promise of being the best on record, and the sun shining on the current made the overflow along the banks look both beckoning and treacherous.

Suzie's eyes were glued to the current in her dreams, and it was running fast. She couldn't help thinking how it's three times faster underneath. She was trying to figure out where the line in the current was between safety and being swept away, like Dick Owens. It had something to do with a person's weight and the depth of entry. She found it haunting.

But most fascinating was Marshal Mezey. Her cheeks flushed pink. Marshal is taller than Mark, but thinner in his arms and waist. He's got a cylinder for a chest with two skinny legs coming down, like a piston. There's nothing there but sticks for legs.

After military school, Marshal came back to high school his sophomore year in a body cast – a full-blown body cast he wore for a year. Some kind of corrective surgery for his spine. The surgery may have helped his spine, but his social life went to hell. And it didn't get any better for him.

One time he was standing in line at Taco Bell, waiting to order, when out of the entire crowd of Friday night customers, a dude from Delano, standing in front of him, stabbed Marshal in the stomach. The red spot on his T-shirt grew bigger and bigger until he was finally rushed to Mercy Hospital. That was one of several random attacks on Marshal alone. Why?

No answers. It was his destiny to be picked on. He was big enough, so it appeared to outsiders that his opponent wasn't picking on someone smaller, but Marshal didn't know how to fight. He had no offense, or defense. He'd stand there with his fist up and proceed to get his ass kicked, time and again. It was like everyone in town knew about him and wanted to take their turn, because he wasn't afraid. But he would have done better if he moved to a town that didn't thrive on fighting.

The standard anti-war vibe for 1969 was "Make Love, Not War."

Marshal was all for making love, and his secret hideaway was safe and at the ready. As he waited at the table for change, Suzie went to use a booth to call Tod.

"Hello, Tod?"

"Oh, man I'm glad you called."

"What's up?"

"We need to talk, and I don't know if this line is tapped," said Tod.

"Why would it be?"

"Well maybe because I had two escapees at the house last night ...see, that's why I hope it's not tapped."

"Who'd be tapping it?" asked Suzan.

"This morning, sometime after you left, obviously, your social probation officer came booming at the door, a fat, bald guy in short sleeves, and rude. He bullied his way around not looking for you but looking for Mark. Mark split out the back. You're gonna have to leave town, now!"

"I'm going to check that. Is that probation officer named Bob Howley?"

"That's what he told me. The shithead."

"He's such a jerk."

"He's not friendly. Bullied his way in here taking a quick sweep around, like he was somebody. Said something about aiding and abetting an escapee from a mental hospital. I told him to get the fuck out until he had reason to take me to jail."

"What he'd say?"

"He said, 'that's where you belong, that's for sure'. Fucking punk."

"Let's meet at the Yokuts Club burial grounds, this afternoon."

"You got Marshal with you?"

"What do you think?"

"That's cool. You're not taking him to Johnny Burnette's house, are you? That's what I'm worried about. Don't introduce Marshal into that fiasco… or crazy whatever it is?"

"I haven't thought about Johnny for at least an hour."

"Good. Don't start now. You sound better. You guys should go to San Jose, or someplace. I hear you can get lost up there. Besides, Marshal and Johnny are not going to get along, you can be sure of that."

"I don't need you to tell me that, okay? We got a place to hide out, where even you can't find us."

"You're going up to Marshal's cabin?"

"How'd you know that?"

"I know Marshal. Meet you at the park. I'll bring the guns."

44. Free to Love

Suzie made another stop in the bathroom of Stan's Drive-In. Stan's was a unique example of 1950's architecture, with its angular flat roof and large windows pointing to the sky. The back parking lot was set up for bell hops to skate to your car for service, sitting under the long eaves that ran perpendicular to the walk-in diner. You had the choice of eating in the luxury of your own car or going inside for fine dining.

The main restaurant was open 24 hours. It was the best burger joint Bakersfield had to offer. They had great eclairs and delicious chocolate Sundays.

The girls' lavatory was in the theme of a locker-room for majorette carhops. Fancy and clean, the vanities were in a separate room, fashioned after the brass tuba with a full-length mirror, stylized after a marching band. When Suzie walked in, she was greeted by a reflection of a twenty-three-year-old misfit dressed in mental infirmary scrubs, covered in Marshal's old leather coat down to her knees.

"I've got to do something about this," she said aloud.

"You gotsa do something bout what, honey," came a voice from behind her.

"About the way I look, I can't believe I look so ...pitiful."

The voice dug into her purse. “Here you go honey, try some of this for those sweet lips. It’s called Ruby Red. It’ll brighten your smile,” said the voice. “Go on, try it, make yourself as beautiful as an iron butterfly.”

“No. I don’t wear make-up,” said Suzie.

“What? Are you crazy? Ain’t you tryin’ to catch a man out there…”

“Well, sort of, I guess.”

“Then sit down here and let me take care of you.”

Suzan recognized the voice. It came from Joyce Jones, a girl she knew back at Emerson Junior High School. They weren’t friends, Joyce being black and Suzan white. That day was still far away, but they admired each other from afar.

“Where you been girl? Looking all scraggly on the outside, but happy inside.”

“So true. But I think you got that backward. I want your dress. Joyce, I need that dress. It’s so beautiful, is that chiffon or cardigan beige?”

“You telling me you’re willing to trade me your scrubs from the …what’s that? Kern County Mental Health? Trade those colors for this rag I’m wearing? That’s some heavy shit. I like that. I wanna be part of that club.”

“Welcome to the club,” said Suzie.

When Suzan emerged from the ladies' room that Christmas morning the church bells were swinging with laughter, ringing in the news that Suzan was a new woman. She felt great. She'd become herself again, no longer pestered by delusional distractions haunting her every move.

Suzan had time to digest the message from Marshal that he would be there for her. She felt confident about him, and that made her feel strong. She smiled that Ruby Red smile. She had on Joyce's dress, only a different style, gentrified by keeping on her scrub pants. That's when she was struck with the conclusion she was in love.

She had to be in love because she had never felt this way before. Marshal was the only one. Suzan looked beautiful. It was her first chance to show off her long blond hair and there it was, only it was sandy-blond, not platinum, more a dishwater blond. She was so excited to see Marshal, she swore to God the first thing she'd do was give him a kiss. They had never even kissed before – how could they have waited so long?

Her eyes swept the dining room, instinctively going to the booth they had been sitting in. He was gone. There was no Marshal. Her face was alive and fresh, then went dead at the sight of the vacant seat. She walked slowly up to the empty booth. The table had been cleared, and there was nothing to remind her of what happened there. It was the birthplace of her love, and now it was gone.

The table was clean and shiny, not a crumb on it. The bill had been paid. She was hoping she had the wrong table, thinking back, trying to recreate the scene but there was nothing. She looked everywhere except under the table – so she looked there: no Marshal.

Suzan suddenly went into shock. Nothing was as it had been. It was wiped clean back to crazy. The love, the feeling of embrace, the happiness of security, the knowledge she was right – was all gone. Everything good had disappeared, and the fear of insanity loomed large instead. She wasn't falling in love anymore; she was falling further insane. It raised its ugly head and grabbed at her mind, tussled her hair strangely, smearing lipstick on her hand. She was back, living the life of a *fractured fissure.*

"Suzie...Suzan!" said Marshal, raising his voice as he approached her from behind, "I got a new coat for you, had it in the car."

"Oh Marshal, I love you," said Suzie, as she took him in her arms and pressed her hand to his face, spreading her fingers across his cheek, she planted her red lips on his and squeezed, then held it for a long-time.

“Hey Mister, get a room why don’t you?” came a friendly comment from the peanut gallery.

Marshal went red around his neck as he scooped Suzie up with a hand around her waist and walked her off to a round of soft applause.

XI

SUZAN'S TESTIMONIAL

45. Suzie Asks for Revenge

The Southern San Joaquin Valley once again provided the same sunny Christmas it has since the beginning of time. The sign along the freeway welcoming all of L.A. to Bakersfield said it all: "Sun, Fun, Stay, Play". No sweeter words were ever said about Bakersfield.

No truer words either. Jastro Park is just north of the 99, a small green space for the community, nestled in the same neighborhood as Bakersfield Racquet Club and Franklin Elementary School. It's also four blocks from the Cornwall Family home. And it's the same park the Yokuts Club Day Camp used to call home for twenty years of service to the Bakersfield community.

Three of the founding co-owners' children were about to meet at the park to discuss what to do with the guns brought to the party by an AWOL ex-Marine – and, oh yes, all three former counselors at Yokuts were being hunted for aiding and abetting an escapee from a mental institution. And there was one more issue they had yet to discuss: what Marshal had been told about Johnny Burnette by Suzie.

It was no betrayal. Marshal simply had no choice. When he was face to face with Mark, he had to tell him the truth about what happened to his sister. He couldn't let Johnny get away with killing Suzie's fetus. What if someday Mark ran into Johnny, and not knowing he had his way with Suzan, Mark might treat him civilly; then how would Marshal feel about not telling Mark the truth? Dealing with issues of false pride was a serious problem.

Mark deserved to know, didn't he? And Suzan wanted Mark to know. But she couldn't say more than she already had for fear of reprisal by her brothers, which is what she wanted. She was going in circles, but she knew one thing; she didn't want to be held responsible.

None of that mattered as things turned out.

They were sitting at the new barbeque tables the Recreation Department had constructed for big parties at the park. Their spirits were bright, considering. It was a beautiful Christmas Day to be in love as far as Suzie and Marshal were concerned.

Tod and Mark were feeling the sun, so they took off their jackets. The blue sky was bountiful above a canopy of green branches gone bare because of winter. The air still had the late morning freshness of dew drops on the chrysanthemums.

Each sibling was lost in their own thoughts. Mark felt like a man because he rescued Suzan, so his job was done. Now he had to watch out for Bob Howley. Tod was a different kettle of fish. There were lots of things he could do but it was Christmas, and he'd like to get high; immediately. Marshal was living a surreal fantasy where things just kept getting better. It was Suzan who was suffering. Happy she united with Marshal, but sad he couldn't fight her battles. It was going to take Mark.

"I have an announcement to make," said Suzie. "It's not nice, so I apologize in advance for bringing everyone down with such a bummer. I wish it never happened, or I could forget about it, because I know it's going to hurt you. But I can't live with the fact I didn't do something about it. I didn't deserve it, I promise you – no one does. Sometimes I think it would be better if I killed myself, I'm such a coward."

That's the kind of admission that gets your attention quick. Marshal could feel this coming and remained determined to hear her out. Mark and Tod's reaction was different.

"What the fuck are you talking about?" said Tod.

Both brothers sat with their mouths open, staring at Suzan for a long time, expecting her to go on. Then they realized what it was all about.

They both said in unison, "Johnny Burnette."

"You got that right," said Suzie. "I've been too mysterious about him because of the way he treated me. He made me feel so small. Now he deserves to fall on his own petard."

"I'm sorry, Suzie." Mark said, "What's that supposed to mean?"

"It means I struggled to get out of my bondage. I kicked and fought, but my mouth was stuffed with a rag and taped shut. I remember Johnny coming from the kitchen with a turkey baster filled with red fluid. It looked like a giant syringe, and he pinned me down face up.

"Then he ripped the gag out of my mouth and force fed the baster down my throat. All the syrup was squeezed down my esophagus to my stomach. I was writhing in pain, holding my tied hands to my stomach. When he removed the baster I started screaming at him, 'You killed our baby!' through my hoarse throat.

"He didn't care. He let me crawl to a corner of the room to throw up what I could. Over and over. Nobody was listening, nobody cared. Johnny sat on the couch to watch the poison take effect. 'The magic of red devils,' Johnny kept saying. 'No one will believe a paranoid schizophrenic like you. I won't allow you to bring another psycho into this world; into my world.'

"He's your own flesh and blood, Johnny."

"Don't say that. He's my mother's flesh and blood too, and she won't allow it. You're not good enough for me or her."

"Not good enough for what?"

"Not good enough to be a mother in my family. There's nothing I can do about that."

"You're the freak," I told him ... "You're the big sissy... you can't do a thing without your mommy. You make me sick."

"Oh, you're going to be sick alright. That's cool," he said.

"You can stop it, Johnny. Call an ambulance."

"It's too late for that now, Suzie. Just relax and let it take you. It'll be over soon..." But he lied about that too. "That shit lasts forever."

This met with silence. Mark and Tod exchanged glances with Marshal, not knowing exactly what to say. Then Tod said, "That mother fucking son-of-a-bitch raped you and bludgeoned your baby. Is that what you're saying?"

"What I'm saying is you're talking to a rape victim. Johnny Burnette killed my last remaining tie with humanity...the fetus lay in a puddle of blood, twenty-one weeks old, my little boy, your nephew Mark; and he had a big dick. I wish you could have seen his dick. You'd have been proud. Johnny said the cops would never believe me, and they didn't. It makes me want to do the same to him."

Tod was standing up now with an savage look on his face – like he couldn't believe the disrespect this guy had shown him. He wanted to punch Johnny in the face right then.

Then Mark spoke. He was ten steps ahead of Tod on the path of vengeance. "Marshal, do you remember how to rig up a suicide chair?"

46. Mark and Tod Blow Up

Suzan knew what she was doing. She felt sharp and on top of things. So, this is what it's like to be in control? She knew what she wanted by pushing the limit with the size of the fetus' dick. But it was true. It was huge! She said it to stir Mark's emotion by reaching down and grabbing his ball sack and saying, "Show me what you're made of."

She wanted revenge. What was her alternative? Settling for more of the same? Living with the injustice of it all? Living, knowing that Johnny had killed their baby and driven her insane? No, no. That was not going to be Suzan's story. It almost was, but not anymore.

Mark had saved her from that story, but she wasn't going away. She had more to say and felt better about telling it now. That was because of Marshal, the man who had everything: money, cars, cabins, guns and ammunition. Marshal would protect her, provide her with food and clothes. But she needed Mark and Tod to take care of this family business.

Once they decided on a plan, they divided up the munitions accordingly. Tod and Mark drove to the end of 24th Steet near Greenacres to shoot and explode the munitions to their heart's content. They made it sound more like the Fourth of July. They realized this was only the second time they had been shooting together, the first time being with Tod's friend, Don, and their cousin Laurie, from New York. Bearing arms was one art you couldn't learn in Yokuts – although you could learn to shoot with a bow and arrow.

Mark and Laurie were only twelve years old at the time. Laurie came to spend the summer from Stony Brooke and it was hot out there in Bakersfield. Laurie and Mark trudged through baking desert sand, and over barbed wire fences, to get to thicker brush and hotter gun barrels, all for the purpose of killing, or perhaps wounding a skunk. Or some other critter that didn't live in trees because there weren't any trees out there, save for scrawny deadwood. At any rate, Laurie put an end to the fun by refusing to participate in shooting at an animal or creatures of lesser stature, e.g. rodents. He demanded to be taken home.

Our cousin Laurie was funny like that. Being the son of George and Betty, he held on tight to his moral convictions, even at age twelve. He was, in fact, unbending. As he grew older and became more active in the Boy Scouts, he finally earned his Eagle Scout Award – a top honor. But he refused to accept the badge when it meant he would have to participate in the ceremony that demanded he believe in God. Laurie refused to say, "Yes," to our Heavenly Father. That rendered him an atheist in the eyes of the Boy Scouts and thus disqualified him from the fruits of his labor: the Eagle Scout Award. (Jesus Christ, Laurie, couldn't you have just said yes?)

Mark and Tod would have shouted out, "Hell yes, we believe in God, and pass the ammunition!"

They couldn't believe their good fortune. "Look at me now, ma! I'm holding an M-60 between my legs. Tod's feeding me the cartridge belt with so many bullets I could take down a herd of elephants, or a pack of wolves – even a flock of sheep. The powder keeps a rat-a-tat-tatting as fast and furious as the ones before them, my forearms jiggling hard from the grip, the sound of metal sliding through the jolt of the hammer, watching the sand pop up and dance."

They had a lot of fun. A great way to spend Christmas.

XII

PAIN FOR VENGEANCE

47. Johnny Law

"Let's drive out to your place, I'd like to see it. Can I drive your car?" smiled Suzan.

"Sure. You think you can reach the pedals?" said Marshal.

"I'm a better driver than you… I don't go crashing my new car into things."

"I was young." Marshal tossed Suzie the keys to his GTX. Since this car was powered by a Hemi engine it was powered to rock 'n roll. Suzie was going to have the experience of power at her fingertips and rumbling under her toes. Suzan was an excellent driver and when she snapped the clutch the wheels made the slightest screech before taking off slowly, and under control.

"Well, I guess you told Tod and Mark," said Marshal.

"I had to tell him. Johnny has to learn,"

"Do you feel you need some vindication?"

"What do you mean?" said Suzan.

"Vindication. Do you feel you need to be vindicated? Will you be made whole after Johnny gets a ride in the suicide chair?"

"I'm not looking for vindication because I didn't do anything wrong. I'm looking for more than that. I'm looking for retribution. I want pain inflicted as vengeance on Johnny. Is that horrible of me?" said Suzan.

"You asked me if I wanted vengeance against that tiger and I said, 'what for?' They're wild animals. Nothing can be done. There's no way to tell how much pain will be required to match the need for vengeance; society has no problem euthanizing the tiger population to make sure it doesn't happen again. That's the cost of human life, right? But Johnny's different. He's a wild animal, with rights. That makes it impossible to match up the vengeance with the pain that caused it in the first place. That basically represents our position for now, right Suzie?" said Marshal. "It's 'retribution' we're after."

"Holy cow, Sherlock! Where'd that come from? ...Clever boy."

Suzie raced the engine and double clutched like a teenager leaving rubber on the island of the gas station. She apologized and cooled her heals again. Man, she was feeling good.

"Marshal, I love you!"

"I wish we could start making out right here, but it'd be hard with you on that side of the console," said Marshal.

"Yeah, well ...come snuggle next to me." said Suzan.

"No, I'm cool. It doesn't look comfortable, but I could try this...no, that won't work, you know... these Hemi's got huge drive trains...at least this long," and he put his hands up to indicate two feet, "that's a lot of thrust," he smiled.

This was where Marshal lost it, not just to break the tension, but because he was so backed up with joy. He started to laugh his hearty ha-ha, then started giggling, before it broke into a mania of laughter that was extremely contagious to Suzan, who was trying to concentrate on her driving

"Wow! I didn't know you had it in you," Suzan said, referring to his size indication.

"That's what she said." laughed Marshal.

Suzie started chortling through her nose and pulled off the side of the road so they could chuckle their heads off. They were in pure heaven. They pulled off directly under the sign at the entrance to the canyon that warned the public there had been nine deaths that year caused by the Kern River.

They must have taken five minutes to enjoy themselves, loving, touching, kissing, hugging, then really hugging seriously until they broke from their brace and decided Marshal could get them to his cabin faster.

As Suzie scooted across to the passenger side, Marshal walked around the end of the GTX, a California Highway Patrol

Car passed by Marshal slowly from the other side of the roadway, flipped a U-turn and parked his black and white behind the GTX.

Marshal froze like a deer in headlights.

"Excuse me, sir, I'd like to see your identification," said the police officer.

"Hey, officer, what'd I do wrong?" asked Marshal, unable to make out the officer's expression, the sun glaring off his aviators.

"You haven't done anything wrong... yet. I'm just checking," said the officer.

"Isn't that against the law?" said Marshal.

"I am the law, smart ass... We got a call about a heavily armed Marine named Marshal Mezey; that's AWOL. You fit the description."

"I guess anybody my age would, but I have no idea what you're talking about, so I'll be on my way," Marshal took a step, then turned and said "but Merry Christmas..."

That's when the officer pulled his Colt .45, classic lawman style, and aimed the barrel straight at Marshal. "Hold it there, buddy."

Marshal reacted with his hands up saying, "No, no, no, no...I'm cool."

Suzie simultaneously leapt from the passenger side of the vehicle, opening the door and yelling his name, "Peter, Peter... Peter ...Don't shoot him..." she stopped to get control of her voice, "He's Peter Inkpen. Check his driver's license. He's my husband."

"Let's see it, buddy," said the lawman, "Your I.D." He glanced at Suzie with an attentive eye while maintaining control of Marshal with his gun. It was all in a day's work for him, even though it was Christmas, it was still routine.

Marshal was more than happy to comply. He slid his wallet out of his back pocket and identified himself as Peter Inkpen. There it was, printed on a valid California Driver's License with his mug on it. There wasn't much more to think about. The officer immediately holstered his weapon.

"I'm sorry ma'am, don't want you thinking you got caught in a Wild West show. You know how it is these days...Angela Davis and everything...Merry Christmas to you too," said the officer.

Marshal said, "Does she look like Angela Davis to you?"

"You know what I mean, you don't know who to trust," said the officer, and in doing so, he let his voice trail off in a way that Marshal knew he was no longer suspected. "The bad guys don't go around with signs on their head."

"I heard you say the man's name you're looking for, and it sure ain't him, I can assure you. That one's mine," she said, first pointing, then running to join the arm of her young husband, her face beaming fresh as a daisy, "He's my husband. I still can't believe I'm so lucky". Suzie gave the officer a smile so magical he believed her.

Suzie cast her spell over the patrolman so he could see Suzan for anybody he wanted her to be, from Janis Joplin to Annette Funicello, even Joan Baez. But she'd settled for Mrs. Inkpen. It cut through the red tape and allowed her to speak freely, as though she was an old friend.

"My name is Suzie Inkpen. Officer, would you like to join us for Christmas brunch?" asked Suzie, hanging on Marshal's arm, making him jump a double back flip with his stomach, thinking, don't ask him that. "We were going to Kernville to have Champagne Brunch at Stacky's. Come join us."

"No, thank you Mam, I'm on duty the rest of the day. I wouldn't mind runnin' that GTX up to Kernville and back, just for the fun of it," said the officer to Marshal.

"You sure could do that, if Suzie and I could take your black and white in exchange," smiled Marshal, crookedly since he had a tough time talking freely with the law. To him, they were pigs, they weren't to be talked to. The police were not to be trusted at all.

"Yeah, that'd be nice," said the officer. "Maybe you two can tell me something. I've got this theory I latched onto since I was a soldier in Vietnam, and that is this: 'We live in a civilization. Wherever there is a civilization, there are laws to protect civilization. It's my job to enforce those laws that civilization has created for itself. Therefore, we are the protecters of civilization, and therefore that makes us law enforcers heroes, right?"

This took Marshal and Suzan by surprise. The thinking man's cop. Wouldn't you know it? He had it all worked out – for himself, and he came in first place. He was the first responder to protect America from itself. When America comes to blows with crime the police become the first responders for justice.

"You were a soldier in Vietnam? You ever see any tigers over there?" asked Marshal.

"No, can't say that I did. All I saw were little slant eyed bastards trying to kill me in their pajamas."

"What's going to happen to the Marine that's gone AWOL?", asked Marshal.

"Well, that's a whole different story, he apparently took a bag of claymores that'll cost him a hundred years when he gets caught. You just wonder, what was he thinking?"

"Maybe he was thinking the military owed him something," said Suzie.

"What could he have lost that nobody else lost over there? You went over to fight because your country needed you," said the patrolman, "That's all there is to it."

"You don't believe that do you? That your country needed you to fight millions of little gooks in the jungles of Southeast Asia to protect the civilization back home?" said Marshal.

"Yes, I did. Readily, never bothering to question the call," said the gallant ex-soldier, who answered the call to duty and lived to say he felt great about it. The old soldier, probably a year or two older than Suzan, said he still felt pride about his enlistment in 1965. But there had been developments since the big surge of 1968, that proved jungle warfare could not be won in Vietnam, and we were winning nothing. There was no payoff. It was all for death. But this Highway Patrol Officer was still full of himself. Happy to be at home, working, and happy to not have tiger claws down his back as a reminder of Vietnam.

"Yep, God and Country. I'll tell you, Mrs. Inkpen, Mr. Inkpen..." He looked them both in the eye, "Other than that... well, criminals like Charlie Manson and Tex Watson are living right down the road, you know...in Hollywood." The patrolman pointed down the road.

"That's so sad," said Suzie, "with Squeaky Fromme."

"Hell, there's nothing sad about it. You want to stay away from those folks," warned Marshal, trying hard not to laugh when he looked at Suzie. He looked back at the policeman, "We won't pick up any hitchhikers."

"Make sure you don't, you never know. This guy that's AWOL from the Marines is probably another serial killer. Being AWOL wasn't bad enough; he decided to steal a bag of claymores to go with it. What do you think he's going to do with that?"

"Sell them?" said Marshal.

"Who wants to buy a bomb that explodes into a million pieces of shrapnel that can kill somebody at 50 yards? It's not much use on the farm, is it? Maybe the *Weathermen* or SDS. That's how deep this goes."

"You think so. He wouldn't think of selling them to Jimi Hendrix, or somebody that could have fun with it," suggested Suzie.

"A claymore?" the officer sounded incredulous, "It's a killing device, there's nothing funny about it!" said the officer, staring them each in the eye again. "Unless you think a truckload full of dead babies is funny."

Both Marshal and Suzan stood with mouths agape. They didn't know whether the lawman had flipped his wig or was just kidding in a very un-California Highway Patrol type of manner. He was taking a chance they were the type of citizen that might see humor in dead baby jokes.

"I'm kidding, in case you're wondering," said the officer, broadening his lips into a California Highway Patrol grin, showing enough teeth to gleam, "Just joking."

They chuckled as best they could to appear happy and well adjusted, which at that moment was very true, for them.

"Since y'all seem well adjusted and 'groovy', as they say, I guess my work here is done. I'll save you the speech I give most young people about the Kern River...other than to say, stay out of it."

48. They Make Peace

As Marshal and Suzan watched the police officer drive away, they felt the air hiss from one end of the car as they were inflated by the helium of the experience. They got so high, they blew up like Michelon tires for the GTX and took off slowly for the canyon, down which the Kern River runs.

For as much notoriety as the Kern River gets for causing deaths, not much is said about the curvy roadway that winds through the granite canyon to Kernville. It has more twists and turns than a rattler and is twice as dangerous, with nothing to stop you if you drive off the cliffside of the two-lane road. You'll fall 159 feet to your fiery death. That happens to someone once or twice a year. Marshal fought the temptation to race his GTX to the cabin. He didn't need to be told; it was ingrained in his head – which was strange because not much else was.

"Wow!" said Suzan, "That was so close. His pointing that gun at you almost made me puke. I saw a flash from his gun that splashed your chest across the car. It spattered me with blood, over what? Goddamnit, what did you do to deserve that treatment?"

Suzie began to cry. Tears rolled down her cheeks as though she had risen to the occasion, and now her actions had worn her out. "I don't think I can live like this Marshal – a half step away from you being killed, over nothing."

Marshal felt the same way. Suzie wasn't happy, so Marshal wasn't happy. Hell, he accepted what came of him. God had already thrown him to the tigers; he expected the wolves would be next. But for Suzan he'd do cartwheels to make her happy. The simple sound of her laughter was joy enough, but here she was crying, her face scrunched up like a weeping rag.

"Hey, Suzie", said Marshal, "Look at me!"

Suzie looked over at him. He was making a funny face that made him look amazingly like a lizard with his ears pulled back, his eyebrows in a V, and a forked tongue slithering in and out. It looked funny – real funny. It took a moment for Suzie's mood to change, but change it did.

"Okay, look at this one, you think you're so funny." Suzan made a face like a little stuffed monkey, with a tiny slit for a mouth and wide-open button eyes. "That make you want put penny in nose?" asked Suzan, fluttering her lashes. This cracked Marshal up and took them into the world of gentle cheerfulness.

It took twenty-five minutes to get to the cabin. Marshal had failed to tell the truth again; the cabin was much more than that. It was seclusive and exclusive, having its master suite perched aloft, up a cedar stairway to the 'heavenly bed' where even its bathroom ceiling had its own constellation. You could lie in bed and watch the water crash through the canyon. It was all so beautiful. Also, there was a phone in every room. Priceless.

That's where Suzan and Marshal landed, in a place they could call their own. It was the first time Marshal could remember lying in bed with a girl, and the first time Suzie wanted to remember being with a man. That's how meshed the gears of their relationship were. They lay on the numerous pillows, a continuum of orange, comfortable with Suzie's head on his shoulder so she could look up at him, or away from his gaze.

"I love you," whispered Suzan.

"I love you," whispered back Marshal.

"What are we going to do Marshal?" said Suzie.

"Well, I say, let's round 'em up and head West," said Marshal, pointing in that direction with his thumb.

"No, I'm serious. No cowboy stuff," said Suzan.

Marshal looked down and saw the blond top of her head, so he spoke softly, "Listen Suzie, I know you're serious, and I wouldn't like it any other way, but we got serious business to attend to with Johnny Burnette tonight. I don't want him to ruin our good time."

"That's what I'm talking about, I'm not so sure I need the vengeance, now. I mean, I've never been on this side where love comes from. I've never been part of generating love. It's a kick – it's friendly here, I love it." Suzie looked up and kissed Marshal.

"I guess that means this is the first chance I've had at being happy," she went on, "and it's because of you, you bug hulk, is what I'm saying. I'm in this spot because you're who you are – you're kind and gentle and more than I deserve. You make me laugh and ... you just let me be me."

"I know I wanted vengeance on Johnny, or 'retribution' for what he did to me and the direction it took me ...a life of insanity isn't all it's cracked up to be. And I'm not blaming Johnny for all that. It was as much the result of trying to get my father off his bucks; but you saw the fruitless fight that was."

"The effort to fight Johnny, while fighting my parents, was too much of a double whammy, and that proved to be my undoing. I couldn't take the fight any longer, so that's when I turned myself into the insane asylum."

"But you came into my life and look at us now. It's a Christmas miracle! I'm healed. I'm totally sane. No more craziness. See me Marshal, I'm not a *fractured fissure*, I'm a God damned Christmas miracle."

"Oh, boy," said Marshal, "I never saw you as a *fractured fissure*, but I'll testify to you being a certified Christmas Wonder."

They were so happy with themselves; they dove under the covers to get busy with what was bringing them so much pleasure.

When they came up for air again, they were faced with the same question, "What are they going to do about the vengeance?" And, "What are we going to do about Marshal being AWOL with a bag of claymores?" Marshal's problem suddenly became bigger than her problem. More urgent, more disastrous. In fact, more overwhelming. What *were* they going to do about that?

"The more I think about it," said Suzan, "You can make a case for being crazy yourself. I mean, think how crazy you'd be to drop out of school, enlist in the Marines, fight in Vietnam, get practically eaten by a tiger, spend seven months in a hospital... It only makes sense you'd be crazy enough to walk out of Camp Pendleton with a bag of claymores. It's what you do with them that will determine if you're crazy or not."

"Yeah, that's the ticket," said Marshal, with that wily grin. "Will you be my attorney? I'd like a cushy little spot there in Patton, next to you, that's where we'll live the rest of our lives at the State's expense. Does that sound perfect? Now, in what kind of crazy fashion shall we disburse the claymores so they're sure to think I'm criminally insane?"

"I think just having them qualifies you for being insane," said Suzie. "We could turn ourselves into the authorities, find the Highway Patrolman and hand him the black bag."

"You said you saw me splattered across the GTX, shot dead by the lawman."

"Yes, that was a horrible image. We must be careful...or you'll be shot for aiding and abetting the *Weather Underground*."

"That's such a stupid name, I don't even get it," said Marshal. "How about we get Tod and Mark on the phone to see what other options we have in this geopolitical atmosphere?"

"No, we're not ready for them yet. I'm scared of what Mark meant by fitting Johnny with a suicide chair. It sounds like more police involvement to me," said Suzie.

"Well, vengeance don't come free. You've got to work at it. But a suicide chair is an easy fit if you know how to tie a hangman's knot. All you need is a neck to put in the noose, let's say Johnny's, and you have 'em stand on the stool with his hands tied behind him. You throw the end of the rope over a rafter and tie it off, nice and tight at the workbench. Now you got Johnny by the neck and he's standing on a stool with his hands tied."

"If you wanted to get some specific information from Johnny, now would be the time to ask. If you don't like the answers you're getting, say, he's not earnest enough, you kick the stool out from under him, so he drops and hangs himself. That's why they call it a suicide chair."

"But as he's hanging there — and this is where it takes talent — he stretches the rope so his very tippy toes can touch the floor when he drops. That way, he can almost save himself, but no, he can't, because you could pull him tighter. You'd find Johnny had a lot more to admit the longer his toes touched the ground. It'd be up to you."

"That sounds awful," said Suzie.

"Yes, it can stretch your throat."

"How do you tie a hangman's noose?" asked Suzie.

"I'll get my rope and show you," said Marshal.

"No, I was kidding."

"Oh."

"When I hear you explain the process, I want to see Johnny's head stretched with his toes earning him a moment of reprieve from choking - but vengeance won't be mine. I don't need it now," said Suzan.

"I could torture him all night and I wouldn't feel this good. My heart wants you. It's shoving out the vengeance to make room for you, Marshal. That's why I'm saying this. My heart wants you in it, there's no room for vengeance. I don't want to think about him. I only want to think of you," said Suzan, and she started to cry again. "And these are tears of joy."

"Let them flow. I love you too," said Marshal, making him the happiest man in the world. He put his hand on the back of her head and began to run his fingers through her hair, "You're so beautiful." He touched her chin as the rays embraced her face. "I love you," he said again, and again. He was captured by her charms as he tried one more time to prove it.

"Wait a minute," she said, "Do you want to make this even better, as if that's possible?"

"Well, heck yeah," said Marshal.

"Let's take showers."

"Can it wait a second?"

"It can wait longer than that."

49. Suzie Examines Herself

After they made a mess in Marshal's grand two headed shower, Suzie hung back in the steamy aftermath to examine herself in the nude. She had the opposite mirrors: front and back, and a third view if she used the make-up mirror to see her profile. And if that wasn't enough there was a view of the river running the full length of the picture window to the outdoors.

It was a nice touch, bringing the sound of water being pushed and pulled by nature's own turbulence. The sun was bright this December's early afternoon, the rays shown through the glass as slanted prisms of light. Outside, squawking crows scolded red tail hawks as the mockingbirds pretended to be owls. This world isn't crazy and mixed up. It's perfect. And the smell of it is so fresh, and new each day. Suzie swore to God it smelled better than a new car.

Suzan studied herself in the mirrors. The full monte. She was as skinny as a model, that's for sure. But she still had a swimmer's build. Her muscles were long, but her strength was in her thighs. She was going to be okay. Perhaps she had been hard on herself.

She made the same monkey face she had shown Marshal. It was funny the way she pursed her lips and blew up her face. The tiny lines stemming from around her lips made her look old. All she could think of was Marshal. He was only 19 and she was going to be 24 next month. It didn't matter, she told herself, stealing a line from her mother, "Everything is as it should be." But was it really?

Suzie's confidence lagged for a moment. Her beauty, if you want to call it that, was in her eyes. They were like the Aurora Borealis. Born from black, they could turn from green to blue and back while you're looking at them. She examined her eyes closely. Yep, they stared back from blue to green, just like *Labradorite,* a natural phenomenon. Her confidence swelled again. She could use these.

Suzie helped herself to some of Mrs. M's sportswear along with some of Marshal's young men's wear and came up with something akin to Bob Dylan and Dinah Shore. Marshal thought she looked great, and that was all that mattered. They were having a great time playing house, being adults, and planning for the future. They both planned on loving each other no matter what, and they were just the type of people that meant it, no matter what. They were two desperate souls.

"Hey Marshal, why don't you show me that swimming hole you were talking about? I'd love to see it."

"Don't you think we should call your brothers? They're supposed to be waiting for us."

"I know. I don't want to because I know they're going to hate my decision. They'll think I'm being weak, not wanting to do anything about it," said Suzie.

"No. I won't let them. We're strong, we're stronger than them," said Marshal.

"Have you ever tried to talk Tod or Mark out of something they think's right to do?"

"No. But give them a call. We have to anyway, it's Christmas."

XIII

SUZAN SNAPS OUT OF IT

50. She Calls It Off

Suzan got Tod on the phone, "We're not having the suicide chair for Christmas this year. I've decided vengeance and retribution are off the table this holiday season."

"Why's that? Marshal forget how to tie a slip knot?"

"No, Marshal's been very exact about that."

"We're ready, ain't that right Mark?"

"Yeah, well, there's nothing happening," said Suzie.

"What do you mean?" said Tod.

"I'm calling off the caper with Johnny Burnette... forever."

There was a moment of panic, then the knowledge that something evil was present and was going to have it his way.

"What are you saying? Who have you been talking to?" said Tod

"I haven't been talking to anybody but Marshal and not even him. I decided for myself that keyholing Johnny isn't going to end my nightmare, it'll just extend it. I've found what I wanted, and needed, and it begins and ends with Marshal. I want to be with him – exclusively. I don't give a flying fuck about Johnny Burnette. He can rot in hell," said Suzan.

Mark grabbed the phone from Tod.

"Listen Suzie, you don't know what you're saying. I understand you want no part of this because you're having fun with Marshal, but this is a criminal act that'll last through time. It's bigger than us and is always going to be there, nagging you when you're done. And I'll tell you something, I don't much appreciate the fact that Johnny's walking around town knowing he killed my sister's son. I won't let him. He's going to face up to that. I got big plans for him, starting with him eating one of those claymores," Mark said.

"Well, that's our other problem. We've got to get rid of those claymores before Marshal gets shot," said Suzie.

"They're not healthy to have around, but I've got a plan that'll take care of both problems," said Mark.

"They're not your problems Mark. They're our problem, Marshal's and mine."

"You're not thinking straight, Suzie. We're talking murder here. Johnny murdered your boy, your own son, and his son, and my nephew – he's got to pay."

"Please Mark, settle down."

"How can you say settle down when you're the one who roiled me up?"

"I'm sorry. It's not like that, Mark. Johnny didn't murder anybody. I made the whole thing up, and I did it because ...I don't know why. I said that because I didn't want to be alone in the snake pit anymore. I wanted someone to listen to me and maybe be kind to me; not just thrown away like yesterday's newspaper."

There was a pause to absorb what Suzie had just said. Surprised, might be a word to describe Mark's non-response. Disappointment that his sister had lied to him about such a deep, personal matter. Glad that it hadn't gone any further. Understanding when it came right down to it. Who could blame her? Then skepticism that perhaps she was lying now about Johnny's involvement. Whatever the case, she was the only one who knew for sure, and forgiveness seemed to be the order for today. Then finally, gratitude that she came clean before somebody else got hurt. She had found Marshal, and he took her to the promised land. Then back to skepticism again.

"Let me talk to Marshal."

Marshal could hear what was going on and took the phone in his natural sheepish way.

"Hello," said Marshal.

"Marshal, what's going on, you know what's going on with her?"

"Well, it's not a bad thing. I guess Suzie decided to tell the truth about Johnny B."

"That's bullshit. She'll come back next week, and it will be Johnny Burnette all over again, it's been going on for years. This is the first time she's been truthful about it, if she is being truthful. What do you think Marshal?"

"Seems like Suzie's got things to say, and I plan on listening," Marshal looked at Suzie sitting next to him and made his lizard face. Then he turned away and said to Mark, "I think Suzie believed her lie about Johnny. That he drugged her and killed her fetus, and did it for his mother, is a bizarre pill to have to swallow. Did you even know she was pregnant? There's things happening here and we don't know what they are...maybe we'll never know. So, when Suzie says she's lying... I don't know. How can you really know what's going on inside a person's mind?"

"All I know is that Suzie wants to leave him alone and I'm proud of that. I'm proud that my future wife can say since she found me there's no need for Johnny B. Let's say Suzie's relationship with Johnny can be looked upon as an allegorical metaphor."

"Marshal, fuck you. I'm sorry I asked, you dumb son of a bitch," said Mark.

Tod grabbed the phone back from Mark.

"Listen, Marshal, let's meet at 5:00 at Stan's. We'll have some Christmas dinner together and sort this thing out…like family."

"Not like my family. Mom and Dad are still holding on to Christmas on the farm," said Marshal.

51. A Christmas Celebration

The Christmas party was in full swing at Stan's Drive-in. The 80-car drive-in was full, and the main restaurant was popping. Tod and Mark managed to commandeer the last big booth in the end. That way they could relax and enjoy the festivities. There was a lounge area by the bar that had a dance floor, and the band, *The Avengers,* were setting up for the sundowner crowd. Testing their microphones. They half expected Suzie and Marshal to be late but here they came, right on time: the two love birds.

"Man, they say true love happens fast, but I didn't see this one coming at all. Are you guys sure it's love and not something that only lasts a day?" said Mark. "Love comes pretty easy this time of year. You never see people breaking up for the holidays."

"Give it a rest, Mark. I'm happy as hell for both of you. No kidding. You look so alive. Not to say you both looked dead before. But it's a pleasant surprise. I love you both. There, I said it. Now let's get some drinks," said Tod, who couldn't believe his own Christmas cheer.

Time had taken the edge off Mark's original outburst. He was coming to realize it was his own false pride he was mad about, although he was too young to understand what *false pride* meant. At nineteen, he thought pride was a good thing, and pride can't be false, by definition, *ergo* how is it even possible to have 'false pride?' It was a question that hung him up more than once. He was learning, or trying to, but it was a slow process. It was a function of the crowd he was running with at the time.

His friends: Vince, Ricardo, Julio, and Mike. Each so-called friend worth the print his name is written on. They were all going down and taking him with them. He could feel them pulling at his tendrils. He'd worry about that later. It was his sister he was concerned about now. If they weren't going to keyhole Johnny, there wasn't any need for Marshal, seeing he was AWOL from the Marines, with stolen U.S. weaponry. That wasn't helping his sister, and it posed a big problem.

As Mark looked across the booth at her now, she wasn't twitchy and scratching, with fingernail marks up and down her arms. Her eyes weren't darting to and froe, jerking her head side to side, looking for people that want to hurt her. Her hair wasn't greasy and unkempt like a rat's nest. It had blossomed into a full peddled flower of blond hair. She was laughing with her lover, fluttering about without a care in the world. They should use love as shock treatment for the insane. If only that was possible.

Marshal was looking his best also. The cowboy's version of tall, dark and handsome. He had on cowboy everything, from the Stetson to his maroon ribbed socks, he was straight out of the Wild West. His tan buckskin coat with the fringe down the sleeves topped it off.

Mark dressed straight Americana in his long legged Levis and plaid shirt, work boots and a Black Power leather coat down to his fingers, with long curly hair. Tod had lost most of his hair taking bennies, so he said, so it was just long in back. But Tod always dressed artfully, picking out accessories that match. This evening he chose a scarlet handkerchief to match his headband and Italian grey suit he purchased at Goodwill. Together they made an interesting crew, even if their conversation proved otherwise.

With Johnny Burnette off the table they decided to eat and be merry. After they had the first round of drinks, they had another, and another. They had Christmas dinner with all the trimmings for $1.50. That included turkey, ham, biscuits, gravy, mashed potatoes, stuffing, cornbread, two starches, and butter. Nobody could do it better than Stan because you got to choose between pumpkin or lemon meringue pie for dessert. Chocolate cream pie cost a quarter more, but Mark thought it was well worth it.

They finished about the same time as the band finished their first set playing *Louis, Louis.* There were few people dancing to this old favorite, but it was still early.

"If you'll excuse me, I'm going to the lady's room," said Suzie.

"Well, I might as well take this opportunity to go myself. Watch our things for us," said Marshal.

That left Tod and Mark sitting in the booth right next to each other, Mark sitting on the outside.

"Hey man, can you give me some room," said Mark, moving his arm around.

"What'd you say?" said Tod, moving closer in on Mark, almost bumping him off the booth bench, making him stand up.

"You're so infantile," said Mark, stretching his legs, looking around the eatery to see who's there. From his vantage point, standing up, he could see beyond the teller, all the way out the doors to the long line of cars on both sides, opting for burgers and fries for Christmas. That's where he saw a new black Jaguar, License Plate: MA BOY, with a guy looking exactly like Johnny Burnette behind the wheel, stuffing his mouth with fast food, wearing a suit and tie. Mark couldn't believe his good fortune, until it struck him: *don't do it.*

That could have been the end of the story, but it wasn't. Mark was learning, but he was not a rapid learner. It was going to niggle him. He was going to wonder whatever happened to Johnny Burnette. We want to know what happened to Johnny Burnette, and there he is.

Well haven't you heard; he's rotting in hell. And no matter where he goes, he must live with the fact of what he's done. Hah! There's no justice in that – and that was Mark's problem. He was still looking for justice, thinking it was something he could earn, never thinking it didn't exist, except as an ephemeral goal.

"Godammit, there he is, I don't believe my eyes," said Mark.

"There's who?" asked Tod.

"Johnnie fuckin' Burnette."

"Where?" said Tod, partially amazed.

"Right out there, eaten a burger in his car," said Mark, taking cover by sitting back down next to Tod. "He's sitting by himself, and he's got on a tie."

"Let's rat pack that motherfucker," whispered Tod.

"How are we going to do that? We need three more guys."

"I'll walk up and distract him; you jump in the back of the Jag and wrap that tie around his neck and pull him over the console ... trap him on the floor...I'll jump in and drive away. We'll take him out in the country and bury him in a field of ants and claymores. That'd take care of both our problems," said Tod.

"How am I supposed to subdue a 6'4" man in the back of the Jaguar, let alone bury him up to his chin in claymores?" asked Mark.

"You can do it. Think of him feeding red devils to our little nephew."

52. Suzan's Celebration

As soon as Suzan hit the restrooms, she had a strange look on her face, but not because she had to pee. She was hoping something would change. Hoping a castle had been built to protect her and Marshal from outsiders; people who didn't understand how they functioned without money. It was hard to say, but they never went unfed. Christmas dinner was always provided, somehow, like magic. That's what she needed now, a rabbit pulled from the hat, or...

Joyce Jones? That was her, standing right in front of her. Joyce Jones: from junior high, in a light blue nylon uniform with the letters "Kern County Mental Health" stenciled across the front, with flaring nostrils, and ruby red lips.

That isn't to say Joyce looked crazy, but don't test her. The flaring nostrils weren't supposed to describe an emotional characteristic as much as describe a girl who could be the daughter of Delroy Lindo and Viola Davis – flaring nostrils, only worth mentioning if they were playing a sad scene. A mixture of snot and tears. But this was not a sad scene, so Joyce played it like Viola, enjoying the opportunity to be witty and cunning, and charming.

"I'm so happy to see you, Joyce," said Suzie, "I was hoping you'd be here."

"I've been waiting for you baby girl. You were supposed to find a way to free me. Did you?"

"No, I found my man, but he turned out to be crazy, like me. He's AWOL from the Marines, has a bag of claymores for sale."

"Claymores? How's he got connections like that? You looking to sell them, huh? I got connections with the underground movement – I'm talking Black Panther Power, baby."

Right then and there Suzan and Joyce gave each other a Black Power handshake that Suzan had learned from a sociological handbook. It was executed like this: you went from the handshake to a thumb-shake, to a finger grab, to a wrist grab, to a shoulder seize, then it's a fist held high to signify solidarity, with the words spoken, "Power to the People." That was the secret *Underground* handshake that Angela Davis introduced as the Black Panthers handshake and anybody who knew it, you could trust to be cool.

53. Marshal's Celebration

Marshal came out of the bathroom and found himself standing on Makena beach. His feet were hot in the white sand with towering waves pounding the shore. Suzan lay on a large beach towel that covered about a quarter acre of sand. "Over here Marshal," yelled Suzan, barely audible. He waved and began plowing through the sand in her direction, shouting, "I see you. Isn't this wonderful, it's so beautiful out here in the sun."

"What'd you say?"

"What?"

"It's gorgeous, so peaceful the way the wind blows and keeps it cool," she said.

"It's perfect," said Marshal.

"Oh Marshal, we were finally able to get away. Tod and Mark couldn't have fixed it up any nicer. The pill house is so cute. And privacy, well, it's so natural. There's nobody here."

"This is what we wanted, right? To be left alone, no one to bother us, or see what we do or fear," said Marshal.

"No one to incarcerate us because we're acting weird. We won't be weird. We'll be normal," said Suzie.

"We're normal, we're normal, we're normal," they chorused in two-part harmony.

The love birds fell together, and pecked, before ravaging each other with love. They could have gotten an award for it, but there was no competition. They both fared well – giving all their body to having a baby. That's what they wanted to make for each other, a cute little...it didn't matter. Boy or girl. They both wanted a child, sleeping or crying, to dote on and teach the ways of the world, somehow providing the child with a lesson they didn't receive themselves about love.

It wasn't that a lesson on love wasn't received, the Yokuts did plenty of talking. But the lesson just wasn't acted upon. The love message failed because it lacked strength of character. When asked to stand tall and weather the storm against the Cornwall family, they each looked the other way. Nobody had the strength of character to make whatever was missing come to life. Jack and Mary hadn't taught Suzie how to use the "strength of character" card. They didn't know how to use it themselves.

Suzie certainly heard plenty of talk about it through Yokuts Club. They made a living off teaching strength of character. It said so in the brochure. But they missed their own mark with Suzie by telling her about what love was, rather than showing her what love can be.

Suzan could have used some strength of character when she was left to turn herself into the insane asylum in Suffolk

County. That took strength of character. Waving goodbye to Suzie as their flight took off from Maquire Air Force Base, taught Suzan her parents had no sense of how to use strength of character to help her. And she sorely needed help.

They probably thought they were using strength of character to refuse Suzan help. That was anti-love. They had other things more pressing to do than send their daughter to the Snake Pit for the rest of her life. They should have taken her with them. So what if she had to sit at home learning to play cribbage with her mom? At least she'd know that they, as a family, had strength of character.

Who am I kidding? If Suzie had gone to Europe, she'd have made her parents' life a nightmare, the same way she did at Betty and George's – rapping her fingers on the wall. Suzan was a restless girl. She fared much better lying with Marshal on the beach doing exactly what she was doing, no doubt about it.

"I love you, Marshal."

"I love you, Suzie. I was thinking, I'm going to ..."

"No, don't say it," said Suzan.

"I'm going to ..."

"Please, don't say it."

"This lifestyle doesn't seem sustainable; you know what I mean?"

XIV

"TO THE MOON"

54. The Peace Sign

"I loved making peace signs when I was in Nam. I made 'em all over the place. We burned 'em in the jungle, made targets and lit them up, shooting streamers into them just for kicks," said Marshal, "Until they started court marshaling us over it."

"Why would they do that?"

"Because they don't want to see nothin' that has to do with peace. We're at war over there, you know?"

"So I hear. But it's just a sign, right? A peace sign?"

"Right on! Don't mean nothin!" said Marshal.

Suzie and Marshal had been lounging on their fictional Makena Beach, enjoying themselves more as they approached the end of their travail. They spread their arms and legs and entangled them together like two King Crabs mating on the acre of blanket they laid on. Marshal was barebacked, showing off his scars, and Suzan had changed into her black bikini.

"You loved to draw them, huh?" she said, "Nobody made you."

"Yeah, I liked it. It made the Sarge upset, but I didn't mind. It soothed me. Especially when I was in the hospital, you know ... just lying there. They're easy to draw ...then I'd decorate them ...leave 'em lying around. I left 'em all over South Vietnam."

"Peace symbols, huh? Who were you promoting? The hippies?"

"Hell, no. I was promoting peace, of course, for everybody. I'll show you how to draw one...it's fun... every part of the peace symbol talks to you. It's like having a lucky charm that symbolizes the Father, Son and Holy Ghost. The Trifecta of Peace," said Marshal.

"No, I don't think so Marshal," said Suzie. "That's pretty much wrong."

"What? Haven't you ever drawn a peace symbol before, the most iconic sign of our generation? I'm drawing one right now."

Marshal strode off the edge of the blanket and stepped into the warm white sand. The sky was shark blue and the ocean whale gray. Suzie crossed her legs pow wow style and watched. There was nobody at the beach, it being Makena Beach, and Marshal continued to talk as he outlined a ten-foot circle with his foot.

"Now here's how you interpret the peace symbol from a Christian point of view, say, before I went to Vietnam. This circle represents His infinite wisdom and guidance for understanding peace. It encompasses everything God knows."

"Okay, wise guy. Lay it on me," said Suzie.

"God's Universe is divided into three parts. There's the Father, who is God, and the Father's Son, Jesus, who is second. The Holy Ghost is third, and is the enforcer of God's rule," said Marshal, proud of his announcement. "This trifecta rules the Peace Symbol."

"Uh-huh," said Suzan, "Is that all? Because I know that's not right."

By this time Marshal had drawn three lines that met in the center of the "O" like a cookie cutter, encircled by the Trifecta. Marshal knelt as he finished making the symbol.

"But now comes the part you never hear about. What does the Trifecta symbolize anyway? Well, Peace, duh! But you've got to think harder than that?" asked Marshal rhetorically.

Suzan continued to stare at Marshal.

"Well, studying the Trifecta like I was on acid in the hospital got me to thinking. I call it the "Inverted Trifecta." It's what led me to become a Naturalistic Mystique, which is what I am now."

"No kidding? You don't say." said Suzie, with a smile, "I didn't know you were so religiously inclined Marshal. You're not going to baptize me, are you?"

"No, just the opposite," said Marshal, "The Father, Son, and Holy Ghost, after Vietnam morphed into Healthy, Wealthy, and Wise, like all is one and one is all. Healthy, Wealthy, and Wise. That's what I'm calling the Inverted Trifecta of the Peace Symbol."

Suzan listened carefully to what Marshal said. This was a side of Marshal she'd never seen before. She paused before saying, "Oh, Marshal, I love you but you've got it all wrong. I mean, what you're talking about has nothing to do with the peace sign. What you've drawn in the sand is not a peace symbol. That's the *Mercedes Benz logo*. It doesn't have a fucking thing to do with peace."

"What are you talking about? A Mercedes Benz logo? It's a peace symbol, everybody knows that. Isn't it?" said Marshal. "That's a peace symbol. It's like a peace symbol."

"Nah, it's nothing like a peace symbol because it's the Mercedes Benz symbol," said Suzie. "The Peace symbol is an ornament that circles four lines, each line telling the story of love and making babies. A true love story about having plenty of babies. Lots of babies that need peace to survive."

"Oh?... well, ...tell me more about that," said Marshal.

“The first line starts at the top of the “O” and goes straight to the middle of the circle. This line symbolizes an egg impregnated by a man. Can you see it? A symbiotic relationship between man and woman, in other words, it’s a symbol of procreation, or, for lack of a better word: fucking. Can you see that in the “O”?

“Sort of,” said Marshal.

Suzie stood over the ten-foot circle in the sand. She wiped the face clean then drew that line to the middle. She and Marshal stared at it together, imagining an impregnation of an egg.

“Now look here,” said Suzie, “this line number two extends from the middle of the “O” and goes straight to the bottom where it becomes a phallic symbol of a Man with an obviously large penis. Can you see that, Marshal?”

Suzan extended the second line down and finished it right when she said the word penis.

“I can see that,” said Marshal.

“Now, can you recognize these last two lines, number three and four, stemming from each side of the penis, like an upside down “V”? Can you see those lines as the legs of a woman embracing the man’s penis between the V of her legs? Or shall I say, ‘in the manner of making love.’”

"That seems pretty obvious now that I'm looking at it." said Marshal. "But it looks more like a man taking a piss."

"Well, that's because you're irascible. Don't be crude Marshal, please. I want you to know about this. You brought it up."

"Okay."

"The most important part is the "O" that surrounds this universal love sign. The "O" symbolizes "Ovaries", without which man cannot exist! Think about that Marshal. If there were no ovaries there'd be no eggs to impregnate, and women couldn't carry their babies, because there'd be no babies. It would mean the end of civilization! The "O" stands for ovaries and a reminder that women carry babies and men should protect them – not bomb them," said Suzie. "You follow me?"

"No, I'm still back on the man and woman fornicating, and calling it the 'Universal Love Symbol.'"

"You're so romantic," said Suzan.

"Does this mean you're my old lady now?"

"Not on your life." Suzie said.

"Why not?"

"Because I want to make babies."

"I can make that happen."

"You haven't yet."

"I will."

"Will you?" said Suzan.

Marshal leaned in close and looked her dead in the eye.

"I'm at your command."

55. So, Says Marshal

Suzan was so rock and roll – so wildly sweet, like a cherry drop. You could taste her just by looking at her. Especially when she wore her hair in a thick braid and smiled with those perfect teeth. She looked fine in western gear too, her cute button nose peeking out from a Mexican poncho. We could have lived in the Snake Pit where we'd be safe amongst ourselves, even raised our baby there if they'd have let us.

But the authorities said there'd be none of that. It irritated them to make us happy. We wanted to have our baby, but that was never going to happen. That's when the whole psychiatry board went nuts over Suzie getting pregnant. As if that wasn't supposed to happen. The Lunacy Czar just cut me loose. They set me free to work in the oil fields and forbade me from ever seeing Susie again. They *forbade me* from seeing Suzan upon threat of being sent to Leavenworth for going AWOL in the first place. How could I ever not see Suzie again? Tell me that.

I'll never forget when Suzan stepped out of her slipper on the floor of the Snake Pit in San Berdoo. That's when I fell in love with her. She was breaking out of Patton that night and asked if I wanted to go with her. She was such a riot; in and of herself. And the next thing I knew I was starring in a Hollywood movie.

What *actually occurred* to Suzan after Tod and Mark risked their freedom breaking her out of Ward 3B was, she was caught again at Johnny B.'s house the very next morning. True story! In the morning when her brothers went to wake her to rebuild her life in San Jose, they found she had caught a cab to Johnny B.'s house to implore him one last time to do "something" for her. That "something" was never determined. Johnny's mother immediately called the police and had Suzan taken into custody. It was back to Ward 3B, next stop, Patton State Mental Health Hospital and the Snake Pit.

And who did she meet in the pit: Me. That was all there was to it. That's what happened during her less than 24-hour escape from the mental institution. It was a re-run of her first apprehension when she threw the cactus plant through Mrs. B.'s window, but this time, the only drama was Suzie's final capitulation to the funny farm. She headed directly to the Snake Pit, from which there was no escape.

It didn't matter anymore to anyone. "The river had run dry." It became clear that Suzie was insane. Tod and Mark wanted out; and I was there to love her. It was all craziness and it hurt. That's what crazy does. It hurts, and it wears you down. We were all losers in the Snake Pit, left with the ugliness that crazy emits. There is no love in crazy. But I was there waiting for Suzie in the end. I had my holster and my Marlboros, and I was the new marshal in town. I had my guns and my claymores to blow this craziness to smithereens.

I loved Suzie. I'd have married her if she'd let me. She was precious and kind and smart. So Johnny wasn't a figment of her imagination, but he may as well have been for as much as people understood. Somehow though, Suzie and I kept riding the same train until we finally hooked up in the Snake Pit. (Or maybe it was on the white sands of Makena.)

Whatever beauty Suzie and I shared in the pit, it was destroyed by reality. The Lunacy Czar had taken care of the problem. I was climbing the 110-foot oil derrick but I wasn't thinking about work. I was thinking about making love to Suzan and the pregnancy it created. Then I thought of how those doctors operated inside her with their tools that scraped away any memory of the fetus, as they tied her tubes in a knot so it couldn't happen again. They sterilized her. Then I thought of myself and how I was forbidden from seeing Suzie ever again. Then I slipped...and fell...a long way down.

XV.

TOD TURNS TO THE HUMANITIES

56. Gambling Our Future on Love

Because I was the eldest and managed to receive my degree in Humanities, e.g., Classical Painting, or "fine art" years before Mark hit high school and Suzie flunked out of college, I naturally assumed the leadership role between us three kids. That was like being a corporal in the Mexican Army: Suzan wouldn't listen to a thing I said.

As much as Mom and Dad may have trusted me to take Suzie by the hand and guide her in the right direction, nothing could be further from the truth. I never spent any quality time with Suzie. She was four years younger than me. She never played any team sport except "Aquanettes," if you can call thirty girls swimming in unison a sport. I had nothing to share with Suzie, like I did football with Mark. She was my sister, and we got along as well as a boy and girl four years apart could be expected to get along while growing up. We lived in the same house. But there was no magic, or panache, to our sibling relationship – just ordinary brotherly love.

As far as I'm concerned, Suzie can rot in Hell with Johnny Burnette because it was all her fault anyway. Her problem was she couldn't get a job and work the system just a little bit. That's all it takes in this great country of ours and she didn't have it. She could have done what I've done my whole life – work a little, then draw unemployment a lot. Maybe work get an ISS check in the future, just for being alive.

I had no interest in breaking Suzie out of Ward 3B, but I had a certain obligation to Mark. I mean, I couldn't say no to her rescue. She's our sister and we got her out of that hole. But it makes me sad she couldn't make it longer than a day. We were triumphant and satisfied at first. We'd set our sister free, and she was going to San Jose for a new start. The authorities would never find her. We thought she could do that on her own. That's how crazy that fool's folly was. And by 'fool' I'm talking about Mark.

What I'm angry about is that after Christmas at Stan's Drive-in I never saw Suzan again. I never went to see her in Patton or visited her after she was released to a community house in Bakersfield. Why not? Because it's so fucking sad. I could never face the disappointment of her living the life of a crazy person. The stigma of it all was too much for me.

The reason insanity is so repulsive is simply because it is. I look at Suzie and see too much of my own life. It's like looking at the face of our mother's corpse, her red lips seamed up with twine. Not a happy face. It's distinct and clear and tells you, "This is the face of insanity, watch me as I eat my Sloppy Joe."

There's no love where insanity lives. There's no room for it within the border of the asylum. Insanity never lets love in once it has a strangle hold on your brain. Suzie wrestled with it as best she could, but she was too weak. Who can blame her? Normally you look to the parents for the necessary love. It's the only natural source for love to cure a psychotic daughter. But Mom and Pop had no time for that depth of love for Suzan. They were busy taking a vacation from love.

I sure as hell couldn't help Suzie out of her jam. I had no resources. So when Mark said he could break her out of that two-bit hole, I was happy to help him. And we were all happy she was free. In hindsight, Mark and I thought we provided that necessary love. We had gone the extra mile to prove something special about how much we loved her. We proved our love by risking our futures and gambling that love would set her free from insanity. Well, we did set her free. Obviously, our love was misguided.

There was a lot of love at stake. And there was nothing else in it for us. It was against the law, and our parents would have flipped out. They would have disowned us. But if everything was right in the world, it should have worked to liberate Suzan's mind from mental illness and the whole experiment would have been a huge success. She could have snapped out of it. But instead, it just made her crazier. I was old enough to know better than that, and I did.

Jack had his master's degree in special education and should have been more sensitive to Suzan's plight. He worked with her closely in Yokuts since she was nine years old. I have an old photograph of her wearing a white T-shirt with Yokuts Club Day Camp written in green letters around an insignia of an arrowhead chipped from obsidian. The kids wore them as standard issue for all campers. It was a nice touch by the old man, like everything else that concerned Yokuts.

Jack was an artistic guy, a craftsman, "a place for everything and everything in its place" type of guy. And ready to enforce his favorite saying type of guy. It just came with the territory. Like clapping his hands as loud as he could early Saturday morning to rouse us out of bed, yelling, "Lot's of work to do today, up and at 'em. Lot's of work to do!"

The photograph is of nine-year-old Suzie standing in pig tails in front of the Yokuts bus. She's wearing shorts, with her rolled-up towel and bathing suit under one arm, and a brown sack with her lunch in the other: the Yokuts bus has pulled up and she's jumping in with Keds tennis shoes, and a big smile saying hello.

The T-shirts were cool though. Besides the arrowhead insignia, Dad painted a cartoon character of an Indian on the bus, with breech skin pants, long hair and no shirt. He's banging the drum attached to his side, with a feather in his headband, and a big toothy grin on his face, and, of course, moccasins on his feet. A happy Yokuts Indian, of the same indigenous tribe of Native Americans who inhabited the Bakersfield region of Kern County. That Indian character was the only replica of the Yokuts culture seen anywhere around Bakersfield, except for the Kern County Natural History Museum.

He could teach them everything else though. He taught archery, making fires, cutting watermelon, diving, dodge ball, handing out milk, cleaning up, passing out gold feathers, telling stories, pumping up balls, forming circles, how to hula-hoop, how to play games, quiet games, throwing children at the plunge, learning about trees, and camping – that's a whole other field, like warding off bears and walking single file, crossing streams, cutting wood, examining sea specimens, the ocean, sleeping outdoors, sleeping in cabins – how to save lives, saving lives, how to be amiable and brave, looking out for others, no fighting, horseback riding, the world around you, making change, being a warrior, being funny, recognizing good from bad, right from wrong, sitting in Pow Wows with our parents watching, putting on plays, all those things and more, is what our Dad taught Yokuts every day.

He was like a dream Dad. Always in good shape and open to questions. He ran the show with a smile and made sure every child was happy. It started out to be as many as you could fit in a station wagon. My Dad would charge ten bucks a head to take a carload of kids to Disneyland in 1955. That's how Mark got involved when he was only five. Dad had room for ten kids to go and only nine signed up, thus Mark got to go on his first Yokuts Club Day Camp trip to Disneyland the first year it opened.

I was at the other end of the spectrum, being nine years older than Mark. By the time it was 1960, I was driving our new Pontiac station wagon as a counselor which was one of three station wagons hauling kids to Santa Monica Pier to have fun at the amusement park.

Suzie was there too, kind of as an add-on. It was like being privileged, but not. It was like participating in privileged games but not being allowed to win. You don't ever get to go home and leave the Yokuts behind until tomorrow, because that's who we were. Kind of like a recreational industry for privileged youth.

Suzie was a cute little girl wearing large glasses. She didn't become noticeable until after she became a counselor, and then she shined. But I'll tell you one thing about Suzie: she always got an A for her conduct at school through junior high on every report card. I'm certain she had "excellent" conduct as an Yokuts counselor.

It's hard to pinpoint where it went wrong between her and Dad because she was no drama queen growing up. She was always a levelheaded gal. But there came a time when her conflict with the old man became identifying, and she would not budge from her position ever since. This incident came to mark the end of their happy Daddy/Daughter relationship.

57. "Snapping"

When Suzan was a senior at Bakersfield High School and her YMCA sorority, called Lambda Kai Tri-Hi-Y, of which she was vice-president, organized a trip outside the YMCA to go to the popular Easter Vacation retreat in Laguna Beach. They were to stay in a motel for three days and party their hearts out. That's not what they said, but it's what they intended to do, and our father said no. There was plenty of time to discuss the trip because she brought it up a month in advance.

The first 'no' to a girl's request to go to the unchaperoned event was to be expected in some households. Suzie was excited about the trip and brought it up again a few days later. It met with the same negative response.

Keep in mind this was a group of young women. There was safety in numbers, perhaps as many as ten to fifteen girls. Several of them were eighteen years old, such as my sister. Dad's answer was still no. These were all "socially responsible" students from nice families who had worked together sponsoring special events for the needy through Lambda Kai. No, was still the answer. All the other girls had gotten permission to go to Laguna Beach over Easter break, but no was the answer for Suzie. Remember Suzan, she was your star counselor, chauffeuring children to the plunge, teaching them lessons, and making Dad money. But Dad said no.

Why not? I wanted to ask him myself but dare not. What are you afraid of? That she may do something to embarrass you, and everyone will find out what a fraud you are – another Dick Owens episode?

Or are you afraid she'll go out and fuck some dude and get pregnant like her mother did with you? God knows that would be a reflection on you, the dude who couldn't keep his pants zipped up. Now here it comes, twenty years later, and you accuse your child of having sex before she can do anything to prove you wrong. Why did you act like that? Why didn't you let her go? You're so afraid of what people think of you and your impeccable image of yourself, which upon further review, we find so tarnished.

Our Uncle George and Aunt Betty certainly were of the opinion you should be horse whipped for your lack of care for Suzan. As for your 'fatuous' statement about the gold shining through eventually? Well, it's been fifty-five years, and I can say flatly, "The gold in them thar hills has never given any sign of shining through for Suzan."

Jack must've been on crack when he wrote that line. What did he think was going to happen with Suzan that would turn to gold? Maybe he just waiting for his ship to sail to

Germany, or for Suzan to turn herself into the asylum, or whichever came first.

Did he think Suzan would either go to work, or be punished for not working and sent to the Snake Pit until she got scared straight? Perhaps he thought eventually she would snap out of it. But it never happened.

I guess I was guilty of that same refrain: wishing, hoping, dreaming, even demanding she change to what I thought she could be.

That's just stupid. It's what you do when you have no time to give love. You can demand Suzan snap out of it, which is senseless. Or you can make it happen through love, which means giving time you will not get back and doing so with no promise it will work. And you must continue to give this special love for a long time.

That sounds like a lot of wild hullaballoos, but it's true. If you want your sister not to go insane, start using love immediately to change her course. It's going to take time, so don't wait until they're diagnosed with *paranoid schizophrenia* because that's a tough nut to crack.

My parents should have let her go to Laguna Beach over Easter vacation, no questions asked. It would have helped build trust. Suzan deserved that much respect from our father, and the love that goes with it. Don't blame your daughter for your mistakes of the past.

XVI

LETTER RE: STERILIZATION

58. Mother Dies

Miss Suzan Cornwall
Unit N-17
Patton State Hosp. Calif.
92369

July 1, 1970

Dear Markie,

I guess mother and daddy are on vacation now. Those lucky ducks! I'm about to leave for dinner so this letter won't be too lengthy. I miss you.

Just finished dinner and took a shower with all the rest of the crew. Gosh I wish I had my own place. Because Don and Vicky [friends of our parents] decided to go to Mexico I won't be discharged for another month, Don and Vicky were the chosen ones to take precedence over me since they had volunteered their home. I wasn't sure you entirely understood what was going on but the only reason they hadn't released me was because they had no responsible adult here in the States to take me.

Just for fun Markie, what would you think if I married Marshal Mezey? You know he was the only guy that cared enough about me these past few years to do something nice for me. Dick Evans would have helped if he was alive. What I actually plan to do is join the airlines, but I just want to know what you'd think if I married ol' Marshal.

I want some babies.

I'm glad you're in Europe with mother & daddy and away from the scummy people in Bakersfield. You're just too nice a person for that Mark, I want to see the best for you and never may you ever be put in a mental hospital.

Write and tell me about your job.

Love

Suzie.

I've tried to live by that advice – staying out of the mental hospital. Tears still well up in my eyes as I read this letter of inspiration from my sister. Writing inspiration from the madhouse. That's how it turned out in the New Year of 1970. I went to Berchtesgaden, Germany to attend University of Maryland, Munich Campus, beginning the Fall semester, 1970. I was saved, and Suzie was not.

I had left Bakersfield and moved to Paso Robles to live with my Grandparents on my mother's side. My Grandma was a loving matriarch, a real grey-haired pioneer of the old spirit who welcomed me into their home – no questions asked. I got a job moving sprinkler pipes on the Deerwood Stock Farm in San Miguel. Grandma Tucker would get me up every morning at 6:00 so she could cook me breakfast with Grandpa before I left for work.

Two months later she awoke feeling a little off, went to the hospital and died. I was afraid people were going to accuse me of killing her just by my living with them. I always appreciated the fact we had those few months together as I became an adult. But her death was a horrible reason for having my mother come home from abroad unexpectedly. My Grandfather, Sid, couldn't live without Grandma either. He took his own life a year later by sticking a hose up his muffler in a closed garage.

I turned twenty the previous March. I remember the day I realized the need for higher education. It was a 118-degrees in the shade in sunny San Miguel, a miserably hot day. There were four of us stacking hay bales in an open-air barn and we were stacking them high. Each bale weighed about eighty pounds so the thought we could throw them around like marshmallows was something your dad said after he watched us work. Fact is, none of us were that strong. Every bale I lugged using hay hooks in 118-degree weather was a fucking bitch.

The way the stacking worked started with me. I was standing on the ground floor and the hay truck had just unloaded its payload of bales in front of me. I'm standing knee deep in front of a hundred bales scattered around me. As the truck pulls away, I'm left there sucking up the fumes of diesel, hay, dirt, horses, alfalfa, horse shit, and flies – the full ranch life. Plus it was hot. Did I mention that?

It was my job to snag the bales and place them on the escalator so they could be stacked up as high as thirty feet. The escalator was like a conveyor belt resembling a bicycle chain. It had teeth for grabbing the bales. It was powered by a gasoline engine and unfortunately the exhaust pipes were directly under my nose. The engine was old, so it shot out black smoke the entire time. A cloud of exhaust would spit in my face and sting my eyes.

That made the ground floor unbearable as far as getting fresh air was concerned. Of the three men working with me, one of them was my age, twenty-years-old. He was married, had a kid and lived on the ranch. He made a life for himself at Deerwood Stock Farm and would live with the consequences of his decision. But the other two men, Keith, 42, and Gary, 40, both were hired hands, like me. This was hard work, and it got me to thinking.

What was the difference between me and Keith, for example? I couldn't see any. He was white, seemed reasonably intelligent, and funny. As things go, I'd say we were exactly alike, came out of the same mold, same height and weight. He was poor, didn't have money until payday, wore Levis and a white T-shirt. I couldn't see any difference between us; he was uneducated like me. I had to ask myself, why should I expect my life to be different from his over the next twenty-two years?

I'll tell you one thing about me, when I was 20 years old I sure as hell was not going to be doing farm work when I was 42 years old. I went home to Grandma's that very night and composed a heartfelt letter to my mother begging her to let me come to school in Deutschland – begging her and promising I would do my best. I never needed something more in my whole life. I asked my mother for an opportunity to prove myself and she gave it to me, happily. I will always be grateful.

I would never have asked my father for the same. Mom always loved me more. I was sorry I would have only one year more to be with her. I will always believe that Suzie's cry for help, and my mother's failure to believe her, is what caused the aneurysm that killed Mother. She had been making plans to return home to Bakersfield when she got sick on a trip to Russia and died. Of course, it was not that easy.

Yes, they were on a tour of Russia when my mother fell ill and had to be treated in a Russian hospital. Her death was never explained to me by my father. While I was attending the University of Santa Barbara, my father told me only that she came back from Russia and was in an American hospital for a month. They were trying to figure out what was wrong with her, when an aneurysm ruptured in her brain and killed her.

She wrote to me from her hospital bed telling me she was fine. She didn't want me to worry because that might interrupt my studies. She was soldiering on. So, I studied and succeeded, but I lost my mother before we ever had a chance to talk about anything. I had a question for the American Hospital in Munich though; "Why'd it take a month to never find out what was wrong with my mother?" But that was a different time, in a foreign place, and my father was in no condition. He was utterly devastated.

59. Meeting Nurse Ratchet

When my mother first came back from Germany to attend Grandma Tucker's funeral, I went to pick her up at LAX. The first place we went was Patton State Hospital to visit Suzan. As we were driving to San Bernadino and I was attempting to tell her the state of Suzie's mental health, when I first observed she was in a state of disbelief.

"Oh, come on Mark, you don't actually believe her, do you?"

"Don't believe what about her?" I said.

"That she's actually insane?

"Yes, I do, very much. I think she's nuttier than a fruitcake," I said.

"No. She's just playing you like she does everybody else," said Mother.

"Well, if she's doing it to everyone, that pretty much means she crazy."

"Don't say that. It's not nice."

"I know it's not nice. I've been living it. You'll see, Mother. She's not kidding. I don't see how you can say that. I mean, she's being held in the insane asylum. It's called the Snake Pit." I took both my hands off the steering wheel to accentuate the point.

"You're being dramatic, I'm sure. I'll talk with the doctor, and we'll see what he says," mother said.

"He says a team of psychiatrist have diagnosed her as a paranoid schizophrenic."

"Well, they think they have to put a name on everything, it's part of the procedure. Okay, we'll call this one Sally and this one schizophrenic."

"Mother, do you have any idea how big Patton is? There're thousands of patients there. I'm telling you, you're not going to see a psychiatrist about Suzie today," I said.

"She's still my daughter and they're responsible for her well-being. I'm sure the authorities will have something to say about that." That's Mother, still holding on to the authorities.

"Well, what do you want to understand?"

"I want to know how Suzie's being treated, the kind of program she's on and when she is expected to be released. You know how these things can fluctuate, some days are bad, and some are good, I guess."

"No. It seems all days would be bad in the Snake Pit, regardless of how much good was going on."

"I'm sorry you've lost so much trust in American institutions."

"No, just the mental institutions. I think the prison system is great."

"Now you're trying to be funny."

"I'm just trying to protect you from what you're about to experience at Patton. I've been there four times since her incarceration and every time I leave, I have tears streaming down my cheeks as I drive away. It makes me sick hearing those voices screaming for help. It's sad to see my own sister as a part of this. And there's nothing I can do about it. I hate seeing Suzie give herself up for this lifestyle, and I hate myself for feeling that way. I just want Suzie back."

There was a long pause. A very long pause – in fact, we paused all the way to San Bernardino and right through the gates of Patton State Hospital to the visitor parking lot where you could begin hearing voices from the Snake Pit screaming for help.

My mother was able to meet the equivalent of Nurse Ratchet in Ken Kesey's *One Flew Over the Cuckoo's Nest.* I wasn't allowed to be present at the meeting, or I should say, my mother wouldn't allow me to be present when she met Nurse Ratchet in her office off the foyer. (We must be careful about what we tell the little ones.) They met for about fifteen minutes and then Suzie went into the office for another fifteen minutes of the chat. When it was over, we both said good-bye to Suzan and pressed on towards Paso Robles to Grandma's funeral.

I remember Mother's demeanor when she walked out of the room with Suzie first and Nurse Ratchet behind her. Mother was wearing a stylish dress suit, white with a no collar jacket like the Beatles wore but trimmed in black. She had her hair cut bobbed, but it was curly black and looked teased. For just coming off an eight-hour flight from Munich she looked incredibly put together, until she came out that door. Then she looked like a woman having a heart-attack but too proud to let anybody know. She carried herself like she was wounded in the chest, but still able to keep her legs moving.

But her nose told the story. It was the only thing on her face pointing up in an aquiline manner, as though looking to the stars for answers. The confrontation caused her to suffer something akin to delirium. The answers she got were contrary to everything she had thought was real. Clearly, she'd been told facts critical to her daughter's well-being. It was about something she wasn't expecting, or perhaps never thought of. What was it? That her daughter was crazy, or that the mental hospital had gone nuts?

They came out of the office sounding very cordial in their small talk. Mother shook hands with Nurse Ratchet in her white uniform, and then said to Suzie that she loved her, gave her a hug and some last-minute advice, and we were gone. That was the last time Mother and Suzie would ever see one another.

That's the problem when your mother passes away young and unexpectedly, before you have a chance to work things out. Had I known this was the last time the three of us would be together, I'd have tried harder to question Mother about this meeting with Nurse Ratchet. But being the youngest and not being allowed in the Ratchet meeting in the first place reserved me a back seat in the family information vehicle.

I was with my mother the rest of the trip to Paso Robles and was able to study her demeanor. She wasn't the same person she was when she arrived at Patton for the meeting. The mere physical presence of the hospital is intimidating. It has a few secrets itself, as tolled by the massive gravesite. It's a sad place, filled with doctors and surgical appliances waiting to be used, waiting for another victim to be coercively sterilized. It's the eugenic way, the scientific solution for social problems: to breed healthy babies.

It was the same policy Patton State Mental Hospital followed to rid the world of paranoid schizophrenics. Only allow guaranteed embryos to be bred, none that have been tainted by the genetically passed schizophrenia. Stop it where it starts.

My poor mother. She never saw it coming. She thought it was going to be like going to talk to the principal about her wayward child and she was prepared for that. She made a living off those types of conversations. She expected to address Suzan's behavior, and to play a role in Nurse Ratchets' admonishments to Suzan, reprimanding her behavior prior to working out a plan directed at Suzan's release. I can only imagine her surprise to hear Suzan had been sterilized. Mary Cornwall's daughter had been sterilized by the people she was entrusted to.

I imagine their conversation went something like this.

"I have an issue of some import, I would like to discuss with you," said Nurse Ratchet, "Well, discuss isn't the word. I would like to tell you about is more appropriate. I suppose if you had been in California, you might have had more input. But at any rate, it's the law, and it's already been done. Suzan has undergone a tubal ligation. That's sterilization surgery. Is that why you've come to visit us today?"

After the hi, hello, how are you, small talk that had been going on, this was a bitter pill to swallow.

"What?" said Mother, "What for?"

"I'm sure you have been made aware of your daughter's history in becoming a patient at Patton State Hospital. I think your airplanes may have crossed paths in the night, with you flying to Germany and Suzan flying home to Bakersfield from Suffolk County."

"Yes, that's true, metaphorically, of course" said Mother, "If only it could have been that simple."

"Yes. Well, were you aware that your son liberated her from the Kern County Mental Health Hospital using violence against one, Ramon Garcia, to make their escape?" said Nurse Ratchet, checking to get the name right from the paper she was reading.

"That must have been a misunderstanding. My son is not a pugilist."

"Is that him standing outside in the foyer?"

"Yes." Mother said.

"Does he have a friend named Marshal Mezey?"

"I know Marshal Mezey. He's the same age as Mark. They went to the same high school. They played together as babies. I know Mrs. Mezey."

"Apparently Mark introduced Suzan to Marshal and during her brief escape between mental institutions she managed to conceive a fertilized embryo. We knew this by talking with Suzan when she never produced a menstrual cycle," said Nurse Ratchet.

Mother didn't offer a peep to break the silence. She just glared at the nurse and waited for the other shoe to drop.

"So," went on Nurse Ratchet, "when we have a 'Ward of the State' as a patient, which is what Suzan has been for the last six months, it is our duty as her caretaker to act swiftly to preserve her safety. The law is clear on this," said Nurse Ratchet, stopping momentarily to be sure the message was being received.

Mother continued to stare at her, not wanting to give away her position.

"It was decided by the panel of psychiatrist handling Suzan's case that she would best be provided for by having the tubal ligation, and by scraping her uterus for all remaining pregnancy tissues, making sure her uterus is empty," said Nurse Ratchet.

There was a long pause as my mother tried to determine if Ratchet was finished. Not quite. She went on: "That procedure was conducted on January 20, 1970. If you have any questions about the care of your daughter, feel free to ask. That's what I'm here for. Of course, please remember Suzan is an adult. You and Mr. Cornwall gave up any rights you may have had to complain. Is there anything else?"

"You're telling me you not only castrated my daughter's ovaries but went ahead and killed the baby she was carrying? What gives you the right?"

"The law," said Nurse Ratchet, "Suzan has become a ward of the State and that means she must comply with State mandates. There are more than three thousand wards in this very building, with over two thousand clinicians watching them. I'm sure you can recognize the need for both the law of eugenics, and compliance with said law, even if it is coerced."

"It's disgusting. You're treating people like property. If she was a four-legged stool and the state wanted all stools to be three legged, you'd just cut off a leg – no questions asked, huh?"

"I can't answer such a hypothetical question. But it must be assumed our legislators had the benefit of the wards in mind when they enacted the law. You knew that when you turned your back on Suzan when she had no place else to go, didn't you?" said Ratchet, in a condescending voice before bringing down the hatchet. "You were aware of the consequences she would face, weren't you? Or were you too busy trying to get away from her?"

"How dare you say that to me. You don't know the first thing about me. We weren't running from her, we were running to our future that we had planned for a long time."

"I know everything about you, Mrs. Cornwall. You're not the first mother to be slapped in the face by her mentally deranged daughter, so to speak. It hurts. You did not deserve it. But that's the face of a paranoid schizophrenic. So get used to it. I don't blame you for turning out Suzan. She never would fit in. It would have taken a Saint to care for her. How could you do that? She was out of control. No, you did the right thing. She has a home here where she can thrive. But it does come with certain conditions, as I have just explained. No children allowed," said Nurse Ratchet.

On our drive from San Bernardino to Pasa Robles we didn't engage in much chit-chat. It was easy to tell Mother didn't feel like conversing. She was deep in thought and tired from her trip. She had just been told how her daughter's body had been violated by the authorities and now she was going to her own mother's funeral. Welcome home Mother. Nice to see you again after a year.

60. Jack Changes His Tune

If a person moves to a foreign country where they speak a different tongue communication between them can change the person for the better. It's a matter of survival. I'm not saying this would have worked for my sister. But it worked wonders for my dad, and no doubt for myself.

Before Jack came to live in Berchtesgaden, Germany, I'd describe my father as the Ogre of Cedar Street, in Bakersfield. A manlike creature condemned to live by the rules and ready to discipline the ignorant fool that didn't abide by his rules. He was an honest man who failed to reap the rewards of honesty because of his stodginess and failure to share.

Jack coddled no one about the family rules. In fact, he liked to shove them down our throats to make sure we knew them. He wanted us to taste them. It was as though the whole world was watching and he feared what they would find. As his children, we had the job of making him look good. All we had to do was follow the rules. Jack always sought the approval of some unknown entity, always pandering to the public, wanting their attention. He always said he didn't care what other parents did, but it was their approval he was looking for.

I watched him struggle with his darker urges when I was ten years old. It was during the summer of 1960, and I'd gone to bed at nine p.m. My mother went somewhere, to a meeting or bridge group, and was expected home late. My father was meeting with camp counselors about Yokuts in the den. When I went to bed there was only the attractive twenty-six-year-old Jackie Jacobs left.

Jackie was a healthy young woman with a gleaming personality in white shorts and sneakers and tan body. They started drinking beer and Dad never drank, so I knew they were having fun. I thought nothing of it because Jackie had been my counselor. As I was trying to sleep, they started playing music like *The Girl from Ipanema*. Suzie was asleep in her bed, and Tod was in the Navy. The music played on, and it wasn't long before I started hearing moaning noises.

We had a two-story house, and my bedroom was at the top of the stairs. I had a direct view down to the den. The moaning persisted. I got out of bed and crawled to the door on my hands and knees to see what was going on. To my surprise, I saw my father sitting in a deep bucket bamboo chair with Jackie on top of him. He was kissing her hard, her butt in the air, her legs doubled back by Dad's sides and humping him with everything she had, trying to bring it to a head. It was very palpable.

I slowly eased back from my view, not believing what I was witnessing. Oh, you don't know how much I wished I yelled, "Hey Dad, whatcha doing down there?" That would have changed our world. Maybe that would have saved our family from his narrative of sanctimonious bullshit we had to listen to. But being ten years old, I didn't have the balls.

I knew I had information that would make my mother cry, and I didn't want that. So I held it to myself. But mainly, I held it because I didn't know what my father might do to me if he found out I knew. I wasn't supposed to be looking, was I? I never asked him.

That's who Jack was. He posed as the greatest father and husband in the world by day and humped my camp counselor by night.

That may catch the eye of a national organization scrutinizing directors of character-building organizations, if there is such a thing. It's a big lump of coal for Jack to explain. But that's only if he gets caught, right?

I had control over the future of Suzie's mental disease right in my hands. I was the only person who had seen Dad's philandering and let it go through my fingers.

It may have helped. Imagine what Suzie could have done with that information? She could have ruined him, squealing him out to my mother. But she would never have done that because she loved her father too much. It's strange, how paternal love works, the loyalty it commands. It's like being the only one who can see the crack in the Liberty Bell. There's a crack there for sure, but the rest of the bell is soundly intact. Why tell anybody?

But then, Jack made the journey to a foreign land and was reborn. It changed him. He was thrown in with new military personnel who knew nothing about him, nothing about Yokuts Club Day Camp, or his work experience, nothing about his family in the States, or people he associated with. These were a different type of men: engineers and Majors with lots of medals, doctors, and Master Sergeants, all living in the same buildings.

Jack started fresh; his peers knew nothing but what he told them. Dad was in heaven in Germany. He was exactly who he wanted to be, with an impeccable record in education, and not dragged down by the small-town fear of being found out.

61. Here's The Kicker

Jack changed his attitude and became the pied piper of children. No doubt he was stung by Suzie turning out to be nothing more than a statistic, the one out of five that suffer serious mental health problems. The need to have his daughter locked away didn't faze him though. What could he do? That was across the ocean and in a different country. He had a hard time showing how much it hurt him, if it did. Jack had no intention of going back to the USA like my mother. He wasn't going with her to help the needy.

This was Europe and he was set free from his American obligation to feel guilty the minute he landed in Deutschland. He was a changed man. Case in point — when I was going to college in Munich he included me and my girlfriend Nancy on a family vacation to Croatia. He actually paid for a separate room so the two of us could have our privacy. That would have been unthinkable back when he lived in Bakersfield.

Here's the kicker. As my father was dying in Nurnberg, I knew he did not have a will. He had remarried a German *frauliene* by the name of Karin, a year after my mother died, and they moved from Berchtesgaden to Nurnberg. He couldn't include Suzie in the inheritance plan under the normal will because any property Suzie was bequeathed would escheat to the State of California of which she was a ward. The estate could be lost in litigation for years. So I went to Nurnberg to be at his side and help him draft his will.

I stayed with him and his German family for a month. I slept on the apartment couch and every day the stench of Grandma cooking red cabbage would seep through the walls. During that time, we spoke plenty; in the hospital, his living room, in the car, driving home to Nurnberg from Chiemsee Lake. Memorable conversations with the snow crunching under our boots, the sun sparkling over the ice. Getting the last good look at the man who bred me as the melanoma ate at his final breath.

"It seems a little suspicious you know, you coming over to help me with my estate plan," said my Dad.

I'd been expecting that one. "There was a time when people thought having an attorney in the family was a good thing," I said, "Can you remember that? You've never had to use an attorney, have you?"

"Humph."

"You never liked to pay an attorney."

"Who does?"

"Well, that's why I'm here, Dad. You'd have waited till it was too late, and then you'd be appointed a ZAG Corp. attorney from the Army, who knew nothing about International, or

California Realty Law, and everything you worked for would be fucked." I said.

"Well, I guess I don't want that," said Dad.

"You've left extremely gracious gifts for your family. Your dream house you had built in Cayucos goes to Tod, and the condo at the beach in Santa Barabara to me. I'm sure Karin can use your legacy in Deutschland, and San Diego. Since you didn't even have a will, how were we supposed to know your final desires?"

"Yeah."

"Why'd you do it?" I asked him bluntly. "You're dying of cancer, you could have quit your job and cashed in years ago? There's been a land boom in California, there still is. But your desire to keep working and living under these conditions baffles me. You're one month from turning sixty-five, what's going on with you?"

Dad looked at me like I was talking in non-sequiturs or maybe I had made a big fat fart, so he said, "What?"

I looked at him with pleading eyes.

"What else was I going to do after Mother died?" he said. "This wasn't the end game we had planned. We weren't planning to work until our retirement dates and then die, leaving it to you. The plan was to finish paying for our dream retirement and start living off it April 20, 1983, the same date as my birthday, next month."

"It was in our plan we'd be living in Germany half the time, and the other half we'd be visiting family in California, with Cayucos as our home base. The rent money from San Diego and Santa Barbara would support my monthly pension. Life could have been perfect, only your mother wasn't here to share it with me. I figured out how to design and build our money boat. We just never got to ride in it," Jack said.

"Why didn't you give some of that boat money to Suzan, back when it could have helped her from floating around the bend, as Uncle George put it, never to be seen again?" After I said that, I realized it was a low blow, but my father managed to sidestep it.

"You don't believe that do you? That's throwing good money after bad. She couldn't do as we asked. She just couldn't. That's all there was to it."

It turned out, for all the name calling Dad suffered from his children for being a cold, heartless bastard, he ended up leaving the kids and new wife with the keys to his castle.

Suzie was right, his estate was sizeable for middle class. But for a man who owned three luxury condos in California (Cayucas, San Diego, Santa Barbara) and one at Chiemsee Lake in Germany, all of them paid in full, with no mortgages; I wonder why, when he died, he was living in Karin's flat in Nurnberg, with her mother and two children. The apartment was on the fourth floor with no elevator, built long before World War II. They are a hearty breed, those *krauts.*

He chose to live so he could save the money he made as headmaster to pay for the condos he purchased after Mother's death. Everything looked promising, except his cancer.

Dad lived with Karin in a German tenement where rent control was stuck at pre-WWII prices. This made it possible for him to use his entire monthly paycheck to pay for the condos. I've seen his endorsed checks. He had finally found a philosophy with Karin that matched his own *weltanschauung.* Afterall, he was in Deutschland and the Deutsch creed rewards frugality, often mistaken as selfishness.

My dad took frugality to an elite level. He looked at the world in dollars and cents and couldn't enjoy life without putting a price tag on it and buying it for less – much less. Dad was the Mr. Scrooge of cheapskates.

And yet he left his beautifully managed estate to his family – excluding Suzan, but not because he didn't love her. It was easy to leave her nothing, because what would she do with a condo? And besides that, it would never have been enough, even if she was bequeathed it all.

62. Jack's Death

The death of my mother is something I haven't written about, or even thought about, or wanted to think about, or sort out, or have come up, or give in to, or be part of my thoughts, or could ever really believe it was true, or be able to handle the truth once I realized it.

It was Mother's Day of 1972 when I received the call from my father in Germany. The phone call was a big deal at the time because the satellites weren't connected as now. It took calling the Red Cross to get the emergency connection overseas. I never understood what the International Red Cross was all about until Mother died. It's a great organization that helps connect people around the world.

When I got the phone call from my father it was sad, to say the least. I could hear the phone crackling in the background from thousands of miles away. Anticipating the news, the last I heard Mother was doing fine, and now this:

Operator: "Mr. Cornwall? ... Mr. Mark Cornwall?"

"Yes, that's me."

Operator: "Hold please, I'll connect you with your party."

There was static in the line as plugs clicked. In the background you could hear the operator speaking, "Mr. Cornwall, I'll connect you now."

"Mark, are you there?" My father asked in a raspy voice, the first hint something was wrong, besides the call itself. We never thought of calling Europe. Do you know how much that would cost? It was prohibitive.

"Hi Dad, yeah, I'm here."

"Hi Mark," he said.

"What's happening with Mother?"

"Oh, it's bad Mark."

"Why? Is she okay?",

"She didn't ...She was ...She's dead!" He shouted into the mouthpiece. And with that he hung up the phone. There were no questions asked, only the message and then I was alone, listening to that crackling silence.

I laid down the receiver deeply hurt, knowing I would never see my mother again. Knowing that I never had the chance to say good-bye. I was alone in my apartment in Santa Barbara and began to cry, or rather, howl at the moon. And I maybe even screamed at the top of my lungs in pain.

The only other time I can remember such a dismal, horrifying moment in my life was about ten years later when my father was dying of melanoma cancer. He had been going through chemotherapy at the German Hospital in Nurnberg — since the American hospital had failed to save my mother. I received word from somebody, perhaps it was Karin, that this was no drill. He was on his way out.

A couple of weeks before I arrived in Nurnberg to see him, he'd been speaking at an assembly at the American Elementary School where he was Principal. Apparently, in the middle of his talk he forgot what he was going to say next. So much so that he was asked if he was okay. Jack obviously was not okay, so they took him to the hospital and there he stayed until I arrived.

When I walked into his room at the hospital it was a great surprise. Nobody knew I was coming, and Dad thought he was facing another day of being part of the walking dead. After he saw me, and recognized I was his son, his face transformed from a bewildered, distant old man, who had lost most of his hair, to the visage of a proud and happy father, smiling. Boy, he was happy to see me. I guess I was the last son from his American dream family of thirty-five years.

Living in Germany thirteen years, most of what surrounded him was Deutsch. German wife, German kids, Grandma, cooking, beer, the *Autobahn Strasse*. Yep, he was happy to see me. Particularly because ever since the memory loss he suffered at the school auditorium, he also lost his ability to speak the German language. Fortunately, Karin had learned to speak English since meeting Dad, and of course the place he worked was an American Elementary School, as part of the UDESIA school system, so there were plenty of Americans at his job.

But when Jack wasn't working, he lived in the same city as the Nurnberg Trials, where the Nazis were tried for their war crimes after the Second World War, so there was always that to ponder, as well as the rubble of the city. But he was in a German hospital room when I arrived, and I guess there's nothing like seeing your own flesh and blood walk into a room of otherwise foreigners.

The best part of going to see the old man on his death bed was when one of Dad's friends from the American School pulled me aside one day said, "Your father has made a miraculous recovery since your arrival. It's so remarkable."

"Oh, thank you."

"I'm not exaggerating – it's like a miracle. His mood is so remarkably elevated. He was so down and now he's so dramatically coherent, and I have to tell you, it's because you came to visit him."

Everyone who has a parent still alive should go visit them before they're on their deathbed. Not for them, but for you. My brother made the choice not to go visit his father on his deathbed and he regretted it, although he never admitted it. I wasn't there before Mother died; however Tod was, and he told me it wasn't a pretty picture. It never is. But oh, if for nothing else, go for one last smile.

I was thirty-three years old and went to visit with no set time to return to Santa Barbara. Every day I would go to the chemo ward with him and Karin, or maybe it was every other day, but that's when I thought up the joke: 'Funny as a chemo ward.' You know, as in "Funny as a truckload full of dead babies." Because there is nothing funny about it. Everybody there is going to die in a matter of a short time. Until then, they're going to suffer tremendously.

My Dad wanted to know if he was going to die straight away or not. An American question, kind of like, "Do I got six months, doc? Or are we going to beat this thing?" We went to speak with his doctor for that purpose only. My father had been frustrated because the doctor was not being straight with him because German people, so the doctor told me, don't like knowing when they're going to die.

The doctor asked me to speak with him alone. He, of course, spoke perfect English, and explained this cultural difference between Americans and Germans. He drew a map of my father's remaining days. With a piece of paper and a pen he drew a line across the page representing how Dad was going to plateau out for a while, then he would dip down, then he would plateau out, then he would dip down, until he died. He had been plateauing since my arrival and had stabilized enough to come home with us.

Unfortunately, coming home meant returning to a fourth floor flat in an old stone building in downtown Nurnberg with no elevator. No elevator! Can you believe that? Not only that, but it was still winter there and it got so cold in the apartment that the water in the toilet would ice over. I know because I would pee on it first thing.

As I was sleeping on the living room couch one morning, Karin came in shouting for help. Jack was having a fit and she didn't know what to do.

I ran to their bedroom and saw my father prone on his back gasping for air. I knelt next to the bed to examine his face. His lips and skin were turning blue, and he was gagging on his tongue. He was having a seizure. I didn't know what to do either, but it came to me in a flash – after I raised my head above my father's body and made a primal scream to the heavens for help. It was a cry from the bottom of my soul for all to hear, that meant "My father's not dying on my watch."

It became immediately clear what to do. I had to pry his lips apart and dig my fingers between his lips which were smacked shut with all dad's might. I used all the strength in my fingers to pry his mouth open. Once they loosened, I worked against the strength of his jaw to gain access to his mouth. I had to pull his tongue from his throat which didn't want to come. When there was enough space, I took a giant gulp of air and blew it down his throat. Then another, and another, as I strained to stop his mouth from clamping shut again.

I could feel his body slacken ever so slightly as the air went in and began its magic of revival. Within a minute it became apparent he was going to live.

Meanwhile Karin had called an ambulance and if there ever was a time to thank God for German efficiency it was then. It was as though they came from the walls, up four flights of stairs and into the bedroom with all the right lifesaving gear, all very clean and precise and hustling their asses off, the way you wanted them to if they were saving your father.

The next time I saw him was a few hours later at the hospital. By some miracle of coincidences, just as I went to the recovery room to sit next to him in his wheelchair, he woke up and the first thing he said to me was in German. He had no idea what had happened. But he had full recovery of his command of the German language. It was like the flip side of a record. He didn't even know he wasn't speaking English. Talk about crazy.

After that experience I realized dying wouldn't be so bad. As it turned out, that was exactly how he died a couple of weeks later. He went into the same gagging routine, only this time he passed on to the other side.

My father never left the hospital again. Since I had been there a month it was time for me to go. I was thankful not to stay around and watch him die any more. That was enough for me.

The last time I saw him he was lying in his hospital bed, looking quite healthy and alert. But knowing this was the last time ever I would see him, made it tough. It's a very sad loss when your father's still alive, lying in front of you, and you have to say goodbye to them like they are dead. It's convoluted. There's no, "see you later." What do you say?

Maybe the German's knew best about not knowing they were going to die. And Dad could see that. But instead of crying, he looked me dead in the eye and shook my hand saying, "See what you're made of, son? See what you're made of?"

My father's last words to me. "See what you're made of?" I could not answer him, except to nod my head. It was that tense. There were no tears, no hugs, no good-byes. I just turned around and walked away, leaving the hospital, Karin, Grandma and the kids behind. But when I think about the look on Dad's face, I can only think of one word: Strength. Strength in the face of death. That's not bad.

XVII

THE GRAND FINALE

63. Tod's Advice for the Love Lorn

I'll give you the bottom line of Suzie's mental captivity: she was going to the Snake Pit, end of story. People think that with a little help here, and a little there, she could have had a normal life and been happy. What a foolish thing to say. She inherited her schizophrenia, and it progressed quite naturally. The disease set in when she was twenty-three years old and stayed the course. She didn't get better. She got crazier and lived amongst the schizophrenics, for which there was no cure. No cure. There was no place for her to go other than the Snake Pit.

So when you vote for the hero of this story, remember I'm the guy who knew where she was going all along.

If you take that advice, it can reduce the mental anguish you suffer when you realize your sister is not just schizophrenic, but a paranoid schizophrenic. Once paranoia strikes, there's nothing you can do. None of them get cured. It's in their DNA.

The best you can hope for is they learn to play board games and keep their mouths shut in public. They still don't fit in and there is still no place for them in our society. I didn't want Suzie to stay with me, but I still loved her.

You know what happened to Suzie don't you? She ended up living with four or five other schizoids being cared for by Filipino care givers in the far end of Southern Bakersfield. That's where she was kept until she died from her second bout of breast cancer when she was fifty-seven years old. She was living in a three-bedroom ranch style home, one of many in the neighborhood. That's as good as it gets for the seriously mentally ill. Very few go home. Tough luck.

They're hard to find too, if you've lost touch with them. The caretakers don't want old family members coming by and disturbing the peaceful existence these patients have found for themselves. Suzie's existence was funded by Catholic Charities. Bless them. They've found as the patient gets older, a visit from a brother or sister can stir the pot of fractured memories and set the patient back significantly. It's far from perfect, but it's a long way from living in the Snake pit at Patton State Mental Hospitable. That's progress, isn't it?

I've never seen Suzan since Christmas of '69, after we broke her out of Ward 3B, and she hooked up with Marshal. I always liked Marshal. Nothing phased him, and there was a lot going on with that crazy bastard. I heard that after he knocked

Suzie up, he killed himself by jumping off an oil derrick after he found out they sterilized Suzie for being pregnant.

That's probably why Suzie warned Mark, "to never be put in an insane asylum!" Yeah, that's good advice. The government ran quite a number on those two mentally disturbed individuals. Why couldn't they have lived together peacefully in the institution? That's all they wanted: to live in the Snake Pit. They both suffered from naivety. So, chalk-up a couple more lives lost in the *fractured fissure.*

When I think about it, our whole family was destroyed by the stigma of mental health. From the first phone call from Uncle George and Aunt Betty to our parents, that put a crack in the metal of the family bell. A crack that continued to splinter, separate, and peel away, until it broke apart. Our family bell could ring no more.

We never again had a family meal, let alone a festive holiday. Us three kids shared our last dubious Christmas in '69, when I shared the orange swastikas on the tree that everybody hated. That's the direction our family gatherings were going, and we never had another one. No Thanksgiving dinner to attend or Easter Sundays to dress up for. No more family obligation to run home for the weekend. Of course, that's what happens when the mother dies and the father lives 8,000 miles away. Now add to that, a sister in the looney bin.

I don't know which came first, the stigma or the falling apart as a family. I wonder what would have happened if Suzie had remained sane and led a normal life of getting married and having children. And imagine if my mother had lived to be the grandmother she always wanted to be, and she came home from Germany liked she planned. And for myself, that I remarried and had children instead of living the artist life that included a stint in prison.

Imagine all of us Cornwalls living normal lives. Do you think any of us would be any happier? Or is that just too hypothetical a question? It sure is for me. It's like trying to imagine you're a totally different person; would you be any happier?

Well, I'd say, since I was imagining it, "Hell yeah! I'd be as happy as a clam at high tide."

XVIII

THE RIGHT TO BE DISTURBED

64. Do Not Disturb

June 8, 1972

Miss Suzan Cornwall
Community House
Patton, Calif.

Dear Mark,

I'm hoping you will do me this favor. Could you please write Dr. Cobb a letter requesting my presence. That is, could you please hope that I may come to Santa Barbara and look for an apartment and a job. Make the dates at your convenience. Please do this as you seem to be my only relative that still has faith. No one else seems to be concerned as much as we are. Or should I say no one else seems to know what is going on.

Love

Suzie

You will have to send money as the state has discontinued my allowance. Maybe you can drive Pat's car and pick me up. I have no money at all.

Or maybe she should have said, "No one else seems to care who we are."

The postmark on the envelope was June 8, 1972, a month after our mother died. Suzan did not come to the funeral. I'm sure she wasn't invited; it was only her mother. I missed receiving the above letter at Santa Barbara, but my landlady forwarded it to me at the American School in Berchtesgaden. That's where I went to watch my father fall apart over my mother's death. He was consumed by so much guilt he couldn't talk about it with me.

What a confusing summer 1972 was. My mother was dead and gone. She had just returned from her father's funeral. Grandpa Tucker had just committed suicide — he didn't want to live without Grandma Tucker. My sister had been sequestered in an insane asylum, my father was shaken to his core, our family home was gone, my older brother seemed crazier than my sister, and I had just finished my sophomore year in college. It didn't appear that things were particularly bright in my future. But my sister saw me as her last bastion of hope. She's pleading for me to keep the faith and write a letter to her doctor, and, oh yes, send money.

Fortunately I was 8,000 miles away in Berchtesgaden. Being that far away absorbs most of the bad feelings I had for not being able to deliver what she asked for. Eight thousand miles was enough miles to come up with 8,000 excuses why I couldn't deliver. I always wanted to try. But in the back of my mind I was thinking how we broke her out of Ward 3B once, and damned if she didn't turn around the next day and get incarcerated again.

It was like déjà vu all over again. Hopeless. And for that, I risked the possibility of being tried and convicted of a felony – aiding and abetting an escapee from a state mental institution. Being tagged with that would have ended my career as an attorney before it ever got started.

But that wasn't to be. I went to law school at night in Santa Barbara and graduated in 1982 from Santa Barbara School of Law. As an attorney, I was a sole practitioner representing plaintiffs throughout my career and was nothing less than "brilliant" until I had my stroke in 2015, which put an end to said career. But before that, when I was still flying high in the law, around 2002, I decided to look Suzie up. I couldn't remember the last time I saw her, but the letter above was the last letter I ever received from her after Mother died.

Not having time for family is an old flaw of attorneys, and the reason for my first divorce. That happened immediately after I passed the bar on the first try. Attorneys, the cold-hearted bastards – they're always on the run. That's what happens when you're busy, I mean really busy, trying to build a career. I had no time to keep up with my mentally disturbed sister over in Bakersfield; until I opened a satellite office on Edison Hwy. that practically put me in her lap.

I had no idea where her lap was at the time, and Bakersfield had grown significantly over the last twenty years. The whole city was blossoming, going from 65,000 in 1969 to 350,000 in 2002. My new wife, D'Arcy, and I went to the police to help find Suzie. I was surprised to find they had an entire unit dedicated to finding older citizens. But they could not locate Suzan anywhere. It was as though she dropped off the grid or been kidnapped, or just plain lost. No one could find her. A couple of weeks went by, and the police still had nothing. I began to think something was wrong, or worse.

Straining my brain, I recalled the name 'Catholic Charities' from my vague recollection of institutions that helped Suzie in the past. I remembered that when State funds ran out, and the schizophrenics were scrambling for sponsorship, Catholic Charities came to the rescue with their aid. I called them up at their Bakersfield office and they had a record of Suzan – in fact, they knew where she was living.

Now we're getting somewhere. But not so fast. There's a lot of vetting that needs to be done. They had made a large investment in Suzan over the last twenty years, protecting her from the outside world by not letting anyone come into Suzie's life to excite her. I don't blame them. I suppose I wasn't the first brother to visit his paranoid schizophrenic sister and unknowingly harangued her with memories of the family, so badly, she could have a total relapse. She was living peacefully at present. There was no room for mistakes.

Catholic Charities directed me to Amelia, the Filipino caregiver, who was much more than meets the eye. She didn't just take care of four to five patients in her home, cooking, cleaning, washing, and feeding them; but she also doubled as an expert on schizophrenic care. She knew when her patients were at their tipping point and how to back them off a cliff when necessary. She was an orderly, a nurse, psychiatric therapist, and mother to all, rolled into one. She let me know the patient always comes first.

Amelia also managed their affairs down to the last hours of the day. She wasn't glad to hear from me because of the threat I posed to Suzie's tranquil existence. I was seen as the one guy who could enter the scene and destroy all that harmony.

But I was her brother, and I needed to see my sister. It had been twenty years. I understood her concerns, but I wasn't going anyplace. After a few vetting phone calls she reluctantly invited me to come see Suzie at their home in Bakersfield, south of town, beyond Billy Goat Acres, on Edison Hwy.

On the day we were to meet, D'Arcy and I drove over to Bakersfield from Santa Barbara and got a room at the Holliday Inn, off Chester Ave. I left D'Arcy at the motel and ventured alone to meet Suzan. It was going to be just me and Suzie. I was excited about seeing her in a strange kind of way, not having any idea what she would do, but knowing it had to be done, and it would be okay. I loved her and knew she loved me.

The last time I saw her was when she was released from Patton State Mental Health Hospital by then Governor Reagan in 1979 on the grounds mental hospitals were cruel and inhumane. There was hope in new antipsychotic medications, and it saved the taxpayer's money to steer the seriously insane persons to local community efforts, i.e. Catholic Charities.

It all became clear as I drove to her half-way house. Same as the places you went when you got out of prison. After Reagan deinstitutionalized the mentally ill as President in 1981 and emptied the psychiatric hospitals nationally into so-called community clinics, things got worse. Sixty percent of those freed from the insane asylum were suffering from schizophrenia and incapable of taking care of themselves. Nevertheless, they were let loose on the streets. That was the beginning of hearing insane people scream obscenities out to nobody on the streets, everywhere. It only added to the homelessness problem. The authorities are hoping to clear that problem up through the 'CARE Court' in 2024 by funding 2.2 billion dollars towards the cause in California. That should class up those community clinics. Good luck!

But there were always patients that were favorites amongst psychiatrists and their staff that were lucky enough to be guided in the direction of Catholic Charities. I like to think Suzan was spared the street life because she was such a gentle soul. It's to those anonymous nurses at Patton State Hospital that Suzie, and I, owe a debt of gratitude for not making her homeless for the last forty-five years.

From 1969, to the point where I started to look for Suzan in 2002, she had spent 33 years of incarceration of some kind. For thirty-three years, her life was surrounded by walls until she didn't need them physically present to confine her. She finally learned the walls are always there for the insane, even if you couldn't see them.

She had accepted her lot in life. But she wasn't thrown in a snake pit with 3,000 others like her anymore. Now she was housed in a pleasant home in the suburbs with four or five roomies. It's a much more humane way of treating the disturbed sector of society – but for 33 years? How much did that cost? Whatever happened with those antipsychotic medications that held so much promise as a cure for the mentally ill?

I'll tell you what happened – it was just more psychiatric bullshit. Promising a cure for what? Being paranoid schizophrenic? Good luck with that. What kind of antipsychotic medication do you have for the fractured family, huh? Maybe we could all take a couple of pills and put the family together again. Because it got blown up in the process of living with the stigma of our sister.

I was getting angry as I turned into the subdivision beyond Billy Goat Acres, no doubt fueled by my excitement of seeing my sister. Our family was victimized by her insanity without ever knowing it. We had all decided the family was not the nucleus it had been for love and comfort. We acted like it was nonexistent, like we didn't need it and began operating as the new norm – no family. It had split us in separate ways, sons hating their father, mother not getting her respect, siblings at each other's throat, all because their sister went insane.

And not once after the parents flew to Germany did the Cornwall's ever sit down to a family dinner. Not once. Even a dinner without Suzie. When our mother died on Mother's Day, 1972, the Cornwall family officially came to an end. I guess they all come to an end at some point but being the youngest of three kids, that meant I got nine years less parenting from my parents than Tod did. And that means nine years less love – if there was any. Oh well.

I had finally arrived at Suzie's place.

I parked in front of the house. There were no cars. I noticed lawn chairs around the front yard. An elderly man was in one of them, sitting idly. He greeted me as I approached the door. The front door was open, so I knocked on the screen door from the outside. I could see down the hallway to the kitchen. There was a light on in the eating area. There were two other patients in the eating area as Amelia came to the door to greet me.

"Hello, I'm Amelia, you must be Mark."

I was wearing a suit and tie, without the jacket, and driving a new black Jag. I was an attorney and wanted to present myself well. I was the prodigal son coming to visit my long-disturbed sister. Amelia continued to address me.

"Just a second, I'll get Suzan."

Five months after this meeting Suzan died. She had breast cancer ten years before and it was thought to be in remission. But one day in early March 2003 I got a call from Amelia telling me Suzie had been admitted to the hospital due to a recurrence of cancer. I was in Santa Barbara.

"Should I come over there tomorrow?"

"No, I didn't say that," said Amelia.

"Well, what should I do?"

"I was just calling to let you know she is in the hospital. Nothing more. I didn't mean to alarm you. She's been there before. I think it's routine, but I don't know," said Amelia.

"We're leaving for the Ahwahnee Lodge in Yosemite tomorrow. It's for my birthday. We have reservations. You think I should cancel them?"

"I think you should do whatever you need to do. I was just calling to tell you there's been a change in her condition and treatment," said Amelia.

"This isn't an emergency, you're saying?"

"No, I'm not saying it's an emergency, based on her health record. But what do you regard as an emergency?" asked Amelia.

This conversation went on like this until I was satisfied that everything was under control, and I could proceed to Yosemite for two days' vacation and see Suzie in the hospital on my way home. What was unforeseen was that I stepped on a rock coming down from a hike to Nevada Falls and broke my right foot. It was a Jones fracture of my fifth metatarsal. I could hear it snap, same as my wife. It was my fault. I shouldn't have been wearing tennis shoes. But the worse part was I couldn't walk, and D'Arcy was too short to help me as a crutch. And because it was early March there was not another hiker on the path to help me back to the rangers' station. I had to walk five miles on a broken foot. Brutal. It was a foreshadowing of things to come.

My sister's condition was foremost on my mind, but now I needed medical attention. The ranger station was only good for aspirin and some crutches.

They suggested I see an orthopedic surgeon. Somehow it was decided we'd go to D'Arcy's mother's house – in Reno. She had everything we needed: including a doctor with the drugs. We drove to Reno and had the foot put in a special cast and alleviated the pain with Percocet. But that took two more days out of our schedule and Suzie had been in the hospital four days now.

On the fifth day we were barreling down Highway 99 towards Bakersfield from Reno and I was feeling no pain. I was sitting in the back seat of the Jaguar with my right leg stretched across the console, next to my wife, who was driving. I was in the back popping pills and drinking whiskey. But I was scared for some reason. I think I'd always felt that I was to blame for what happened to Suzie, as unreasonable as that may sound. I wanted to see her. There were things I wanted to tell her.

I'd only seen her twice since we reunited. At our second meeting I took her to lunch at a local drive-in called Joe's Drive-in. It was very similar to Stan's Drive-in, but this was a different time and place —with no girls on skates. It had been thirty-four years since I broke her out of Ward 3B.

I broke her out. I did it! It had meant that much to me. I would rather have gone to prison than not break her out. There was no more meaningful event in my life than the moment I broke Suzan out of Ward 3B. It meant "I love you." It was a "Harmonic Convergence" of love, that included my brother. It took me fifty-five years from writing this book to figure that out. Fifty-five years to understand and appreciate that fact.

I couldn't have lived with myself had I not taken that action. I don't know why. I would probably feel different had I been caught and prosecuted. But the fact that I had made the attempt meant something, even though Suzan decided to nullify the deal. I was happy to have served her and almost forgot that moment after repressing it all those years.

As I watched my sister eating her Sloppy Joe in the car at Joe's Drive-in, I grew disgusted. She ate as though she had never eaten a Sloppy Joe and was only five years old. I began to wonder why people who are mentally ill have such a hard time eating their food. Meat and sauce squeezed out of her bun and coleslaw landed on her lap and in the car. All of which went unnoticed by Suzan. I tried to help her by wiping her mouth, but it was to no avail.

But Suzan didn't mind. She was enjoying herself, and who cares if the food went everywhere? No one minds if a baby throws their food on the floor. Or do they? Why did I mind if Suzie wanted to eat like a monkey?

This was Suzan being crazy, which is what she was. Accept it or let it go, was the answer. I went back to the hotel that afternoon and told D'Arcy she was never going to meet Suzie. I didn't tell her why because I could never tell people, even my wife, about the why of Suzan. D'Arcy was used to living with my stigma and did me the favor of not asking why. Just going to meet Suzan was a big enough deal for one day. I shouldn't have to tell her it was because of the way she ate her Sloppy Joe. I was ashamed of myself for thinking that. I held it in, dealing with the stigma the same way I had since I was nineteen. I was fifty-three years old and obviously, I couldn't accept it or let it go.

I was going to talk to her now. We were to meet at Kern County General Hospital, the same hospital I broke her out of Ward 3B. Only this was the newly renovated and twice as big hospital as the former one in '69. I was excited to see her and share my feelings of love.

We parked in the handicap zone and D'Arcy got out and went to the front desk as I managed to pull myself together. We were late after making the seven-hour drive down old Highway

99. We had contacted them the day before so they would be aware we were coming as fast as we could. I was slowly getting out of the car. I had to get out of the back seat and put my shoe on, then struggle with my crutches to get out of the parking lot and over to the long walkway heading to the front office. This was going to take forever.

I got to the head of the walkway and had to take a break. As I was standing there, I saw D'Arcy come out the big double glass doors with a nurse by her side carrying a piece of paper. It looked like they were coming to get me, so I started up again. But the nurse had such a look of despair on her face I stopped where I was at. I looked over to D'Arcy and thought I saw her shake her head slowly. I looked back at the nurse and waited for her to approach.

"I'm sorry Mr. Cornwall. But your sister passed away in her sleep at 6:15 this morning," said the nurse.

Thank God, she died in her sleep. But not surrounded by family.

65. The Last Harrah!

Amelia escorted me and Suzan to two chairs in the middle of the lawn so we could talk in private. Well, that would be after Amelia could hear the gist of our conversation and decide if I was a friend or foe. She stood within earshot of our conversation long enough to become annoying, and I couldn't wait till she left so we could talk privately. It took about ten minutes of small talk to be left alone.

"It's been a while. You look great," I said.

"Yeah, it seems like only yesterday," she said, "How you been doing?"

She didn't talk the same. Her cadence was slower, like she had a mouth full of marbles and was sucking on one of them. Her smile was friendly. It revealed she'd taken care of her teeth, but her skin had gotten pasty from no sun during the summer. Who could blame her? I couldn't stop smiling, I was so excited. Her eyes were a startling blue from what I could see of them.

"It's been a long time," I said.

She did look good, all things considered. Her hair was well groomed, although scraggly because of the split ends. That's where the grey mixed with her original blond goldilocks. She looked poor, of course, because she was. She chose to wear an aqua-marine blouse, and shorts past her knees; and donned a large white floppy hat to keep the sun off her face. Maybe it was me, but I thought she looked beautiful - so much better than she ever looked while in the care of Patton State Mental Health Hospital. She no longer had that look of faraway eyes. Not that day.

It was about noon that Fall day, when we took our seats in the lawn chairs in the front yard. I was happy it was Fall or it wouldn't have been that comfortable sitting out under the scorching sun.

"How have you been?" asked Suzie.

"I got married a couple of years ago to a girl named D'Arcy. You'd like her. She doesn't wear make-up either."

"Oh yeah, is she cute?" and she gave me that cockeyed grin, with one-eye closed.

"Yeah, and she's funny too," I said.

"Well, I'm all about being funny," she smiled, and then asked, "You seen Tod lately?"

"I haven't talked to Tod for years…at least ten years or so. You know Tod, he's hard to talk to."

"How about at Daddy's funeral?"

I was surprised she brought Dad up.

"Not even there," I said, "He gave a speech about Dad, calling him "J C", …that stood for Jesus Christ …Uncle Sam liked to have wacked him upside the head. But when he said something bout Adolph Kraft, and changing his name to Kraft, who was Uncle Sam's real Dad, our mother's real father, Uncle Sam said he'd have something to say about that."

Suzie laughed, but I thought she was being polite and probably thinking about something else. But she was thinking, "I remember Uncle Sam and Martha had a little girl that was mentally retarded. Her name was...I can't remember – but she had a name for everyone. Mother was Movie Star, Tod was Honey, you were... Roy Rodgers."

"Who were you?" I asked.

"I can't remember that either," said Suzie. We both pondered that one for a second.

"You were Sister Sue," I said.

"That's right, Sister Sue." This time she chuckled.

"God, I wish I could remember her name. I remember there was talk, when we were young, about whether Sam and Martha should send her to a home to live. They decided to keep her with them."

"They had the opportunity to choose their lifestyle when she became a teenager. They had to give up a lot to raise her," I said, still not remembering her darn name... Sandy! That was her name. Sandy Tucker."

"Sandy, yes, of course. She was such a different child."

"She was funny alright. If she didn't like somebody she called them a 'black cow.' She ended up living forever because she had all that love. Martha and Sam should have gotten more credit," I said.

"I wish I could have gotten some of her paternal love. It couldn't have done me any harm," she said.

"I've been sending you love, Suzie. I'm sorry I didn't come get you."

"You're not my parent, Mark. I didn't expect anything from you. You didn't bring me into this world. I'm not here because of you."

"I wanted you to have the world. Not be locked up from society your whole life."

Suzan smiled and said, "The only thing life produced for me was a big hole."

"What?"

"All life's produced for me is a big hole; that's all I've produced from life. There should be a picture of me in the dictionary with a big hole as my face."

"What do you mean by that?"

"It's my mantra – life's a big hole. I didn't say shit hole. What I mean is, I can dig and dig and still come up with the same dirt I started with; the same dirt I started with is there in the end. It's a statement about dirt; the stuff they used to throw on you when you're dead. I've worked digging my hole, one day at a time, one day after the other, scraping my life's work from the sides of my hole. But it always ends up being the same black dirt. It doesn't matter; it's always a big black hole. And a hole's not a pit like I was thrown into when I was 23. A hole is an escape route that breaks through to the other side where life is perfect. It just never happened."

It made me sad that it had come to this, trying to make sense out of my sister's ramblings. There had to be meaning in her thoughts, but I couldn't figure it out. She was trying to teach me something. She went on.

"I lived in another house that was closer to downtown, and I used to walk everywhere. Ten, twenty miles a day, no kidding. I walked all around town. People got to know me as the lady in the green coat, cause that's what I always wore, even in summer. Can you believe that? Not the crazy lady, but just the lady. I learned something important. If the peace sign can be mistaken as a Mercedes Benz logo, then you can be seen and mistaken for something else. There's alchemy to it. You may be seen as something you're not."

Suddenly a tear drop swelled in my eye. It alarmed me, something bad was coming. It wasn't about the pea green coat I knew she had been wearing since she was fifteen years old. I was thinking about how often she must have cried, laying in the snake pit at night, alone, with no friends or allies, and nothing she could do about it. She was watched like a convict, and not because she was wearing a green overcoat, but because she was a paranoid schizophrenic that needed to be drugged. Pea green overcoat or schizophrenic? Or maybe she was too tough to cry. I never got a chance to ask her.

It was beyond belief that Suzan became a leader by surviving the system with her integrity intact. Amelia told me Suzan spent her canteen money buying ice cream from the ice cream truck that came through the neighborhood every day. She bought it for all the other patients she lived with. She was so generous to those around her. "What'll it be, strawberry, chocolate, Drumstick, or Mr. Softie?" It was the little things that counted. She had nothing more to give. She taught her friends to be kind to your kind.

"I've been thinking, Mark."

I started to cry uncontrollably. My eyes leaked like sieves. I was trying to hold it back, but it was impossible. I felt raw guilt over Suzie being in this condition, living in Bakersfield in a home she shared with others who couldn't make it on their own. I cried because it was my fault. I had never felt such emotion for loss before, even when my mother died.

But what was I crying about? The people she lived with now were her new family. But did they love her? I should have been happy for Suzan.

And yet, I cried so much I couldn't talk. The tears just kept coming.

Finally, I eked out, "I'm sorry. I can't help it."

I'll never forget her consoling words. They're hard for me to even write down. But she said: "That's okay. Sometimes it's good to cry."

And so it was that Suzie became my hero. I looked at her smiling at me, like she knew it all. "Man must suffer to be wise."

XIX

EPILOGUE

66. The Brothers Agree

When I was twenty-seven years old, I decided to do what I always wanted to do and that was go to law school. I wanted to be one of those guys hanging around the courthouse with a suit on, taking care of business. I was limited to the "checkbook" school of law, aka, Santa Barbara College of Law, which allowed me to attend school at night. I spent the next three and a half years enjoying the curriculum as I worked my way through law school. My father didn't pay a dime for my higher education. Why would he? I was 27 years old. And I was married, had a little girl, a mortgage payment, and a new car.

As I was educating myself so I could mature beyond my twenties, Tod educated himself by making new friends in the drug world. Well, they weren't all new. It was more a continuation of his art into alchemy. Specifically he dealt with cocaine. Exclusively he was branded by cocaine. Cocaine had become his best friend, and he never left home without it. By the time I graduated from law school, Tod had gotten busted for smuggling and distributing cocaine. That earned him a five-year prison term in a California Correctional Facility. He spent most of his incarceration time in a work camp.

That really pissed me off. It was like getting a snowball smashed in my face for Christmas. So now I am stigmatized by my sister being incarcerated in Patton State Mental Hospital and my brother stigmatized me by being incarcerated in a criminal institution. I had two stigmas stacked against me and what I wanted to know was how and why that happened. How could two out of three children, who grew up in such a promising home environment, turn into such non-contributing members of society. For all practical purposes, their personality flaws made them outlaws.

Tod got screwed from the very beginning when the nurse misspelled his first name by leaving the extra "d" off his birth certificate when he was born in Santa Barbara. My parents decided to live with the mistake; thinking it made Tod special. And special was right.

I had gone through the normal period of love and adoration for my older brother. He had received nine years more parenting than me, from the same parents. Although you would never guess they were the same parents given the stories Tod told. When I was nine years old, Tod joined the Navy, and he was my big brother hero. I couldn't have been prouder of him! I remember visiting him with my parents at the naval base in San Diego where he was learning to be a "signalman" on the bridge of a ship. Or three years later, when we visited him at college in Isla Vista, I got a sweatshirt representing UCSB. Tod was my superhero. He even brought me home a 10-speed bicycle from the University for my thirteenth birthday. Who knows where he got that bicycle. But it was cool.

Then he married Lisa and you know the story from there. He was married and divorced. And that's where he stayed - at around 27-years old. Tod couldn't make the mature jump out of his twenties. He lagged in his art as others moved forward in their occupations. He never quit being a *sand skunk* as his relationship with women will attest. He never married again.

I don't know what happened to Tod, but his failure to cultivate a lasting relationship with anybody goes way beyond the scope of this book. Our family had been fragmented. None of us kids stuck together. There were no bonds. Fortunately, our parents didn't live to see what became of the family. Sometimes I wonder if we weren't made to hate each other.

Then there was a turnaround in our story. Everyone had died except me and my dear brother, and you could count on one hand the number of times we had spoken over the last fifteen years. We had shared some unkind words. The kind you always remember until you forget and then it's not worth dredging up again. I was still angry over Tod getting popped for cocaine and wiping it on me. After Dad died, Tod went to live in his house in Cayucos. He would have otherwise been homeless if not for Dad. We decided we would go our separate ways.

When Tod called me for help, he was having an extended stay in the Cayucos Senior Hospital, suffering from the equivalent of a gunshot wound to his belly. He had an open wound the size of a fist in his gut, which was the result of something blocking his colon. He had the wound split open in the hospital for over a month. He was healing from the inside out after missing the sutures that held his gut together. It was an ugly, bloody looking hole, keeping him from moving around.

There was only one thing Tod could do while lying in bed and that was use the telephone. With that technique in hand, Tod opened the address book he'd had since being a teenager and called every person he knew to ask for help. I don't know how many people he knew, but he called them all. I was apparently the last one on the list. The deal he offered was, in return for $50,000, the person would act as Tod's health care provider until Tod died. He needed that job filled to get out of the hospital. Not a single person was interested in taking the money. Naturally, I wanted to see the $50,000 first. It turned out to be only $20,000 he had hidden in his bank box, but I took the job anyway. One look at him told me he didn't have long to live.

I loved my brother but sometimes I hated him. That's all I can say. I'd have taken him home even without the $20,000, but it was challenging. It was nearly impossible to get him out of the hospital bed, into the car, and back into the bed at his house. Tod had become a morbidly obese man with no strength in his lower body. His body weight was nearly 300 pounds the month before, and now he weighs 225 pounds with a donut of fat flesh hanging from his belly. He suffered from a host of chronic diseases, but right in the middle of his belly was this gaping hole. We must have worked for an hour in the parking lot trying to get him from the wheelchair into the passenger seat of the vehicle. He couldn't get his right knee passed the door-jam. He just couldn't do it. And I was shoving as hard as I could.

Comparing Suzie's proclivities to Tod's indiscretions, or Suzie's mental disease versus Tod's criminal disease, the only difference I could see is Suzie had an excuse. Her DNA didn't allow her to do otherwise. She was going to the snake pit. The problem for her was nobody understood her disease or how it should be treated. They could only isolate her with 3,000 other patients like herself who had no other choice but to live with their kind in mammoth institutions.

Tod was a horse of a different color, as they say. He had choices and continuously chose the wrong one. If it was a choice between working for a living or trying to figure out the other way to survive, he chose the other way every time.

"Why were you like that Tod. Why'd you hate working so much?

"Well, I guess I just loved smoking dope more."

"You ever think it had to do with Suzie going insane."

"Me, hating to work? No, I already had that figured out by the time Suzie went crazy. I was busy with Lisa by then. I didn't have time for Suzan."

"I guess nobody did." I said.

"Our parents sure didn't waste their time on her, those lucky duckies," said Tod.

"True that. I had a great time climbing in the Bavarian Alps after I moved there. Climbing the *Watzman* was a big deal for me. It opened a whole new way of life for me. Going to school in Munich, learning to speak German, changed my entire *weltanschauung*. Traveling around Europe with my rucksack and climbing Mt. Olympus in Greece, instead of attending the 1972 Olympic Games, changed me. Those experiences took the boy from Bakersfield and gave him a Renaissance cap. It made a new man out of me, interested in academics and climbing mountains. I found the older I got; the only way I could eke out any happiness in life was through climbing mountains. Big mountains. The biggest in the world. The highest summit on the seven continents.

I started with the highest mountain in the world – Mt. Everest, in 1983. I met Ed Hillary at his school on the Khumbu. Then it was a slow burn for five years before I climbed Denali in Alaska. I climbed Aconcagua the following year in Argentina. Mount Blanc and the Matterhorn took a few tries in Europe. Then it was Mt. Cook in pristine New Zealand, and the romantic Kilimanjaro in Africa, where I took D'Arcy and later married her. I may never climb Mount Vinson in Antarctica though. I'm running out of time."

"Yeah, I remember when you went to climb Mt. Everest. You trekked from Kathmandu to the icefall at base camp. That's a 200-mile trek over the Himalayas," Tod said.

"I worked mountain climbing into my legal career as best I could. I could always massage a month a year to go mountain climbing. That Everest climb took three months. That doesn't leave much time for do-overs. It took me three trips to Zermatt to finally summit the Matterhorn. That's cost, plus three seasons of climbing time. Thank God I saved the easiest mountain for last. I'm going to write a memoire and call it *My Seven Summits*."

"That should put some hurt on Dick Bass's *Seven Summits*. It's one thing to go out and climb those mountains but another thing to write about them, don't you think?" said Tod.

"Well, that's what I plan on doing."

"I don't doubt you. I just can't wait to see what you say about me."

"You won't be around to read it," I said.

"You don't know that." said Tod.

About the Author

Mark S. Cornwall resides in Summerland, California. He's been an author for a decade but before that he spent 33 years as an attorney. His career was stopped short by a stroke which his doctor said, "really kicked his ass." He transformed himself into the author he always aspired to be.

Lawyers do a lot of what they call writing – for judges and appellate courts as their audience. It's more akin to professional copying, by rote. There's no room for wit or passion, let alone creativity. "The facts, mam, nothing but the facts." Writing is best left to the ...writers.

So with that in mind, here is the written truth about his ***FRACTURED FAMILY***. The final installment of the Cornwall memoir trilogy.

www.ingramcontent.com/pod-product-compliance
Lightning Source LLC
LaVergne TN
LVHW050922080826
845145LV00001B/167

* 9 7 8 0 9 7 7 8 5 1 4 5 4 *